PENGUIN PLAYS

JOHN GODBER: FIVE PLAYS

John Godber was born in 1956, the son of a miner. He hated theatre and literature as an adolescent and originally wanted to be a sportsman. Instead he decided to train as a drama teacher at Bretton Hall College and read drama and theatre arts at Leeds University. He then went on to gain his M.A. and Ph.D. He began as a probationary teacher at his old school, Minsthorpe High, in Yorkshire and was Head of Department by the time he left in 1983. He has been a regular attendant at the Edinburgh Festival since 1977 and has won four Fringe First Awards. His work was brought into focus through the National Student Drama Festival and in 1984 he became Artistic Director of the award-winning Hull Truck Theatre Company. His plays have been seen in many languages across the world. *Up 'n' Under* won the Laurence Olivier Comedy of the Year Award in 1985, while *Bouncers* received seven Los Angeles Drama Critics Circle Awards. Among his other plays are *Blood, Sweat and Tears*, *Shakers*, *Salt of the Earth*, *The Office Party*, *Happy Families*, *On the Piste* and *April in Paris*. He has written screenplays for television, and his other television work includes episodes from *Crown Court*, *Grange Hill* and *Brookside*. In 1987 he wrote and co-directed the BBC 2 six-part series *The Ritz* and its sequel, *The Continental*, and in 1991 he devised the BBC 2 series *Chalkface*. In 1988 he was made a Doctor of Letters by Hull University.

JOHN GODBER

Five Plays

Penguin Books

PENGUIN BOOKS

Published by the Penguin Group
Penguin Books Ltd, 27 Wrights Lane, London W8 5TZ, England
Penguin Books USA Inc., 375 Hudson Street, New York, New York 10014, USA
Penguin Books Australia Ltd, Ringwood, Victoria, Australia
Penguin Books Canada Ltd, 10 Alcorn Avenue, Toronto, Ontario, Canada M4V 3B2
Penguin Books (NZ) Ltd, 182–190 Wairau Road, Auckland 10, New Zealand

Penguin Books Ltd, Registered Offices: Harmondsworth, Middlesex, England

Up 'n' Under first published by Amberlane Press 1985
Bouncers first published by Chappell Plays Ltd 1987
Teechers first published by Samuel French Ltd 1988
September in the Rain and *Happy Jack* first published by Penguin Books 1989
This collection first published 1989
10 9 8 7 6 5 4 3

Printed in England by Clays Ltd, St Ives plc
Filmset in Monotype Ehrhardt

CONTENTS

INTRODUCTION

The five plays in this collection have much in common; they are also quite different in many ways. Apart from anything else, these plays significantly mark my graduation from amateur scribbler to so-called professional writer. All of them place the actor at the centre of the theatrical experience; that is, none of the plays demands a box setting – all of them require simply actors and an empty space. By the same token all the plays have an inherent theatricality: they are of the world of theatre and, I am proud to say, cannot easily be translated in tele-sense. As far as a common theme is concerned, I suppose all five plays deal with aspects of working-class life and, to a greater or lesser extent, working-class leisure time. All the plays are very cheap to produce, and there is for me a deep irony in this. As a school teacher I had limited resources and consequently wrote plays to fit into the back of my car; when I became Artistic Director of Hull Truck I had to design plays that would tour and would fit into the back of a truck. It must also be said in passing that all five plays give back the imagination to the audience – they ask the audience to engage in the theatrical event.

Three of the plays are autobiographical, one more than the other two. *Teechers* is the only truly autobiographical play. I had been a drama teacher for five years, and although I had written a play about education while I was still teaching, it was not successful. After some five years out of teaching I was able, I think, to give a more balanced overview of my experience in comprehensive education. *Happy Jack* and *September in the Rain* are autobiographical but not in the strict sense. Both plays are about my grandparents and chronicle their lives. All the incidents in the plays are based on fact, but I could not separate these stories from my own life, for they were continually being retold in our household – they were the myths of my childhood.

Up 'n' Under was a kind of formula writing. I needed in 1984 to write a play that might attract a homogeneous audience to our theatre in Hull. As Rugby League was an enormous force in the city and no one had written about the sport (it being, incidentally, one of the few working-class-developed sports), I set about writing a play about rugby. It was not intended to be a comedy, but it was funny, and it won the Olivier Award for Comedy of the Year. In the following year *Bouncers* was nominated for the same award, though, as far as I am concerned, it is not a comedy either – it is a social phenomenon. Because I wrote the play very quickly for a group of friends who wanted to perform, the structure of the play is elastic; it has no real narrative drive; it is elliptical and cinematic.

When I was writing it I had no real sense of what I was creating. Only now, in retrospect, can I see that *Bouncers* highlights many of my fundamental beliefs about the theatre. The play demands high-energy performance, which also facilitates moments of pathos. It has a running time of around ninety minutes, the length of the average feature film. Its scenes are short and sharp. Direct audience address is used to change location quickly. Movement plays a large part in the play. It can be staged with or without an interval.

I believe in the theatre, but I believe only in a theatre that is theatrical. I also believe that if the theatre is to survive, it must not ape television, though it can borrow ideas and techniques – for example, *Up 'n' Under* has a slow-motion action replay, *Bouncers* a rewind and fast forward, *Teechers* a scene of slow-motion violence.

I remember, as a student, reading a statement by Piscator about box sets and realistic theatre. He said, 'We can't expect a man to sit and look at one set for three hours when he can fly around the world in eight.' I suppose that I had this in mind when I wrote the plays. All of them move very quickly. All of them ask the members of the audience to pay attention and to use their imagination.

J.G.
June 1989

BOUNCERS

AUTHOR'S NOTE

Bouncers is about working-class Britons at play. It is both a warning and a celebration. The style is deliberately elliptical and sharp, necessitating a performance style that depends as much on energy as it does on technique. Fast, clean and rhythmic movements are married with acute and natural social observations in order to create a nightmarish vision of the disco world. *Bouncers* occupies the nighttime, and the darker elements of the play should act as a constant undercurrent.

The play requires strong, physically versatile and above all flexible actors. This flexibility can be applied to the script. Any document about recent affairs is clearly in danger of becoming a museum piece. As a consequence, my own productions of *Bouncers* often change in reference, in length and in temperament. In short, *Bouncers* contains many truths about the nature of night life, but one need not necessarily show them all. The play can run from forty minutes to an hour and a half. Keep it alive for today. Make it work for your particular actors, in your particular space, and you will have a first-class production of *Bouncers*. Directors of the play should never think of Chekhov; rather, they should think of cartoons and cinematic techniques. The play was conceived for an audience that regards the theatre as box sets, big red curtains and tedious actors. The theatre can certainly be all that – but it can also be *Bouncers*.

J. G.
January 1987

CHARACTERS

LUCKY ERIC
JUDD
RALPH
LES
MARCO

Bouncers was first presented by Hull Truck Theatre Company at the Assembly Rooms, Edinburgh, on 10 August 1984, transferring to the Donmar Warehouse Theatre, London, in September. The cast was as follows:

LUCKY ERIC	Peter Geeves
JUDD	Richard Ridings
RALPH	Richard May
LES	Andrew Dunn
MARCO	Chris Walker

Directed by John Godber

It was subsequently produced by Hull Truck Theatre Company and Armand Gerrard Management at the Arts Theatre, London, opening on 22 July 1986.

ACT ONE

A provincial discothèque. The stage is bare and no props are used apart from a couple of beer kegs and four handbags. During the course of the action, the four bouncers, RALPH, JUDD, LES and LUCKY ERIC portray over thirty different characters. The switches of roles should be fast and sharp, emphasized by music and lighting. Disco music and lighting should be used to full effect to create the atmosphere of the place.

As the audience enters, the music plays, the lights flash and the bouncers establish the mood of the evening; walking up and down the aisles, generally surveying people, ushering them to their seats, passing the occasional threatening comment, etc. Gradually, they make their way to the stage. We focus in on LUCKY ERIC, *the wise old owl of the bouncers, who addresses the audience in time to the rap which plays in the background.*

LUCKY ERIC: Ladies and gentlemen . . . we present *Bouncers*.
We welcome you to a vision
Of the eighties urban night life
To stag nights and hen dos
To drunken crying girls and gallons of booze
It's celebration time – come on
It's always frustrating
For the oldest swingers in town
Yes, all human life is inevitably here
In a midnight circus
And I must make it clear
That the beer is pricey, the music pulsating
The atmosphere is intoxicating
We four will try and illustrate
The sort of thing that happens late

At night in every town
When the pubs are shut
And the beer's been downed . . .

> (LUCKY ERIC *joins the other bouncers in a line across the stage and they begin the rap. They carry out a complicated dance routine as they sing.*)

I SAID A HIP HOP
A HIPPY A HIPPY
A HIP HIP HOP AND DON'T YOU STOP

ALL: I SAID A HIP HOP
A HIPPY A HIPPY
A HIP HIP HOP AND DON'T YOU STOP

> (*They then move straight into the lyrics of the 'Bouncers' Rap'.**)

LUCKY ERIC: DOWN AT THE DISCO IS THE PLACE TO BE
THE LIGHTS ARE SO BRIGHT LIKE A COLOUR TV
THE MUSIC IS LOUD AND THE BEER FLOWS FREE
IT'S A DISCO PLACE FOR YOU AND ME
NOW ON THE DOOR YOU PAY YOUR MONEY
THE PLACE IS PACKED THE PLACE IS FUNNY
LOOK AT THE GIRLS

ALL: MMMM. . .

LUCKY ERIC: SMELL THEIR HONEY
THEIR HEADS ARE HAZY
THEIR LIMBS ARE LAZY
AND ALL THE YOUNG GIRLS DANCE LIKE CRAZY
COME ON
PUT ON YOUR CLOTHES

JUDD: FROM THE C&A

LUCKY ERIC: DO UP YOUR HAIR

LES: DOES IT FEEL OK?

LUCKY ERIC: I SAID GO

ALL: YES

LUCKY ERIC: I SAID GO

---

* The 'Bouncers Rap' single is available from Hull Truck Theatre, Spring Street, Hull HU2 8RW. Alternatively, the Sugarhill Gang's 'Rappers Delight' would provide the right rhythm needed.

ALL: YES
LUCKY ERIC: I SAID GO TO THE PLACE THAT IS THE BEST
    NOW THE DISCO PLACE
    THE DISCO BEAT
    IT'S THE KIND OF BEAT
    THAT MOVES YOUR FEET
    IN THE HEAT
    THE BEAT
    YOU CAN'T DEFEAT
    IN THE HEAT
    THE BEAT
    YOU WATCH THE MEAT
    YOU WANNA STAY COOL
    YOU WANNA STAY NEAT
    THE DISCO STREET
    THE DISCO BEAT
    COME ON
    WELL YOU FINISH WORK
ALL: WELL IT'S FRIDAY NIGHT
LUCKY ERIC: AND YOU'VE GOT YOUR PAY
ALL: SO YOU FEEL ALL RIGHT
JUDD: INTO THE PUB
LUCKY ERIC: WHAT DO YOU DO?
ALL: DOWN EIGHT PINTS
LUCKY ERIC: YOU DON'T CARE
ALL: COS IT'S FRIDAY NIGHT
LUCKY ERIC: I SAID HIP HIPPY
    GIP GIPPY
    HIP GIP HOP BOP
    DRINK THAT SLOP
ALL: AND DON'T YOU STOP
    GET DOWN GET UP
    GET IN GET OUT
    GET DOWN GET UP
    GET IN GET OUT
    GET DOWN GET UP
    GET IN GET OUT

JUDD: THE BOUNCERS ARE MEAN IN THEIR BLACK AND
    WHITE
RALPH: THE FELLAS ARE PISSED AND THEIR FISTS ARE
    TIGHT
LES: BUT THE CHICKS ARE LOOSE
ALL: COS IT'S FRIDAY NIGHT
LUCKY ERIC: WE GOT SOUL
ALL: RAPPY
LUCKY ERIC: WE GOT SOUL
ALL: RAP RAP
LUCKY ERIC: WE PLAY LOTS OF OTHER STUFF
JUDD: THAT SOUNDS LIKE . . . [*crap*]
ALL: SHUDDUP
    GET DOWN GET UP
    GET IN GET OUT
    GET DOWN GET UP
    GET IN GET OUT
    GET DOWN GET UP
    GET IN GET OUT
LES: IF YOU COME DOWN HERE
    WEARING JEANS
JUDD: YOU CAN'T GET IN
ALL: KNOW WHAT HE MEANS
    GOT TO HAVE A TIE YOU GOTTA HAVE A SUIT
    YOU GOTTA LOOK CUTE OR YOU'LL GET THE BOOT
    YOU GOTTA HAVE A TIE YOU GOTTA HAVE A SUIT
    (*Repeat to fade until only* RALPH *is still singing loudly by himself and looking like a real idiot. Sudden switch to the sound of a telephone ringing.* LES *becomes a smooth-talking radio DJ.*)
LES: You're listening to Radio 1 with Steve Wright ... Hello, Steve. It's Gervaise here. Keep your tongue out and I'll call you back. All right?
ALL: 1059. 1083.
LES: Yes. That was *The Bouncers*. Strange name for a group, that one. What do you think, Mr Sinden?
JUDD: (*as Donald Sinden*) I need alcohol. I need cigarettes, satin

knights and a knighthood. Nobody speaks when I am on stage.

LES: Yes. That record is going down very well in the discos so I shall certainly be playing it tonight at my gig in Littlehampton.

RALPH: Yes indeedy. Dave Doubledex here.

ALL: Get the picture.

JUDD: Let's have that off.

> (*Suddenly the scene changes and the bouncers become female customers in a ladies' hairdressing salon.* RALPH *sits under a hairdrier, reading a magazine.* LUCKY ERIC (*'Maureen'*) *is having his hair washed by* JUDD (*'Cheryl'*). LES *is off stage.*)

That Steve Wright gets up my ring ... and he's so popular because people keep ringing him up. Do you listen to it, Maureen?

LUCKY ERIC: No, Cheryl, love. It gets on my bloody nerves. I like that Bruno Brooks and Gaz za za Davies.

JUDD: This new Alberto Balsam should do wonders for your hair, Maureen.

LUCKY ERIC: Do you think so?

JUDD: Oh, yeah.

LUCKY ERIC: I want to look nice for tonight.

JUDD: Going anywhere special?

LUCKY ERIC: It's Rosie's twenty-first. It should be a good do.

JUDD: I hope it is, love.

LUCKY ERIC: You know her. She comes in here. She works at our place. Four of us are going down to Mr Cinders.

JUDD: Oh, I've heard some good reports about that place.

LUCKY ERIC: Yes. It's all right.

ALL: Yes. It's all right.

LUCKY ERIC: It's the best place round here.

JUDD: It's all plush, isn't it?

LUCKY ERIC: Yeah. You've got to get there early to get in. It gets packed out. Like the black hole of bloody Calcutta.

> (LES *enters the salon, out of breath. He has become 'Rosie'.*)

LES: Chuffin' hell. Talk about being rushed off your feet. Look at the time and I've only just finished.

LUCKY ERIC: What've you been up to, Rosie?

LES: An order came in at ten to four . . .

LUCKY ERIC: Chuffin' cheek.

LES: Friday and all. And my bleeding birthday.

LUCKY ERIC: Cheeky getts.

LES: Can you fit me in, Cheryl?

JUDD: I can't, I'm afraid, love. I'm chock-a-block till seven.

RALPH: I told her to book.

JUDD: I'm going out myself . . . Dragonara Casino.

LUCKY ERIC: Gambling?

JUDD: Well . . .

LUCKY ERIC: Bloody 'ell.

LES: I'll just have to be late, that's all. I'll nip over to Barbara's.
    She might be able to fit me in. I'll see you down here later,
    Maureen.

LUCKY ERIC: All right, love.

LES: Tara, loves.

ALL: Tara.

LES: Tara, everyone.

LUCKY ERIC: She's a dizzy sod, that Rosie.

RALPH: (*Getting uncomfortable under the hairdrier*) How much longer,
    Cheryl?

JUDD: Bloody hell. She's on fire!

LUCKY ERIC: Cheryl.

JUDD: Bloody hell. I wish you'd get your hair cut.

LUCKY ERIC: I've got a new sort of skirt thing. It's nice, a bit tight,
    but so what? Ski pants as well.

JUDD: C & A?

LUCKY ERIC: No.

JUDD: Top Shop?

LUCKY ERIC: No chance. Got it from Chelsea Girl.

JUDD *and* RALPH: Chelsea Girl.

JUDD: Oh, yeah. They're lovely. I've got one in a sort of maroon.

LUCKY ERIC *and* RALPH: Maroon.

JUDD: I got them in the sale.

LUCKY ERIC: How much were they?

ALL: Barbers –

    (*Although the scene remains exactly the same we are now in a*

barber's. JUDD *is a brusque barber.* ERIC *is in the chair.*
RALPH *reads a dirty magazine.*)

JUDD: Come and get your hair cut if you dare.

RALPH: Jesus Christ! Where is he?

LUCKY ERIC: I can't see him.

JUDD: I'm over here, lads. Right. Who wants what? You young lads
    want a proper haircut. Well, for a quid you can have the
    Norman Invader look. Very popular with the thugs. Or for
    three fifty you can have the Elephant Man cut.

LUCKY ERIC: What's the Elephant Man cut?

JUDD: It makes one side of your head look bigger than the other.

RALPH: Funny barber.

JUDD: You said it.

RALPH: I wouldn't let him near me.

LUCKY ERIC: Why?

RALPH: Look at his own hair.

JUDD: (*Ignoring them*) Or you can have the Tony Curtis haircut
    look.

LUCKY ERIC: Hey, what's the Tony Curtis haircut look?

JUDD: All off. Totally bald. Egghead cut.

LUCKY ERIC: Tony Curtis doesn't have his hair cut like that . . .

JUDD: He does if he comes in here. Funny, eh? Funny, lads, eh?

LUCKY ERIC: Just cut it, will yer and cut the gags.

       (LUCKY ERIC *gets in the chair and* JUDD *begins to cut his
       hair.*)

JUDD: Going somewhere, are we?

LUCKY ERIC: Disco.

JUDD: How old are you?

RALPH: (*Looking at a magazine*) Juddy hell! Look at the body on that.

LUCKY ERIC: I'm nineteen.

JUDD: Got a woman?

RALPH: I hope that she's down there tonight.

LUCKY ERIC: I might have at two o'clock.

JUDD: Make sure that you don't get an ugly one.

RALPH: There's only ugly ones left at two o'clock.

LUCKY ERIC: Bollocks, Jerry.

JUDD: Watch the language, you.

RALPH: What are you doing to his hair? He can't go out like that
... Hey, you can keep away from me, you bleeding maniac.

JUDD: Anything on?

LUCKY ERIC: No, thanks. What time are we starting?

RALPH: Time they do open.

    (LES *enters*.)

LES: I'm here, you dreamers.

LUCKY ERIC: Kev, ready for the big night?

LES: Ready as I'll ever be.

RALPH: Hey. I am dying for it. I've starved myself all week.

LUCKY ERIC: He's a dirty sod.

LES: Seven o'clock in the Taverners', right?

LUCKY ERIC *and* RALPH: Right.

LES: All right.

LUCKY ERIC *and* RALPH: All right.

LES: Where's Terry?

JUDD: I'm here.

    (JUDD *switches from playing the barber to playing 'Terry'. The
    scene changes to a street corner where they all wait for 'Terry'*)

ALL: I thought he was the barber.

JUDD: Just finished a mindless day of wood stackin', talking about
the races at Chepstow, the dogs at White City and the problems
of getting Leeds back into Europe ...

ALL: (*Chant*) United!

JUDD: ... ready for the nighttime. Mindless girl-watching and a
chance perhaps of the old sniff of perfume and feel of inside
thigh; milky-white thighs and bloodshot eyes. It's no surprise
that I'm dying for it.

ALL: See you down there at seven. Terry – Jerry – Kev – Baz –

JUDD: Be young –

LUCKY ERIC: Be foolish –

LES: But be happy –

ALL: Be da da da da da da da da ...

RALPH: And be careful not to catch it!

ALL: Bollocks!

    (*The actors now become the lads getting ready for the big night
    out.*)

LUCKY ERIC: Baz, that is it. Friday night, fit for a fight. Get down there. Have a skinful. Might have a Chinese, or a chicken in the basket. Maybe a hot dog. Might risk it. Got my dole money saved up. Try and pull some skirt. Give her a pup.

RALPH: I'm looking cool. I'm looking great. Wish I didn't have that spot. (*Squeezes an imaginary spot.*) Gotcha!! Blackheads. Slap some Clearasil on my face. Not bad, Jerry. Not bad at all, mate.

LUCKY ERIC: Hope I don't get stabbed again.

JUDD: Time is it?

LES: Jesus Christ . . .

RALPH: Ten to seven.

LES: Gonna be late.

RALPH: Time for another quick check.

> (*They all stand in a row and check the various parts of their bodies.*)

LUCKY ERIC: Hair?

LES: Check.

JUDD: Tie?

LES: Check.

LUCKY ERIC: Aftershave? Cliff Richard uses this.

ALL: (*Sing*) 'Got myself a sleeping, walking . . .'

RALPH: Check.

LUCKY ERIC: Talc on genitals?

LES: Check.

LUCKY ERIC: Clean underpants?

RALPH: Well . . .

LES: They'll do.

LUCKY ERIC: Money?

JUDD: Double check.

LES: Condoms?

LUCKY ERIC: Checkaroonie.

JUDD: Breath?

> (*They all breathe out and try to smell their own breath.*)

ALL: Ugh! Beer should drown that.

JUDD: Right. That's it then. We're ready. Catch the bus at the end of our street.

RALPH: Ding ding.

LES: Fares, please.

LUCKY ERIC: Bollocks.

JUDD: Get down town to start the pub crawl. When we get there it's packed already. I see me mates. Baz, Jerry an' Kev an' me into the Taverners'.

> (*During the following sequence the lads attempt to get served. Their actions should convey the bustling, pushy atmosphere of a pub.*)

Four pints, please!

ALL: (*As they down the first pint of the evening*) *One!*

LES: Course I'm eighteen.

LUCKY ERIC: Get some crisps.

JUDD: Four bags of beef.

RALPH: Look at the tits on that.

ALL: (*To audience*) Social comment.

JUDD: Four pints, pal.

ALL: *Two!*

RALPH: Hey, who's pushing?

LUCKY ERIC: Are you being served?

LES: Hey up, bastard.

RALPH: Four more pints, pal.

ALL: *Three!*

JUDD: Got any pork scratchings?

LUCKY ERIC: Hey, watch me shirt.

RALPH: Look, who's pushing?

LES: Packed, in't it?

JUDD: Let me get to them bogs.

LUCKY ERIC: Excuse me.

RALPH: Four pints.

ALL: *Four!*

JUDD: And a whisky, love, please.

ALL: *Five!*

LUCKY ERIC: Excuse me, love.

LES: I gave you a fiver.

JUDD: Fat gett.

RALPH: Four pints, four bags of beef, four bags of salted peanuts and four whisky chasers.

ALL: *Six! Seven!*

JUDD: Have you got any cashews.

LUCKY ERIC: Hey, twat, I've been stood here a month.

LES: Can we have some service down here?

RALPH: I'm next, love.

LUCKY ERIC: Shut your mouth, skullhead.

JUDD: I'm being served, love, thanks.

> (*The four lads recoil as they see beer spill all over* LUCKY
> ERIC's (*'Baz's'*) *trousers.*)

LUCKY ERIC: Oooh! Look at that. Somebody's spilt beer all over
my suit.

JUDD: Daft gett.

LUCKY ERIC: It's brand new.

LES: It'll dry.

JUDD: How many have we had?

RALPH: Ten.

JUDD: Time for another.

LUCKY ERIC: I've only had nine.

RALPH: Are we off?

LUCKY ERIC: D'you think we'll get in?

JUDD: Should do.

LES: Hope there's no trouble.

LUCKY ERIC: There's four of us.

ALL: Yeah.

RALPH: Come on. Let's get down there, pick something up. Right?

ALL: Right.

LUCKY ERIC: Hang on.

LES: What?

LUCKY ERIC: Piss call.

ALL: Oh, yeah.

> (*They all turn their backs as if peeing and then turn back to
> face the audience.*)

JUDD: We'd better split up.

LES: Why?

JUDD: The bouncers.

LUCKY ERIC: Don't let you in. In groups.

RALPH: OK. Me and Kev. Right?

JUDD: Yeah. And me and ... (*Realizing who he's paired off with*) Oh, shit!

> (*Just as they are about to move away they all freeze. Pause. They once more become the girls we saw earlier in the hair-dresser sequence.* LUCKY ERIC '*Maureen*', LES '*Rosie*', JUDD '*Elaine*', *and* RALPH '*Suzy*' *all stand together in a circle having a laugh and a drink in a pub. They are all dressed up in their brand new clothes ready for the night out. This should be communicated to the audience through their actions. They introduce themselves one by one.*)

LUCKY ERIC: Maureen. Massive but nice. Fat but cuddly. Not a bag, but likes a drink and a laugh. A bit busty.

LES: Rosie. Birthday today. Tall and slim, hair all permed. I had it done at Barbara's.

LUCKY ERIC: It's nice. It really suits you.

LES: Thank you.

LUCKY ERIC: Cow.

LES: I've had a drink. I feel a bit tiddly. Hey, it will end in tears. Hello love.

LUCKY ERIC: Hello.

LES: Have you lost a bit of weight?

JUDD: Plain Elaine.

LUCKY ERIC *and* LES: It's a shame.

JUDD: Left school at sixteen with one CSE in metalwork. I'm on the dole.

LUCKY ERIC *and* LES: It's such a shame.

JUDD: Enjoys a good night out but doesn't expect to get picked up though. Handy in a fight ... come here, ya bastard.

RALPH: Rosie, Maureen, Elaine ...

ALL: Suzy ...

RALPH: ... sexy ... I've got stockings on under my dress. Do you wanna look? You cheeky getts! Go on then. Anybody's for half a lager. Goes under the sunbed ... brown all over. I bet you would fancy it, big boy. Ooh, he's nice, that one.

LES: I'll say he is. Yeah. Right Who wants what?

JUDD: I'll have a pint of Guinness ... no, only a joke. I'll have a brandy and lime.

LUCKY ERIC: Well. I'll have a lager and black because if I have any more I'll be on my back.

LES: As usual.

LUCKY ERIC: You cheeky sod.

LES: Sorry.

RALPH: I'll have a pina colada.

LUCKY ERIC: Christ. Listen to her.

RALPH: Well, I'm eighteen.

LES: She doesn't bloody care. I feel a bit sick.

LUCKY ERIC: You'll be all right when we get down there.

LES: Are we getting the bus?

RALPH: Well, I'm not walking it in these shoes.

ALL: They're lovely.

RALPH: I know.

JUDD: I'm gonna put a record on.

ALL: Ya da da da da da da ya da da da da.

> (JUDD *walks up to an imaginary jukebox, represented by* LUCKY ERIC. LES *and* RALPH *join* JUDD *around the jukebox.*)

RALPH: Put that on, 3A. I like that.

JUDD: No. It's crap.

LES: I think you should put Wham! on.

JUDD: I'm putting on a funky disco record.

RALPH: I'm afraid you are not, because I like this one here by Sister Sledge. (*Singing, as the record*) 'I was walking down the street one day, I heard a voice, (*repeat as if the record is sticking*) I heard a voice . . .'

> (*Sudden blackout and freeze. The actors walk to the side of the stage. A dark and foreboding sound filters out from the speakers. The pace has been fast and hectic up until this point, but now the stage is quite still. We are outside the club. Eerie, disturbing music plays as we move into a mime sequence during which the bouncers come to life. During this sequence each actor should create and display a kind of larger-than-life character for each bouncer. It is at this point that the individual characteristics of each bouncer are established. Ordinary mannerisms and gestures are grotesquely exaggerated as, one by*

one, the bouncers step forward to introduce themselves through mime. JUDD, for example, walks slowly and cautiously to the centre of the stage, looks around, takes a hand exerciser out of his pocket and begins to do a series of exercises. He does so to the point of exhaustion, his face grimacing as the seeping pain of lactic acid invades his forearm muscles. He puts away the exerciser and has a moment's silence to himself. He takes a comb out of his pocket and begins to carefully comb his hair. When he has completed this highly meticulous activity he puts the comb away and enjoys another moment's contemplation. He spits on the floor, rubs the spit into the ground with his foot and then cracks his knuckles. All these actions are executed with the greatest attention to detail and are outrageously heightened, as indicated above. Once JUDD has finished his sequence, RALPH moves centre stage and repeats the ritual. Once finished, he stands by JUDD. LES joins them, once more enacting the ritual. Finally they speak. Each word is delivered with much more emphasis than would appear necessary as they acknowledge each other.)

LES: Judd?

JUDD: Les.

RALPH: Les?

LES: Ralph.

RALPH: Judd?

JUDD: Ralph.

(LUCKY ERIC *joins the group.*)

LUCKY ERIC: Ralph?

RALPH: Lucky Eric.

JUDD: Eric?

LUCKY ERIC: Judd, Les.

LES: Lucky Eric. All right?

LUCKY ERIC: Yeah. Why?

LES: Cold innit?

RALPH: Yeh. Bitter.

JUDD: Any trouble last night?

LES: Usual. Couple of punks got glassed.

JUDD: Nothing special then?

RALPH: No.

LES: I wanted to have 'em, but Eric said no.

LUCKY ERIC: You're too violent, Les. You can't control yourself.

LES: You don't have any fun, Eric. That's your trouble. Gerrin' past it.

LUCKY ERIC: (*Totally manic*) Don't you ever say that I am getting past it! Ever!

JUDD: Many in?

RALPH: Packed. Early rush, then it'll tail off.

LUCKY ERIC: That's Fridays for you.

JUDD: I got a basket meal for nothing yesterday.

LUCKY ERIC: When?

JUDD: Yesterday.

LES: Who gave it to you?

JUDD: That girl.

LUCKY ERIC: Oh, yeah?

RALPH: Nice one she is, nice tea bag.

JUDD: Not bad.

LUCKY ERIC: Yeah, all right in the dark.

RALPH: A bit fat around the buttocks if you ask me.

LUCKY ERIC: Sommat to grab, innit?

JUDD: Chicken it was. Tender.

LES: And chips?

JUDD: No chips. Fattening!

LUCKY ERIC: Short legs.

RALPH: Yeah, right.

LUCKY ERIC: Optical illusion, that is.

JUDD: What? That chips are fattening?

RALPH: How come?

LUCKY ERIC: Makes her arse look bigger.

LES: Nearer to the ground.

RALPH: Good centre of gravity, chickens.

LUCKY ERIC: How's the judo?

RALPH: Not bad, thanks.

LUCKY ERIC: Still training?

RALPH: Yeah, twice a week. And you?

JUDD: Couldn't train hamsters.

LUCKY ERIC: I trained you though, didn't I? Every day, power-lifting. I bench-pressed 354 pounds yesterday.

LES: Who?

LUCKY ERIC: Me.

LES: When?

LUCKY ERIC: Yesterday.

LES: Get pillocked!

LUCKY ERIC: No pillock, Thomas. No pillock.

JUDD: I've seen him do it.

LES: Yeah?

LUCKY ERIC: Could have done two raps.

JUDD: 354 pounds, that's, er, twenty . . .

RALPH: That's heavy, Judd.

LUCKY ERIC: What can you bench, Judd?

JUDD: Something.

LUCKY ERIC: Still wrestling?

JUDD: No.

LES: Still on the dole, are you?

JUDD: No.

RALPH: Doing a bit of nicking?

JUDD: No. Well, a bit . . . I'm doing a bit of Rugby League . . . Sunday League stuff . . . I've started training for it.

LUCKY ERIC: It's a bit quiet out here tonight, isn't it? . . . Too quiet.

RALPH: It'll soon liven up when the pubs turn out. They'll all be streaming down here, like sheep.

ALL: (*Chanting*) Here we go, here we go, here we go. (*As if downing another pint*) *Fourteen!*

RALPH: Bastards!

LUCKY ERIC: What time is it?

JUDD: Well, the big hand is on nine . . .

LES: Early doors yet. No need to start gerrin' aggressive.

RALPH: Yes, they'll all be coming down here, looking for a woman.

LES: Yeah, a big buxom woman.

JUDD: Or a small petite woman.

LUCKY ERIC: Or a bloke.

JUDD: Yes, there's usually one or two of them about and all.

LUCKY ERIC: Is there?

LES: They're all right, you know, really.

RALPH: No, they are not all right, you know, really.

LES: They are . . . they are the same as us. They've got the same feelings, the same sex drives.

LUCKY ERIC: Have they, Leslie?

LES: Yes, they have, cos one of my best mates . . .

RALPH: Hold on a minute, Les.

LUCKY ERIC: What are you on about, Les?

LES: Now listen. I was just about to say . . .

RALPH: Yes . . .

LES: That one of my best mates . . .

RALPH: Yes . . .

LES: Once knew a fella who once, and only once, worked in a club for gay people.

LUCKY ERIC: Tell us another one. You can't be too careful these days, Les.

RALPH: Each to their own. That's it. Each to their bloody own. You have just got to let people get on with what they want . . . that is my philosophy for life.

LUCKY ERIC: Fair enough Ralph. Fair enough. I like to hear a man express his philosophy. Fair enough. (*Pause.*) You can borrow my handbag any night, sweetie.

RALPH: Steady on.

LUCKY ERIC: Yeah?

RALPH: Steady on.

LUCKY ERIC: Or what?

RALPH: Are we trying to start something, Eric?

LUCKY ERIC: Could be.

RALPH: Are we trying to encourage a conflict situation?

LUCKY ERIC: Might be, Mr Inner Calm.

> (RALPH *takes up a strong stance and invites* LUCKY ERIC *to hit him.*)

RALPH: Come on then . . . there . . . now . . .

> (LUCKY ERIC *makes a move as if to hit him, but stops. It is a hoax.* LUCKY ERIC *stands and laughs at* RALPH. *The other*

bouncers see the latent danger but, as this is a regular occurrence, they are not unduly disturbed.)

Power-lifters. I've shit 'em.

LUCKY ERIC: Judo. Puffballs.

(*They back off. There is a moment's quiet.*)

JUDD: Eric, Eric ... Remember that Rugby Union trip that came down?

LES: Zulu warriors?

RALPH: None of that tonight, I hope.

JUDD: Caused chaos.

LUCKY ERIC: Bloody idiots.

LES: College boys.

ALL: (*Sing*) 'She's a rag shag-a-bag, she's an automatic whore.'

JUDD: Chuffheads.

RALPH: College, my arse.

LES: They came down here doing their college antics, hitting each other over the head with beer trays, dropping their trousers every five minutes.

JUDD: Like I said, one or two of them about.

LES: Justin.

JUDD: Rupert.

LUCKY ERIC: Chaps.

RALPH: Beer races, Zulu warriors. It was like bloody bonanza down here by the time they'd finished. Chairs all over the bloody place. We had to call the cops; let them deal with the maniacs.

ALL: (*Chanting in an upper-class accent*) Jolly boating weather, fa la la la la ...

RALPH: Supposed to be bleeding educated.

LES: And then one of these awful pickets threw a stone at the policemen's horsey.

LUCKY ERIC: No.

LES: Yes.

RALPH: Animals to a man. Style, no style. (*Indicating himself*) Style. And they thought it was funny. I remember talking to one of them.

(JUDD, LUCKY ERIC *and* LES *become the students.* RALPH *has to deal with them.* JUDD *stands on a beer barrel. The students are preparing for a beer race. They line up to perform the beer race.*)

LUCKY ERIC: Here we go, Justin. Beer race. *Un, deux, trois.*

LES: My go . . .

(LUCKY ERIC *and* LES *drink and pour beer over their heads.*)
Now your turn, Justin . . . oh, he's fluffed it. Get them down, Justin.

(JUDD *'Justin' has fluffed the exercise and consequently has to take his trousers down to the Zulu warrior song.*)

LUCKY ERIC *and* LES:: 'Get them down, you Zulu warrior, get them down, you Zulu chief . . .'

(RALPH *approaches to sort them out.*)

RALPH: Oi!

JUDD: What, my good man?

RALPH: Leave it out.

JUDD: Leave what out?

RALPH: You know what I mean, just leave it out.

JUDD: Relax, friend, we are only having a bit of a laugh.

RALPH: It's not funny.

JUDD: Relax.

RALPH: Don't do it.

ALL: (*Sing*) 'When you want to go to it . . .'

RALPH: I said, it's not funny. Now you and your mates can just get out.

JUDD: Excuse me, sir, but are you addressing me?

RALPH: Yes.

JUDD: I object to your tone.

LUCKY ERIC: Ditto.

LES: Ditto.

RALPH: Where are you from?

JUDD: St Luke's.

ALL: Ra!

RALPH: St Luke's what?

ALL: Ra!

JUDD: Christ, mate, we're a college. St Luke's.

ALL: Ra!

JUDD: We're on a rugby tour. Been playing Cheltenham.

LES: Ra!

JUDD: Not Ra. Rotters.

LES: Oh, sorry. Rotters, rotters.

JUDD: You know what it's like, get a stinking skinful, piss in a bucket and try and get one of the drunken chaps to drink it.

LES: Well done, rotters.

RALPH: I think that you've had enough, don't you? Come on, out you go.

JUDD: Don't touch me . . .

RALPH: Look, don't start it . . .

JUDD: Don't touch me or there'll be a bloody riot in here tonight.

> (RALPH *hits the student. We come out of the scene and he addresses the bouncers.*)

RALPH: I couldn't help it. He was just provoking me, so I let him have one. A hip throw. That's what started it.

LES: Animals.

JUDD: They have these special nights, you know. Rugby clubs. Sex and all that, live.

LES: Yeah?

JUDD: I thought of joining.

LUCKY ERIC: I was just thinking.

JUDD: What with?

LUCKY ERIC: My brain, Judd, up here. Where you keep budgie food and dubbin. I've got a brain.

JUDD: You ought to be on *Mastermind*, Eric, if you've got a brain. Fancy having a brain and doing this job. At this rate you're going to end up on *Krypton Factor* or sommat.

LUCKY ERIC: And at this rate you're going to end up on a life support, Judd.

LES: Leave it out, Eric.

RALPH: You're very tetchy, Eric.

LUCKY ERIC: Oh, yeah?

RALPH: Yes. You're very very tetchy.

LES: What were you thinking about, Eric, with this brain that you've got?

LUCKY ERIC: I was just thinking: women.

LES: Oh, yeah, and what about them?

LUCKY ERIC: They're weird!

LES: They're not as weird as having a beard up your arse.

RALPH: What on earth are you trying to say, Eric?

LUCKY ERIC: Different attractions. Strange.

JUDD: What's strange about women?

LUCKY ERIC: They laugh at you when you're naked.

RALPH: I was just thinking as well. I mean, where is everybody? I'm freezing to bloody death out here. Why's that?

JUDD: Because it's cold.

RALPH: Because nobody's turned up yet, so let me get me hands on somebody, warm them up a bit.

JUDD: They'll all be gerrin' some beer down their bloody necks, stood about in plush pubs, slopping beer down 'em. Either that or they're watching the bloody telly, come down here about half eleven, tight-fisted sods.

LES: It's still early.

RALPH: I'm going inside in a minute.

(LUCKY ERIC *has been gazing into the night*.)

LUCKY ERIC: Look at them lights, look at all those lights.

JUDD: 'The City by Night', by Lucky Eric, 'An Artist's Impression'.

LES: Piss artist.

LUCKY ERIC: Them lights are like people, just like people's lives.

LES: What's he on about?

LUCKY ERIC: Them flats, people live in them flats.

JUDD: He's a bloody genius, you know.

LUCKY ERIC: Couples, huddled together in one or two rooms.

RALPH: Mom, he's nicked me Meccano.

LES: Shut up.

LUCKY ERIC: Carrying out relationships.

JUDD: Aye aye, here we go. Getting round to sex.

ALL: *No, no, no . . . Yes!*

LUCKY ERIC: In them flats, somebody'll be having a shag right now.

(*Pause, while the idea sinks in.*)

LES: Lucky bastards . . .

LUCKY ERIC: All over the world people will be dying, and conceiving children and growing vegetables and shagging.

LES: Lucky bastards.

RALPH: Don't let it get to you, Eric.

LES: Don't get depressed.

LUCKY ERIC: And we're stood here out in the cold like four daft pricks.

LES, RALPH *and* JUDD: (*Shouting*) Lucky Eric's first speech!

> (*The three bouncers fade into the background as the lights dim and a spotlight comes up on* LUCKY ERIC. *He delivers his speech with total sincerity.*)

LUCKY ERIC: The girls are young. Some look younger than the others. It worries me. It does. I'm not thick. You think that we're thick. We're not. *I'm not*. Got to be eighteen. I turn a blind eye. We live by rules but we all turn blind eyes. I don't know whether or not it's a good thing . . . still at school half of them. They come down here Friday, Saturday, saving up all week the money they've earned working part-time in the super-market. What else is there? With their made-up faces, floating about on a cloud of Ester Lauder, wearing Impulse and footless tights, or flashing wrinkle-free flesh, of schoolgirl knicker dreams, flesh of sunburnt leg; hairless leg, shapely, untouched by human hand, leg. I sweat a lot. Wouldn't you? Two drinks and they're going; legs opening to any particular denizen of the night with car keys and Aramis-splashed face, maybe even Old Spice. Drunken, free, giddy, silly girls, wanting to be women, done too soon. Vulnerable, cruel world the morning after, or the month after when the curse hasn't taken its spell! I wanna touch them, squeeze them, keep them safe. Smell like pomander, a lingering smell. Pure and dirty, innocent and vulgar; it all withers, washes away. Eighteen going on thirty-five, because they think they've got to, because they're forced to . . . I dunno.

> (*Lights come up and the other bouncers take up their positions and start to talk once more – all as if the speech had never occurred.*)

JUDD: Ever had any strange sex, Leslie?

LES: No. Never.

RALPH: I have. I've had some of that.

LES: Yeah? What was it like?

RALPH: Strange.

LUCKY ERIC: I nearly had Chinky once.

JUDD: Oh, yeah. Army, was it?

ALL: 'Shun . . .

RALPH: In Malaya, was it?

(*They all make Malaya noises.*)

LUCKY ERIC: No . . . Fish and chip shop down Blenheim Terrace. Nice woman; didn't understand a word she said, though.

LES: That the language of love, Eric?

JUDD: Number 34 with rice, eh?

RALPH: 69, knowing Lucky Eric.

(*They all laugh maniacally.*)

LUCKY ERIC: Couldn't go through with it.

JUDD: Why?

LUCKY ERIC: Married.

LES: He's crazy.

JUDD: I'm in the mood tonight.

RALPH: Tell us something new.

JUDD: I could shag a rat.

RALPH: The power of the spoken word.

(*Lighting suddenly changes and loud music booms. We are transported into the nightclub.* RALPH *plays the DJ.*)

Hope that you're all having a greeeaaat time down here at Mr Cinders. Remember that on Tuesday, yes, that's Tuesday of next week, we'll be having a video special. So do come along and enjoy that extravaganza. I shall be giving away a few bottles of champagne very shortly for a number of people who are celebrating their twenty-first today; key of the door and, let's hope, key of another special place. Are there any nympho-maniacs down here this evening? Yes, there are. Well, I'll be playing something for you very soon, and it will not be a record. OK, OK, let's just stop the music for a moment, and put up your hand, yes, put up your hand if you are a virgin. I don't believe it, ladies and gentlemen, there are no virgins down here this evening. Looks like it's going to be a night to remember. This is Shalamar . . .

(*The music plays loudly. The four actors now become*

'Elaine', 'Rosie,' 'Suzy' and 'Maureen'. They pick up their handbags and walk with great dignity into the middle of the dance floor. They then all place their handbags in a pile on the floor and begin to dance around the bags to the music.)

ALL: (*With the song*) 'When you love someone, it's natural not demanding . . .'

LUCKY ERIC: Maureen – short but nice, fat but sickly.

LES: Rosie – feels a bit tiddly.

JUDD: Elaine – sweating like a racehorse, wants to sit down.

RALPH: Suzy – sexy and flashing it about a bit.

JUDD: Christ, I'm sweating.

LES: Ya what?

JUDD: I'm dripping.

RALPH: I am.

LUCKY ERIC: I feel sick . . .

RALPH: You what?

LUCKY ERIC: I feel sick.

LES: It's too warm.

JUDD: Ya what, Rosie?

LES: I feel dizzy.

JUDD *and* RALPH: Happy birthday.

LES: Shut up.

LUCKY ERIC: I think I'm gonna spew.

JUDD: Oh, isn't she pathetic?

LUCKY ERIC: Let me get to the toilet.

LES: What's she had?

RALPH: Five barley wines.

LUCKY ERIC: Hang on a minute. I feel all right now, it was just indigestion.

JUDD: (*To the audience*) And then, as if by magic, the drunken tears, and Rosie discovers twenty-firsts are not all fun . . .

LUCKY ERIC: Her boyfriend, Patrick, is seen kissing another . . .

RALPH: With several large shorts imbibed, the tears and mascara begin to run.

LES: He's left me for another, over in a dark corner snogging, and French kissing, tongue job to say the least. I feel myself get all angry and upset inside but I've already had enough drinks to fill a bath. The hate turns inside to self-pity and the tears begin to flow and with it the mascara. And soon my face looks like a miner's back in the showers, rivulets of black Max Factor. And then the friends . . .

ALL: That's us.

LES: . . . begin to comfort me and offer me advice on how and what to do.

JUDD: Burn her face off.

LES: Oh, don't be daft, Elaine.

LUCKY ERIC: Castrate the philanderer.

RALPH: Finish with him.

LES: Then the plague begins to spread, the tears begin to flow and all advice becomes sobbing woe. Look at him sitting there as cool as a cucumber. I've been going out with him for two days . . . it's pathetic.

ALL: Pathetic, pathetic, pathetic . . .

> (*Loud music comes up.*)

RALPH: I love this. I've gorra dance.

LUCKY ERIC: Oooh, it goes right through me.

RALPH: It goes right through me an' all.

LES: What hasn't?

RALPH: I heard that, Rosie.

LES: I'm sorry, Sue.

ALL: (*With song*) 'Ooh wee . . .'

> (*Lights change and we are suddenly outside the club once more.* LUCKY ERIC *and* JUDD *are the two bouncers, patrolling the doors.* RALPH *and* LES *play a variety of characters trying to enter the club.*)

LUCKY ERIC: Seems to be going quite steady.

JUDD: Yeah. Look out, a couple of young lads here.

> (RALPH *and* LES *appear on the scene.*)

RALPH: Jock.

LES: And Birdy . . . all dressed up, very smart.

RALPH: But we look a bit rough.

LES *and* RALPH: Hey, come ed, come ed.

LES: Hey!

RALPH: What?

LES: *Brookside*, yeah.

RALPH: Hey!

LES: What?

RALPH: Bleasdale, yeah.

LES: Hey!

RALPH: What?

LES: Beatles, yeah.

LES *and* RALPH: Yeah yeah yeah!

LUCKY ERIC: Evening, fellas.

LES *and* RALPH: Evening.

JUDD: Where you from?

LES: About.

JUDD: Oh, yeah?

LUCKY ERIC: Not from round about here, are you?

RALPH: No, not round about here.

LUCKY ERIC: Oh.

LES: Is there a problem?

JUDD: No, no problem.

LES: Great, we're in, come on.

LUCKY ERIC: Are you out sort of celebrating like?

RALPH: Yeah, you could say that.

LES: Yeah, we're celebrating, yeah.

LUCKY ERIC: What, a stag night, is it, lads?

LES: Yeah, that's right, a stag night.

JUDD: Sorry, lads, can't let you in.

RALPH: Why?

LUCKY ERIC: No stag night parties allowed in.

LES: You what?

LUCKY ERIC: You heard.

RALPH: Jesus Christ.

JUDD: Sorry, fellas, but rules is rules.

RALPH *and* LES: Please.

LUCKY ERIC: Go away.

RALPH *and* LES: Come ed, come ed, come ed.

     (*They go off.*)

LUCKY ERIC: Soft bastards.

JUDD: Always works.

LUCKY ERIC: Stag nights. It's always a good laugh.

JUDD: No wonder they're losing custom in here.

    (RALPH *and* LES *now become 'Mark' and 'Brian'*)

RALPH: Mark – drives a Mini, car keys in hand, open-neck shirt, even in winter.

LES: Brian – very cool, did some karate, thinks he's Bruce Lee. More tea, Mr Prize Fight?

RALPH: No, thanks, Mr Lee.

LES: Evening.

JUDD: Evening.

RALPH: Evening . . . waiter.

LES: What a marvellous joke.

RALPH: I know, and it just sort of came to me.

JUDD: Where are ya going?

LES: In there, my good man.

JUDD: Oh, yeah?

RALPH: Yeah.

JUDD: You're not.

LES: Why?

JUDD: Look, don't get clever, sunbeam.

LES: '*Look*'?

JUDD: Listen, bastard, do you want dropping?

LES: Come on then, let's go down to Tiffs . . .

RALPH: Under the circumstances, a rather good idea. Taxi.

    (*They exit*)

LUCKY ERIC: (*With mounting laughter*) Tiffs . . . Tiffs . . . Tiffs . . . It's shut!

JUDD: (*Laughing*) Shut!

    (RALPH *and* LES *enter again, this time as punks. They spread their hands above their heads to create spiky hair, spit, spew, pogo, etc.*)

Where are you punks going?

LES: In the discothèque, man.

LUCKY ERIC: Not dressed like that, you're not. Go home and change your tutu.

RALPH: Hey, man, don't mess with my tutu.

LUCKY ERIC: Don't call me 'man' . . . forkhead.

RALPH: Come on man, we're not going to cause any trouble in
    there.
        (*He spits.*)
JUDD: I know you're not cos I'm not going to let you in.
        (*He spits on* RALPH.)
RALPH: Hey, did you see that?
LES: Yes, I did, and I think it was a very good shot ... come on,
    let's go and have a pint of piss in the cesspit ...
RALPH: Hey, Ruffage.
LES: Yes, Ashley.
RALPH: *Do* you know what they are? ... they are fascist pigs ...
    they've spoilt the whole evening and I am shortly intending to
    write a song about the experience.
LES: Go on then.
RALPH: Fascist pigs.
LES: Fascist pigs.
RALPH: (*Singing*) Oh, you fascist pigs ...
LES: (*Singing*) Oh, you fascist pigs ...
RALPH: What do think of that then?
LES: They're lovely lyrics.
        (LES and RALPH *pogo off upstage. The actors suddenly
        change position so that* LUCKY ERIC *and* JUDD *become the
        lads, 'Terry' and 'Baz' and* RALPH *and* LES *become bouncers
        once more.*)
LUCKY ERIC *and* JUDD: (*Chanting*) Here we go, here we go, here
    we go ...
LUCKY ERIC: Watch these two, Terry.
JUDD: Why's that, Baz?
LUCKY ERIC: Might be a bit awkward.
RALPH: Evening, lads.
LUCKY ERIC: Evening.
LES: Are you members?
JUDD: You what?
RALPH: Members only tonight, lads, sorry.
JUDD: It wasn't members only last night.
LUCKY ERIC: Or last Friday. Play the game, fellas.
RALPH: Only pillocking, lads. In you come. Thirty-eight quid each.

JUDD: You what? Hear that, Baz?

LUCKY ERIC: It's only thirty bob.

LES: Let them in, Ralph.

RALPH: In you come . . .

  (LUCKY ERIC *and* JUDD *enter the club, and walk upstage.*)

  Why did you let them in?

LES: I'm going to do that fat one.

RALPH: You're weird, Les.

LES: Oh, yeah?

RALPH: With the greatest respect you're very weird.

LES: I know.

  (*They all now become the lads.*)

LUCKY ERIC: Baz –

JUDD: Terry –

RALPH: Jerry –

LES: Kev –

  (*They all take another imaginary pint and slop it down.*)

ALL: *Sixteen!* And a vindaloo!

LES: In the toilets –

LUCKY ERIC: Lav –

RALPH: Bog –

JUDD: Shit house –

  (*Standing upstage centre, they are in the club toilets. Each of them passes wind and there is a delight of visual scatalogical jokes. Finally, they are ready to urinate.* LES *narrates, conveying the atmosphere, while the others act out the situation.*)

LES: At about twelve o'clock, the toilets are the hell-hole of the disco.

ALL: Scenes from Dante's *Inferno!*

LES: Keeping your feet on the slippery tiled floor is a feat in itself. Many an affair has been ruined by loose footing; one quick slip and you're up to your hip in urine . . .

  (*One of the actors slips and drowns.*)

When you actually reach the urinals, your Hush Puppies are soaking, seeping through to your socks. In the urinals, there is by this time a liberal smattering of tab ends, and the odd soupçon of sick. In the sink there's probably a Durex packet, with the condoms still inside, some forgetful stud having left them. The smell is nauseous; you stand, holding your breath, trying to pee, reading the wall, trying your best not to catch anyone's eye.

LUCKY ERIC: (*Reading*) 'You don't come here to mess about so have a piss and . . .' Oh, charming . . .

JUDD: (*Reading*) 'Follow this line . . .' (*Follows a line, moving slowly.*) 'You are now pissing on your foot.'

LUCKY ERIC: 'Rearrange this well-known phrase: shit Mrs Thatcher is a' . . .

RALPH: I've got it! Mrs Shit is a Thatcher.

JUDD: Don't be stupid. It's . . . Shit Thatcher, Mrs is a . . .

LES: Here's one. 'Save water, piss on a friend.'
      (*They start to look at one another's genitals.*)

LUCKY ERIC: (*To* RALPH) What the hell is that?

RALPH: It's mine.

LUCKY ERIC: Jesus Christ!

JUDD: What's up?

LUCKY ERIC: Look at that.

JUDD: Bloody hell.

RALPH: What's the matter with you lot?

LUCKY ERIC: (*To* LES) Hey, seen this?

LES: What?

LUCKY ERIC: Look at that, I've never seen one so big.

LES: Bleeding hell . . .

RALPH: Haven't you seen one before?

LUCKY ERIC: It's like a baby's arm with an orange in its fist.

RALPH: Let's have a look at yours then.

LUCKY ERIC: Gerra way, you pervert.

JUDD: It's not natural.

LES: It is an offensive weapon. He could mug somebody with it.

RALPH: Oh, yeah.

LES: Come on, let's get back on the dance floor.

LUCKY ERIC: Do you fancy a bit of a laugh?

ALL: Yeah . . .
      (*Laughter. They become bouncers once more.*)

LUCKY ERIC: Ralph, get the kettle on ... Les, get the chocolate
  biscuits out ...
JUDD: Why?
LUCKY ERIC: It's the interval.

ACT TWO

RALPH, JUDD and LES *enter and form a line, centre stage.* LUCKY ERIC *joins the line, inspecting the audience.*

JUDD: (*To the audience*) What are you laughing at?

LUCKY ERIC: Do you think they're ready for it?

LES: No. But they're gonna get it.

> (*Loud disco music plays.* RALPH *becomes the DJ once again. The others become the lads, by now fairly drunk, attempting to dance while the DJ speaks.*)

RALPH: Yeah! Wow! Things are really happening down here tonight. Have some fun, yeah, have some fun. Tell you what, girls ... tell you what we'll do ... the first girl who brings me a matching pair of bra and knickers, yes, a pair of knickers and a bra, there'll be a bottle of Asti Spumante and a fortnight's free entry, get it, entry, to Mr Cinders. So come on girls, get them off and bring them up to me, marvellous Michael Dee, the DJ with the big B ...

> (LUCKY ERIC *plays a very drunk heavy-metal freak. He approaches the DJ.*)

LUCKY ERIC: Hey!

RALPH: I don't care what size they are, girls, as long as they are clean.

LUCKY ERIC: Hey, man!

RALPH: Yeah.

LUCKY ERIC: Hey, man!

RALPH: What's the problem, man?

LUCKY ERIC: Play sommat decent.

RALPH: This is decent.

LUCKY ERIC: Play sommat decent.

RALPH: Go away, man. Get it together.

LUCKY ERIC: It's rubbish.

RALPH: Everybody's gerrin' off on it, man, you know. I mean, what're you saying? You're talking crap.

LUCKY ERIC: It's shit.

RALPH: Well, that may be your opinion but everyone seems to be enjoying it.

LUCKY ERIC: Hey, man, ya got any Deep Purple?

RALPH: (*Over the microphone*) Bouncers to the DJ . . . bouncers to the DJ . . .

LUCKY ERIC: Hey, man, have you got any Yes?

RALPH: Who?

LUCKY ERIC: Hey, they'll do, man. I saw them at Knebworth. They've got a better stack than this tinny shit . . . how many watts have you got, man? . . . Hey get off me . . .

　　(LES *and* JUDD *appear as bouncers, ready to cart him off.*)

JUDD: Come on.

LUCKY ERIC: Tell him to put something decent on.

JUDD: Take it steady, pal.

LUCKY ERIC: Do you like Status Quo?

JUDD: No, but I like Perry Como. Now get out.

　　(*The bouncers throw him out of the club. All four now become bouncers again. They are back on the door. It is growing late. They begin to sigh heavily, looking down the road to see if anyone is coming. By now they are bored and cold.*)

RALPH: I think that the snot up my nose is frozen.

LUCKY ERIC: Very interesting.

RALPH: Aren't you cold?

LUCKY ERIC: No, I've got blood in my veins, not water.

JUDD: All fat, that's why.

LUCKY ERIC: Listen what's talking.

JUDD: That's muscle.

LUCKY ERIC: That's shit.

RALPH: That's enough.

LUCKY ERIC: Roll on two o'clock.

JUDD: Have we got any films in?

LES: Yeah. A bluey. It'll make your nose run, it's that blue.

JUDD: Where did you get it?

ALL: Video shop.

> (*Scene change to the video shop.* LUCKY ERIC *and* RALPH *are looking for videos.* JUDD *plays the shop assistant.*)

LES: Have you got any of them video nasties?

JUDD: No, no, no, no . . . Yes.

LES: Oh . . . what have you got?

JUDD: I've got *Rambo One, Rambo Two, Rambo Three* to *Thirty-seven, Friday the Thirteenth, Friday the Fifteenth, Monday the Twenty-third, October the Ninth, My Mother's Birthday, Bank Holiday Sunday* and most of the religious holidays in Three D.

RALPH: *Queen Kong*, the story of a sixty-four-foot gay gorilla.

LES: Yes, that's it, something a bit blue.

JUDD: I've got light blue, dark blue, sky blue, and navy blue.

LES: Navy blue?

JUDD: Or something with animals . . .

> (*They all grunt and gurgle like animals.*)

LES: I'll take the one with animals. The boys should enjoy this.

> (*Back outside the club.*)

LUCKY ERIC: Perverts . . .

JUDD: At two o'clock the disco shuts . . . free drinks all round.

LES: At least we've got a video now.

RALPH: Yeah, you can say that again.

LES: At least we've got a video now.

JUDD: Which beats the old projector we used to have . . . three-quarters of an hour fixing up the bloody projector. Then with sweaty hand in tight polyester, we'd watch the twitchin' and the screamin'. Like fish in a barrel, we'd fidget and jump watching plot and orifice explored.

> (*All the bouncers have a drink. They then mime setting up the projector, ready to watch the blue movie.* RALPH *and* LUCKY ERIC *act out the film.* LUCKY ERIC *plays a buxom Swede taking her clothes off, about to have a shower.* RALPH *plays the postman. Sleazy background music and strobe lights should give the scene a cinematic feel. The other bouncers provide a commentary.*)

RALPH: (*As the doorbell*) Bing bong . . .

LUCKY ERIC: Whom de iz eet?

RALPH: It ist me. Nobby, ze Swedish postmant . . .

LES: Hey up. It's Nobby, Swedish postman.

LUCKY ERIC: Come on ze in, Nobby. I'm unt der shower, unt . . .

LES: (*Excitedly*) Go on, Nobby, lad . . .

RALPH: Ver ist der usband?

LUCKY ERIC: Engagedist unt ont dert buziness . . .

LES: Husband away on business . . .

JUDD: Go on, Nob!

LUCKY ERIC: I am zo lonely wit my usband in Oslo . . .

LES: Aye, aye . . . she's lonely with her husband away on business in Oslo. I can understand that. Can you, Judd? A woman alone and all that.

JUDD: Gerron with the film.

LUCKY ERIC: Oh, I've dropped the soapen on the flooren.

RALPH: She's dropped the soapen on the flooren.

LES: She's dropped the soap.

JUDD: Go on, Nobby, my son . . .

>   (*As* LUCKY ERIC (*'Nobby'*) *is about to move the action
>   freezes as if the film has jammed. Strobe stops.*)

Give that projector a boot.

ALL: Boot!

>   (*Strobe restarts. The action is now played in reverse, as though
>   the film is being rewound, up to the doorbell ringing at the start.
>   We snap out of this scene and the actors are all bouncers again.*)

JUDD: It's not fair.

LUCKY ERIC: Porno films . . . a waste of time.

JUDD: It pays your wages.

LES: There's something wrong with a bloke who doesn't enjoy a good bluey, that's what I say.

RALPH: I think that's a fair comment, Les.

JUDD: Eric doesn't like them. He thinks it's degrading.

LES: What's degrading about it? They get paid for it. I mean, it's not exactly as if they're doing it for peanuts.

JUDD: I'd do it for peanuts. I'd do it for nothing. What a job? Eh? What a job? It's not exactly a matter of being a good actor, is it? Just get in there, get stripped off, get stuck in . . . Not a bad job, Eric, eh? Beats this shit.

LUCKY ERIC: You're an animal, Judd.

JUDD: Keep talking . . .

LUCKY ERIC: An animal . . .

JUDD: How's that?

LUCKY ERIC: Don't you know?

ALL: (*Very softly*) Lucky Eric's second speech.

>(*As* LUCKY ERIC *speaks, the others can act out the scene. Background music should play.*)

LUCKY ERIC: I'm sat in this pub, just an ordinary pub, and it's Christmas. Everybody's had one over the eight. And there's a group of lads, football supporters, that type. Eleven stone, walking about like they think they're Frank Bruno. And there's this girl, nineteen, twenty, and she's drunk, and she's got it all there, the figure, the looks. The lads are laughing, joking with her. 'Give us a kiss, eh?' and she does. Well, it's Christmas, I think, well, it is Christmas. I sat watching for an hour. She was well pissed. They all had a go, kissing her, feeling her, lifting her skirt up. Nobody noticed, pub was packed. Merry Christmas they'd say, and line up for another kiss and a feel, each one going further than the other, until I could see the tops of her thighs bare. And in that pub, she had them all, or they had her, six of 'em, in a pub. Nobody noticed, nobody noticed but me. It was a strange feeling, a weird feeling, I remember walking over to where they were. I was aroused more than ever before in my life. I'm so powerful, so powerful. I stood in front of them, looking at them. The first head was quite hard, but the others were soft, like eggs; they hit the wall and smashed. The girl stood up. 'Give us a kiss,' she said. 'Give us a kiss.' 'Go home,' I said. 'Please go home . . .'

>(*Lights come up.*)

LES: So what's the plan then?

JUDD: Inside?

LES: Yeah.

RALPH: The usual.

LES: What if there's a big fight? Rush in, eh? Get some kicks in.

LUCKY ERIC: Don't be a twat all your life, Les, have a night off.

LES: A few kicks never hurt anybody.

JUDD: Look at all those lights ... them lights are like people ... they are like people's lights ...

LUCKY ERIC: Anybody could do this job.

LES: Bollocks!

LUCKY ERIC: No, they could, it's a matter of ego.

LES: Isn't that Frankenstein's mate?

RALPH: That's Igor.

LES: Same, innit?

LUCKY ERIC: His brain's – painted on.

LES: But he's handy though, Eric.

LUCKY ERIC: I'm telling you. It's all image.

RALPH: Eric's got a point. I once heard some talk of a nightclub in Manchester that employed a woman.

JUDD: Bollocks ...

LES: Pull the other one ...

RALPH: Straight up is this. She was a big fat woman.

JUDD: I know her.

RALPH: Whenever somebody was making an arsehole of themselves, she'd go over and tell 'em not to be so stupid, tell them to pull themselves together. She never had any trouble either.

JUDD: Can't see that happening down here. She'll probably get glassed.

LES: Or picked up.

ALL: *Ha ha ha.*

> (*Inside the disco.* RALPH *becomes* '*Suzy*', LUCKY ERIC *becomes* '*Baz*', LES *becomes* '*Kev*' *and* JUDD *becomes* '*Elaine*'.)

LUCKY ERIC: It's ten past one. Baz is well gone.

LES: Kev is ready to try it on, with anyone with two legs and two tits. Two teeth, anything.

JUDD: Plain Elaine has got a pain in her head, she's ready for bed.

RALPH: Suzy is sexy, she's been flirting about.

LUCKY ERIC: What about those two? Come on let's get in, have a bash.

LES: Just gimme a sec. I'm dying for a slash.

> (LES *moves off*. LUCKY ERIC ('*Baz*') *now walks up to the girls.*)

LUCKY ERIC: Now then, girls, all right, are we?

JUDD: Piss off, fatty.

LUCKY ERIC: You can't get around me that easy.

JUDD: You're ugly.

LUCKY ERIC: That's nice . . . What's your name?

RALPH: Suzy. I'm drunk, you know?

LUCKY ERIC: Wanna have a dance?

RALPH: What about my friend?

LUCKY ERIC: I've got a mate, he's just gone for a slash, he'll be back in a dash. Come on, shall we go? . . .

JUDD: Hey, I hope I'm not gonna be left here?

RALPH: I'm only going for a dance, Elaine, that's all.

> (LUCKY ERIC *and* RALPH *move upstage as if to the dance floor and freeze.* LES *comes back from the toilet and is faced with* JUDD *('Elaine').*)

LES: Where's Baz?

JUDD: Is he fat?

LES: A bit.

JUDD: He's just got off with my friend.

LES: The lucky gett! Go on, pole it. He always gets the pretty ones.

JUDD: D'you wanna dance?

LES: Who, me?

JUDD: Come on, I like you.

LES: Gerroff me.

> (*Both couples now take up a smooching position. They begin to think aloud.*)

LUCKY ERIC: God! She smells great, her chest's really warm. I can just about feel her arse. I think she's drunk. Oh no, I'm gerrin' a hard on. She's rubbin' herself against me.

> (LUCKY ERIC *moves his body in order to dance away from* RALPH *('Suzy').*)

RALPH: I don't know where I am, I'm sinking and spinning, round and round, round and round . . .

JUDD: So am I.

LES: This is bad news, I hope nobody sees me. I think Terry's drunk anyway. She's strong is this one. She's breaking my bleeding back. I just hope that she doesn't fall over. I can feel her fat.

JUDD: If he makes a move or tries anything with me I'll break his arms. He's nice and cute though, I'll say that much. I think he likes me . . .

LES: She is the ugliest girl I've ever met . . .

LUCKY ERIC: I think I've pulled a cracker this time . . .

RALPH: I'll let him take me home but I'm not having sex.

LUCKY ERIC: I bet she goes like a rabbit.

LES: I hope she doesn't try and kiss me. I'll spew.

LUCKY ERIC: Wait while I tell all the lads.

RALPH: His breath smells awful, I think he must smoke.

LUCKY ERIC: Yes, I'm in here, no trouble.

RALPH: He's really too big, a bit of a joke. He's not what I'm after, not handsome and slim. I'll tell him I'm going to the loo, that should lose him . . . I'll have to nip to the toilet.

LUCKY ERIC: You what?

RALPH: I've got to go to the toilet.

LUCKY ERIC: What for?

RALPH: Don't be nosy.

LUCKY ERIC: Don't be long, will yer?

RALPH: You wait here, don't move. I'll be back in a tick.

LUCKY ERIC: Right.

> (RALPH *walks away from* LUCKY ERIC. LUCKY ERIC *freezes as he looks at his watch*.)

LES: Listen.

JUDD: What?

LES: I'll have to go now.

JUDD: Why?

LES: I should have turned into a pumpkin ten minutes ago.

JUDD: Oh, yeah.

LES: Look, can you let me go please . . .

JUDD: Give me a kiss first . . .

LES: I can't.

JUDD: Why?

LES: I've got something that I don't want you to catch.

JUDD: What's that?

LES: Me, I've got a terminal disease.

JUDD: You haven't, you're only saying that.

LES: Like fuck I am!

JUDD: You're stopping here with me or I'll chop your face off . . .

LES: Oh, Christ . . . get off, you old bag.

ALL: (*Shout*) *Fight!*

> (*They all now dash to the centre of the stage, as bouncers and lads, grab each other and generally give the impression that there is a fight going on.*)

LUCKY ERIC: Come on, you two. Leave it out. Get them out, Judd. Fire exit.

JUDD: Let's do the bastards.

LUCKY ERIC: Let's just get them out.

JUDD: I'm going to do mine.

LUCKY ERIC: Don't.

JUDD: Who are you talking to, Eric?

LUCKY ERIC: You, you daft bastard.

JUDD: Oh, yeah.

RALPH: Hey, no need to fight over us, lads.

LUCKY ERIC: Piss off . . . There's no need to do them over, just leave them. They're pissed up anyway.

JUDD: Who do you think you are, Eric?

LUCKY ERIC: Nobody.

JUDD: You get up my back.

LUCKY ERIC: Look, Judd, don't set me off.

JUDD: You weird bastard!

LES: How weird?

LUCKY ERIC: I said, don't set me off.

JUDD: You shouldn't be doing this job. You should be bouncing at Mothercare. You're soft.

LUCKY ERIC: (*Now quite manic*) Don't set me off.

JUDD: Soft inside.

LUCKY ERIC: Don't set me . . .

JUDD: Soft bastard . . .

> (*This is now too much for* LUCKY ERIC *to take. He attacks* JUDD *with a finger.* JUDD *quivers. Suitably violent music comes up as all the bouncers suddenly become psychopaths for a few seconds. They all stop dead.*)

LUCKY ERIC: Sorry, Judd. Sorry.

ALL: Lucky Eric's third and final speech.

(*A spotlight picks out* LUCKY ERIC.)

LUCKY ERIC: We have these 'Miss Wet T-shirt' and 'Miss in String' evenings. Eighteen-year-old beauties displaying their orbs through string vests or firm outlines on wet cotton, naked, some of them, save their skimpy knickers. All of them somebody's daughter – mothers, some of them. And the glossy Polaroids on the doors outside show more hideous topless antics. Breasts in beer glasses. Breasts smeared in shaving foam. Breasts oiled and on show. And Michael Dee, the DJ, kisses and sucks as if they were his own. Slimy bastard. I see the girls selling themselves for five minutes' fame. I can see the staid state of exploitation. I can even smell the peaches of their under-arm roll-on. The working class with no option left, exposing its weakness. I feel very sad ... I feel very protective. I might pack it all in. I might pack it all in, fuck off and go and listen to Frank Sinatra.

ALL: Come on, Eric ... that's enough ...

(*Blackout. We return to disco.* RALPH *plays the DJ.*)

RALPH: Someone has just handed me a piece of paper from the dance floor and on it, it asks me to dedicate this record to Sharon and David, who are out there getting it together. So tell him you love him, Shaz, and tell her you love her, Davs. After all, a little white lie never really hurt anyone now did it? ... But let's be serious for a moment, shall we? All of you girls out there tonight at Mr Cinders, later on when you're really getting it together, spare a thought for me and for our doormen who couldn't even pull a muscle. They'll certainly be going home lonesome tonight ...

LUCKY ERIC: You're dead, pal.

RALPH: Just having a joke, Eric ... so remember me, marvellous Michael D, your love doctor ...

ALL: Jerry – Terry – Kev – Baz –

(*The bouncers become the lads. It is now getting late, they are very drunk, and making efforts to pick up a girl ... Five minutes until the club closes.*)

RALPH: I was right, you know?

LUCKY ERIC: What d'you mean?

RALPH: There are only ugly 'uns left at two o'clock.

LUCKY ERIC: I had one, but she walked off.

LES: Was she drunk?

JUDD: Must have been.

LUCKY ERIC: Thanks.

LES: What about them four, over there?

RALPH: You what? She must weigh about seventeen stone.

LUCKY ERIC: Better than nothing.

LES: She'd eat me.

JUDD: She'd eat us all.

LUCKY ERIC: What do you say to someone that big?

LES: Sod off. You're big.

JUDD: Sod off, ya pig.

OTHERS: No no no. He said big . . .

JUDD: Sod off, ya big pig . . . it wasn't me that said that, it was me brother . . . and I haven't even got a brother . . .

LES: You have, he's in *Star Trek* . . . You're right, you know, there are only scrag ends left at two o'clock.

JUDD: Sod you lot, I'm game.

ALL: And me.

(*The lads begin to dance with imaginary women.*)

RALPH: Hey, you don't sweat much for a big girl, do you?

LUCKY ERIC: Can I borrow your face? I'm going ratting tomorrow.

LES: Do you want a drink? The bar's over there.

JUDD: Give us a kiss, come on . . .

RALPH: Didn't I used to go to school with you?

LES: Does your dad race pigeons . . .?

LUCKY ERIC: Does your shit stink?

ALL: Ooohh.

(*Slowly the lads change back to the bouncers. It is closing time and the bouncers encourage people to leave, see them off, etc.*)

LUCKY ERIC: Good night.

LES: Night, love, take care.

JUDD: Good night.

RALPH: Night . . .

LUCKY ERIC: Take it nice and steady.

LES: (*Looking at an imaginary woman*) Look at the arsehole on that.

RALPH: She's had a skinful . . .

JUDD: She's got handles on her hips.

(LES *becomes a punter, leaving the disco.*)

LES: I've had a great night, fellas . . . I've had a wonderful evening.

LUCKY ERIC: Come away from him, mate.

LES: Does anyone know where I can get another bottle of champagne?

LUCKY ERIC: You've had enough.

LES: Just one more bottle of champers, and everything will be tickety tickety boo.

JUDD: Tickety tickety fucking boo.

RALPH: Nut the posh bastard.

JUDD: . . . Nut.

LES: Good night. (*As a bouncer*) Yeah, goodnight, sir.

JUDD: Watch this, I'll nut him.

LUCKY ERIC: Good night.

RALPH: Have a safe journey home.

(LES *becomes a bouncer once more.*)

LES: Good night. She's down here every night is that one.

JUDD: I thought I'd seen her before.

LES: She's been hanging around me like flies round shit.

LUCKY ERIC: You said that, Les, not us . . .

LES: I think she's after something.

RALPH: 'Eat shit. Five million flies can't be wrong.'

LES: What?

LUCKY ERIC: Nice to hear that old one again. Good night, love . . .

ALL: Good night . . . Good night . . . Good night . . . Good night . . . Good night . . .

JUDD, LUCKY ERIC *and* RALPH: (*As lads*) Here we go, here we go, here we go . . .

(*Change of scene to an empty shopping precinct.* LUCKY ERIC *becomes the owner of a hot-dog stand. The other bouncers play the lads.*)

LUCKY ERIC: Hot dogs. Hot dogs with onions. Beefburgers. Cheeseburgers. With or without onions. Hot dogs . . .

(*The lads approach the stand.*)

Right then, fellas. What d'you want? Hot dogs? With or with-

out? Cheeseburger? With or without? Or with red or brown
sauce?

LES: Two pints of lager, please.

LUCKY ERIC: Oh, oh, well, we have got a little joker here, haven't
we?

RALPH: Do you do pizzas?

LUCKY ERIC: Very funny.

JUDD: I'll have a kebab. Got any kebabs?

LUCKY ERIC: Yeah. I've got some kebabs.

JUDD: I'll have a kebab.

RALPH: Yeah, and I'll have a kebab.

LES: And me . . .

JUDD: Three kebabs.

LUCKY ERIC: With onions?

JUDD: Yeah. Three with onions.

   (LUCKY ERIC *mimes putting sausages into hot-dog rolls.*)

LUCKY ERIC: Three quid, lads.

JUDD: Great stuff.

LUCKY ERIC: You want sauce?

RALPH: Quick service, innit?

LES: Yeah.

LUCKY ERIC: You want any sauce?

JUDD: Chilli?

LUCKY ERIC: Red or brown?

RALPH: Hey. This ain't a kebab. It's a hot dog.

LUCKY ERIC: Listen. If I say it's a bleeding kebab then it's a
bleeding kebab. Right?

ALL: Right, boss.

LUCKY ERIC: Now sod off!

   (*Scene change to the lads now waiting for a taxi.*)

   Baz –

JUDD: Terry –

RALPH: Jerry –

LES: Kev –

ALL: Waaaaaaaaaaay!

JUDD: Have you seen the length of this taxi queue? I'm friggin'
freezin'.

LES: I wish I'd've put a big coat on.

RALPH: Oh, no, look at that . . . I've got spew all over me shoe.

LES: I have.

JUDD: I have.

LUCKY ERIC: I've got shit on mine.

ALL: Waaaaayyyy!

JUDD: Innit dark?

LES: Well, it is half past three.

JUDD: Half past bloody three and we're stood out in the cold, freezin' to bloody death.

LUCKY ERIC: Just think, *if* I'd've got off with that Suzy I'd be in bed now snuggling up to her brown, tanned, sunburnt, soft body.

ALL: Whaaaaaaaaaaaaaaay!

LES: Innit quiet? All asleep, and tucked away in their little boxes. Innit quiet? Listen, listen to the city. Quiet, innit? All those people asleep. It's like being in a painting.

LUCKY ERIC: I'm dying for a slash.

RALPH: Do you feel pissed up?

JUDD: Who?

RALPH: You?

JUDD: (*Considering the possibility*) No. Not now.

RALPH: No, I don't.

JUDD: I did about an hour ago. I've sobered up. I think.

LES: It's the cold.

LUCKY ERIC: I'm having a slash.

   (*He begins to urinate.*)

LES: (*Pretending a taxi is approaching*) *Taxi!*

LUCKY ERIC: Oh, shit! (*He attempts to do up his flies.*)

LES: Only a joke.

JUDD: I've spent thirty-five quid.

RALPH: Yeah?

JUDD: Jesus Christ, I've spent thirty-five bleeding quid.

RALPH: I have.

JUDD: That had to last me till Wednesday.

LUCKY ERIC: Feel better after that slash.

JUDD: Thirty-five quid! I didn't even get a kiss or a feel of tit. Pissing hell, I'm depressed.

RALPH: We all are.

LES: (*To audience*) Another social comment?

JUDD: No, no. Keep it going.

LES: All right, it's up to you ... I've spent forty quid – next week's board money. My mam'll have a fit.

LUCKY ERIC: I've spent ... er ... I've forgot what I came out with. I've only got thirty-seven pence left.

JUDD: Yeah, but thirty-five quid.

RALPH: (*Hailing a taxi*) Taxi! St John's flats ... Waaaaaay!

LES: Hey, look, it's them four birds!

(*Whoops of delight as the taxi arrives. They mime getting into the taxi and it screeches off. They sit moving as though in a car. One of the lads lights a cigarette and begins to smoke. One of the others begins to feel sick.*)

RALPH: I feel sick.

(*The actors convey the sensation that the car is speeding away and taking corners at fast speed.* RALPH *begins to retch.*)

Tell him to stop.

LUCKY ERIC: I want another slash.

RALPH: Tell him to stop or I'm gonna be sick.

JUDD: (*As though to the driver*) Will you stop? He says he's not stopping cos it might be a trick.

LUCKY ERIC: A trick? What's he want me to do? Rupture my bladder?

LES: I feel a bit spewy. Tell him to slow down.

RALPH: Tell him to stop.

JUDD: I've told him.

LES: Let some air in here. It's like a wrestler's jockstrap.

(LUCKY ERIC *urinates out of the window. It all blows back into the others' faces.*)

LUCKY ERIC: I'm doing it out of the window.

LES: Don't be so bloody stupid.

LUCKY ERIC: Hey, lads, I'm slashing out of the window ...

RALPH: Errm ... I've been sick down his back.

JUDD: Window ... dick *shut!*

(*He shuts the window.*)

LUCKY ERIC: Aaaargh!

(*The car suddenly screeches to a halt.*)

ALL: Home.

(*Scene switches back to the bouncers at the club.*)

RALPH: Look at the bleeding mess.

LUCKY ERIC: Animals.

(JUDD *sings nonsense into the microphone.*)

LES: Look at the amount of beer that's been left. A waste is that, waste.

(*They stand around contemplating the mess.*)

JUDD: Shall we get packed away and get the video on?

LUCKY ERIC: Eager tonight, Judd, aren't you?

JUDD: I wanna see the filth.

LUCKY ERIC: You are too sensitive, Judd, that's your problem.

RALPH: Look at the mess. Hey, there's a pair of knickers over here.

LES: Keep 'em, they might fit you.

JUDD: I'll give you one pound twelve for 'em.

LUCKY ERIC: Have you seen the bogs?

LES: What's wrong with them?

LUCKY ERIC: Two urinals cracked. It's all over the floor.

JUDD: What is?

RALPH: (*Still rummaging around*) Anybody want a basket meal? One here, still warm.

LUCKY ERIC: Ah, ah . . . look at this.

LES: What?

LUCKY ERIC: Another fiver.

JUDD: Jammy bastard.

LUCKY ERIC: That's four nights on the trot.

RALPH: That's why they call him 'lucky' Eric.

JUDD: Are we gerrin' the video on or what?

LUCKY ERIC: He is a pervert.

RALPH: Well, I don't know about you lads, but I'm shagged.

LES: And me.

JUDD: I wish I was.

LUCKY ERIC: I wish you was and all, Judd.

RALPH: Innit peaceful? Listen how quiet it is.

JUDD: My ears are still buzzing.

LUCKY ERIC: My brain's buzzing. I'm going deaf.

LES: You what?

LUCKY ERIC: I said ... Oh, very funny, lads. You lads are definitely on the ball at this late hour.

JUDD: Hey, are we gerrin' this chuffin' video on or what?

LES: Yeah. Ralph, get some cans and we'll have a couple of hours. Are you stopping, Eric?

LUCKY ERIC: I'm not a pervert.

JUDD: Look what I just found.

LUCKY ERIC: What?

JUDD: A ten pence piece ... Come on ... Look, he's dying to stop.

LUCKY ERIC: No ... I'm gonna get off home.

JUDD: Just watch the first bit.

LUCKY ERIC: No, I'm not stopping.

RALPH: Come on, Eric, spoil yourself.

LES: Yeah, come on.

LUCKY ERIC: No, I ...

JUDD: Come on, man ...

LUCKY ERIC: Well, OK. I'll stop for the first three hours.

JUDD: Right. Where's that video with animals in it? Gerrit on!

LES: All right, Judd.

> (*They put on the imaginary video. It is Michael Jackson's* Thriller. *Music comes up and the lights fade to green, as the bouncers all don monster's teeth. They proceed to do a complicated rip-off of the* Thriller *video; moving forwards and backwards, grotesquely slouching their shoulders, clapping their hands, etc. Note: the* Thriller *video should be carefully studied in order to achieve just the right elements of parody. Eventually the lights come up and the music stops. The rap music from the start of the play comes up once more.*)

ALL: I SAID A HIP HOP

A HIPPY A HIPPY

A HIP HIP HOP AND DON'T YOU STOP

DOWN AT THE DISCO WAS THE PLACE TO BE

THE LIGHTS WERE SO BRIGHT LIKE A COLOUR TV

THE MUSIC WAS LOUD AND THE BEER FLOWED FREE

IT WAS A DISCO PLACE FOR YOU AND ME

NOW ON THE DOOR YOU PAID YOUR MONEY

THE PLACE WAS PACKED THE PLACE WAS FUNNY
YOU SAW THE GIRLS
MMMMM ... SMELLED THEIR HONEY
THEIR HEADS WERE HAZY
THEIR LIMBS WERE LAZY
AND ALL THE YOUNG GIRLS DANCE LIKE CRAZY
COME ON
BUT NOW IT'S OVER YOU GOTTA GO HOME
THERE IS NOWHERE ELSE TO ROAM
BE CAREFUL HOW YOU WALK THE STREETS
THEY'RE THE MEANEST STREETS IN THE WHOLE DAMN
    PLACE
COME ON
WELL FRIDAY NIGHTS AND SATURDAYS TOO
WE'LL BE DOWN HERE, YES, WITH YOU
AND YOU
AND YOU
AND YOU ...

LES: Thank you and good night

> (*Music comes up as the bouncers take their bow. They then usher out the audience much in the same way as they greeted the audience at the start, improvising suitable comments.*)

TEECHERS

A Classroom Comedy

AUTHOR'S NOTE

Teechers was designed to be played by three actors, multi-role-playing twenty other parts in a play-within-a-play format. Everything about the production was reduced to the basic essentials: actors, stage, audience. I wanted to produce a play that relied on the same bare essentials that a drama teacher might have in school: kids (actors), a few chairs and desks (the set), and an audience. With these basic ingredients anything can happen in a drama lesson; indeed the characters in *Teechers* illustrate that once talent has been tapped in school the result is often staggering. Multi-role-playing is also, it must be said, an economic as well as an artistic consideration. Maybe if I had twenty actors at my disposal I would have produced a different play? In this version of the play the twenty multi-roled parts have been listed in order that twenty actors (kids) could perform the play if so desired. However the play is performed, actors or students, it is important to remember that *Teechers* is a comedy, a comedy that illustrates many anxieties in education today. Comedies must primarily be funny; here is a comedy, I think, which is also deadly serious.

The set

Nothing is required in the way of a set except for three plastic briefcases, old newspapers for the staff-room scenes, a broom for Doug, and two chairs and two open-top desks for the various other settings, all of which should be easily obtained in school. When produced by three actors, character differentiation is helped by the use of funny noses (which the kids would have bought cheaply from W. H. Smith's). Clearly, when the play is produced with a larger cast a proportional increase in props is to be expected.

The music

Any incidental music in the play should be contemporary chart music.

CHARACTERS

SALTY   A school-leaver, bright and fresh-faced, rather dirty in appearance

GAIL   Loud-mouthed and bossy, attractive and full of enthusiasm

HOBBY   Shy. Should be very large, must be bigger than the other two. She is doing the play despite herself

NIXON   New drama teacher, young and casual

MRS PARRY   The headmistress, large and loud, a real eccentric

MR BASFORD   The deputy head, a typical child-hater, a nasty piece of work

MISS PRIME   Dolly bird of a PE mistress

MS WHITHAM   A fussy and hopeless teacher, desperate to leave

MS JONES   A moaner, rather fat, someone who wants to leave but no one will employ her

DEANIE   A teacher who thinks all the kids love him, a bad dancer

DOUG   The caretaker, a miserable old man, he hates kids and drama

OGGY MOXON   The cock of the school, looks much older than he actually is, the school bully in a modern age

PETE SAXON   A large, frightening youth with tattoos, appears foolish

MR FISHER   Head of PE

BARRY WOBSCHALL   A small boy who never brings his PE kit

PIGGY PATTERSON   A boy who is always telling on others. He always runs to his lessons

RON   A boy who never does PE

MR HATTON   Helps with the youth club dance

DENNIS   Oggy's side-kick

MRS COATES   Headmistress at St George's

MRS CLIFTON   Head of Governors at St George's

TEACHER A
TEACHER B

The action takes place in a comprehensive school hall.
The time is the present.

Teechers was first performed by the Hull Truck Theatre Company at the Edinburgh Festival 1987, with the following cast of characters:

SALTY
    also playing TEACHER B, NIXON,   Martin Barass
PETE SAXON, OGGY MOXON, MR
FISHER, MR HATTON, DEANIE

GAIL
    also playing TEACHER A, MS   Gillian Tompkins
WHITHAM, OGGY MOXON, MR
BASFORD, MISS PRIME, BARRY
WOBSCHALL, DENNIS, DOUG,
MRS COATES

HOBBY
    also playing MRS PARRY, MS   Shirley Anne
JONES, MR BASFORD, RON, PIGGY   Selby
PATTERSON, OGGY MOXON, MRS
CLIFTON

Directed by John Godber

ACT ONE

A comprehensive school hall.

A wooden stage. There are two double desks upstage. Upstage right is an old locker with a school broom leaning against it. Downstage centre is a chair; left and right two single desks and chairs angled downstage, and three bags. A satchel, plastic bags and sports bags are near the chairs and desks. They belong to SALTY, GAIL *and* HOBBY *respectively.*

Some music plays and SALTY, GAIL *and* HOBBY *enter, recline on the chairs and desks and look at the audience for a moment before speaking.*

SALTY: No more school for us, so you can knackers!

GAIL: Salty, you nutter.

SALTY: What?

GAIL: Swearing.

HOBBY: Shurrup.

SALTY: So what?

HOBBY: You daft gett.

SALTY: It's true.

GAIL: Just get on with it.

SALTY: Nobody can do us.

HOBBY: We've not left yet.

SALTY: Knackers.

GAIL: Oh, God, he's cracked.

HOBBY: Shurrup.

SALTY: I've always wanted to be on this stage. I've always wanted to come up here and say, 'knackers'. I bet you all have. Whenever I see Mrs Hudson come up on this stage to talk about litter or being a good samaritan or corn dollies or sit down first year stand up second year I think about that word. Cos really Mrs Hudson would like to come up here and say, 'knackers school'. She would.

GAIL: Are we doing this play or what?

SALTY: It's like when she gets you in her office, all neat and smelling of perfume, and she says, 'You don't come to school to fool around, Ian, to waste your time. We treat you like young adults and we expect you to behave accordingly. I don't think that writing on a wall is a mature thing to do.'

HOBBY: That's good that, Salty, just like her.

SALTY: Yeh, but really she wants to say, 'Hey, Salty, pack all this graffiti in, it's getting on my knackers.'

GAIL: Are we starting?

SALTY: Anyway, why am I bothered? No more school, no more stick, no more teachers thinking that you're thick . . .

GAIL: No more of Miss Jubb shouting like you're deaf as a post, 'Gail Saunders, how dare you belch in front of me.' Sorry, miss, didn't know it was your turn . . .

HOBBY: Brilliant . . .

SALTY: Hey, no more full school assemblies sat on the cold floor of the sports hall freezing your knackers off . . .

HOBBY: No more cross-country running, and cold showers and towels that don't dry you.

GAIL: Oh, and no more scenes in changing rooms where you daren't get changed because you wear a vest and everyone has got a bra . . .

HOBBY: No more Mr Thorn sending letters home about how I missed games and was seen eating a kebab in the Golden Spoon.

GAIL: No more sweaty geog teachers with Brylcreem Hush Puppies.

SALTY: No more trendy art teachers, who say, 'Hiya' and, 'Call me Gordon' . . .

HOBBY: We haven't had an art teacher called Gordon.

SALTY: I know.

GAIL: No more having to run the fifteen hundred metres with a heart condition.

SALTY: No more.

HOBBY: Cos today we're off. Twagging it for ever.

GAIL: Let's start, Salty.

SALTY: Hang on, before we do start, we all want to thank Mr Harrison, our new drama teacher. Before he came to this

school, last September, us three didn't do sod all, not a thing.
He got us into this, he's good bloke. You are, sir. I know that
he's been offered a job at a better school . . . Well, good luck to
him . . . Before Mr Harrison came here, the teachers had given
us up for dead . . . We were average.

HOBBY: Lillian is average. She opens her book well, and likes a
warm room.

GAIL: Gail is stagnant to inert, and fights when cornered. Average.

SALTY: I don't feel average today. I feel top of the class . . . thanks
to sir.

HOBBY: I never thought I'd be doing this. I hated drama, only took
it for a doss about . . .

SALTY: Right, don't forget to keep in character, and, Hobby, always
face the front.

HOBBY: I will do.

GAIL: And speak up.

HOBBY: I will do.

SALTY: A lot of the stuff in the play was told to us by Mr Harrison . . .

GAIL: And even though you might not believe it, everything what
happens in the play is based on truth.

HOBBY: But the names and the faces have been changed.

SALTY: To protect the innocent.

GAIL: We're going to take you to Whitewall High School. It's a
comprehensive school somewhere in England . . . And they're
expecting a new teacher to arrive.

HOBBY: There's fifteen hundred kids at Whitewall and it's a Special
Priority Area which means that it's got its fair share of problems . . .

SALTY: All we want you to do is use your imagination because
there's only three of us, and we all have to play different
characters . . .

HOBBY: And narrators . . .

SALTY: And narrators.

HOBBY: So you'll have to concentrate . . .

SALTY: Oh, yeh, you'll have to concentrate . . .

GAIL: Title . . .

SALTY: Oh, shit, yeh . . . And it's called *Teechers*.

(*A sudden burst of music. They become teachers, with briefcases and files, walking about a number of corridors. The lights become brighter.*)

Morning.

GAIL: Morning.

HOBBY: Morning.

SALTY: Morning.

HOBBY: Morning.

GAIL: Morning.

PARRY: Stop running, Simon Patterson.

TEACHER A: Morning, Ted.

PARRY: Morning, Roy.

TEACHER B: Morning, Mr Basford

ALL: Morning, Mrs Parry . . .

PARRY: Good morning . . .

WHITHAM: You are chewing, girl, spit it out. Not into her hair, into a bin . . .

TEACHER B: I don't call that a straight line, do you, Claire Dickinson? No? Neither do I.

PARRY: I know that was the bell, Simon Patterson. The bell is a signal for me to move and not for anyone else.

(*Music.*)

NIXON: I'm Jeff Nixon, the new drama teacher. I'm looking for Mrs Parry's office.

HOBBY: Up the steps in the nice part of the school, first left.

(SALTY *exits.*)

GAIL *and* HOBBY: (*Together*) Mmmmmmmmmm.

GAIL: He doesn't look much like a teacher, he looks like somebody who's come to mend the drains.

(SALTY *enters as* NIXON.)

NIXON: I knew at my interview that Whitewall had a bad reputation and no drama facilities. But like a sheriff with my brand-new degree pinned to my chest I bounded up to Mrs Parry's office . . . She was busy . . . With Mr Basford, the Deputy Head.

(GAIL *dons a facial mask, nose and glasses, which all the cast wear as* MR BASFORD.)

BASFORD: I don't believe you're doing this.

PARRY: I run it and I shall do what I like.

BASFORD: After all the work I've put in, now you turn around and tell me that I'm not Coco . . . Great. It's a bloody liberty.

PARRY: Mr Basford, I'm sorry . . . But there is nothing else to say . . . I need a younger person. I'm sure you'll have a great deal of fun in the chorus.

BASFORD: In the chorus. I wouldn't be seen dead in the chorus.

PARRY: It's that or nothing, good day, I have another appointment. Mrs Parry, or should I say Cordelia Parry, BA, M.Ed., was a huge attractive women. She carried herself very well but had awful dress sense, and would often mix pink with yellow. She was of large frame with a voice to match. Mr Nixon? Jeff Nixon?

NIXON: That's right.

PARRY: Hello, nice to see you again. Coffee?

NIXON: Please. Mrs Parry's office was a cavern of theatre posters . . . She certainly had more than a passing interest.

PARRY: Drama! Bare boards and a passion. Wonderful. This is my all-male production of *The Trojan Women*, and this is me as Ophelia.

NIXON: Behind her head was a photo of a much lither Mrs Parry in an amateur production of *Hamlet*.

PARRY: I'm doing *The Mikado* in the spring term, Mr Nixon.

NIXON: I knew exactly what she meant.

PARRY: I'm looking for a Coco . . .

NIXON: It must be difficult.

PARRY: Mr Basford usually takes the leads in our local G. and S. productions but I'm afraid he was rather tiresome last year in *The Pirates* . . . We're looking for new blood . . . Well, that's given you something to think about, hasn't it?

NIXON: It certainly has.

PARRY: And so to business, Mr Nixon.

NIXON: The meeting went on for another twenty minutes, but I got the message. Keep an eye off for the teacher-eating girls and the thuggish boys . . . they'll have you for breakfast.

GAIL: But one thing struck him about Mrs Parry. She really did care about the kids at Whitewall.

PARRY: As we walked from my office, that is Mrs Parry's ... I wished Jeff all the luck with his probationary year, and took him towards Mr Basford's room, home of the timetable. Here we are.

NIXON: The gigantic timetable was screwed to the wall. It was so colourful, so meticulous, it was a work of art, like something from the Vatican. A life's work had gone into making it.

PARRY: The nomenclature is fairly straightforward. You will be N.I., Mr Nixon, and drama will be D.R. As you'll be having your lessons in the Main Hall, drama with you in the Main Hall, would read N.I.D.R.M.H. If you have a first-year class it could read, N.I.D.R. M.H.I.Y.X. Period one. Fairly simple.

NIXON: Elementary, Mrs Parry.

PARRY: If you have any problems at all, Jeff, don't hesitate, come up and see me straightaway, I'm always available. And don't forget about *The Mikado*. I know how much the theatre must be in your blood ... It could be your big break ...

NIXON: So I tentatively said 'yes', to a small part in the chorus, and although Mrs Parry was disappointed that I didn't want Coco, she said that I would certainly enjoy my time in Titipu.

A corridor.

GAIL: Excuse me, sir?

NIXON: Eh?

GAIL: Sir, I'm lost.

NIXON: Well, where should you be?

GAIL: Sir, I don't know, I can't work it out on my timetable. I'm in tutor group I.D. But I'm in teaching group I.Y.5 and I should be in block 4.3.B doing biology. But 3.Y.Y.6 are in there with Mr Dean doing history. He says that I should be in 3.1.D but I've been there and the class is empty. Sir, I've been looking for my class for forty minutes.

NIXON: What have you got next?

GAIL: PE in the gym.

NIXON: Do you know where that is?

GAIL: Yes, sir.

NIXON: Well, I suggest that you go and wait there, then at least your class'll find you.

GAIL: Right. thanks, sir . . .

NIXON: Oh, before you go. Have you any idea where 9.I.B is?

A pause. We are now in the form room.

HOBBY: When you're a hard nut and fifteen you always have to give teachers a bad time. It's part of the rules of the game . . . And when there's a new teacher you can be even tougher. In our class we have seen off three tutors in as many weeks.

GAIL: Miss Bell had a breakdown, but said she was pregnant.

HOBBY: Then we had a supply teacher who was always crying . . .

GAIL: And then they sent old Mr Willcox who was deaf so that was a laugh, we used to say anything to him.

HOBBY: And now they've sent us a new teacher. A brand new, sparkling clean, not even out of the box teacher . . .

TEACHER A: They're only going to be in school for two more terms . . . Send them the new bloke Nixon . . . He can cut his teeth on 7.Y.Y down in 9.I.B . . . It's out of the way – if they eat him or burn him alive we can forget about him.

SALTY: In 7.Y.Y there was me, Salty, Gail and Hobby who you know, Kevin Mears – who spoke funny . . . All right, Kevin?

GAIL: Not bad, Salty, all right . . . I've been down to our Malcolm's, he's got a brilliant BMX. We had a great game of rally cross.

SALTY: Kev was fifteen going on three. There was John Frogett who never wore any decent shoes.

GAIL: Sally Wrenshaw.

HOBBY: Vicky Marshall.

SALTY: Walter Jones.

GAIL: Fancy calling a kid Walter . . .

SALTY: And Trisha Foreshore who had been through nearly all the kids in the school . . . except me.

GAIL: Salty, that's not true . . .

SALTY: It is.

GAIL: It is not.

SALTY: Right, you ask Benny Good.

GAIL: I wouldn't ask Benny Good what the time was . . . He's a big mouth and a liar . . .

HOBBY: Oh, come on, get on with it.

SALTY: And Trisha Foreshore who was known, but it might not be true, as being a bit of a goer.

GAIL: That's better.

HOBBY: When they sent you a new teacher, it was like getting some foster parents ... When Nixon arrived we were bored and disinterested.

NIXON: Hi ... Is this 9.1.B? I'm Mr Nixon ... It's a bit chilly in here, isn't it? Can you two lads come down from the book-shelves. I don't think that they were meant for sitting on, were they? If you don't mind – just come down. And if you could stop playing table tennis that would also help. Can everybody sit on a seat and not on a desk? That's better ... Right ... My name is Mr Nixon.

(*Gail and Hobby laugh.*)

The entire class burst into laughter. I didn't see that I'd said anything funny. My name is fairly straightforward and I've only got one head. I turned to the blackboard and saw that some joker had drawn some enormous genitals on the board. I looked at the class, they were still laughing. 'Bollocks' is not spelt with an 'x'.

HOBBY: I don't like him.

GAIL: You've got to give him a chance.

HOBBY: Why, do you like him?

GAIL: No, but ... We even gave Miss Bell a chance.

HOBBY: He's trying to be too smart ... I hate teachers who call you by your nickname.

GAIL: Yeh, but you hate being called Lillian. Everybody calls you Hobby.

HOBBY: So what, that's no reason why he should, he's new.

(*A school bell rings. Each actor goes to a desk, as kids. They address the audience as staff.*)

A number of classrooms.

WHITHAM: Right, quieten down, quieten down, said Maureen Whitham, scale two humanities, as she pathetically tried to control a class of thirty. Please be quiet. If you don't keep quiet I'll have to get Mr Basford ... Be quiet ... Shut up ... Hush ... Shhh!

NIXON: As I walked through the maze of a school I heard and saw many different types of teaching.

WHITHAM: Please, don't throw the books about, it's one between three, now everyone be quiet ... BE QUIET.

NIXON: It was like a menagerie.

(HOBBY *becomes* MR BASFORD.)

BASFORD: Nobody speaks in Mr Basford's lessons. That's why I have the best maths results in the school. Nobody talks, you can't work and talk, nobody can, not even me, and I'm a genius.

NIXON: Most classes had some sort of noise coming from them.

WHITHAM: Right, said Maureen Whitham, as she hopelessly tried to settle her class ... I'm going to get Mr Basford ... Oh ... Silence, that's better.

NIXON: Mr Basford's class worked in absolute silence, with absolute commitment. He also had the best kids.

BASFORD: Don't let the bastards grind you down, hit 'em low and hard ... low and hard. Kids respect discipline. If they don't get it at home, they get it in my lessons. Hush down ... I can hear someone breathing ...

The main hall.

NIXON: I arrived at my first lesson five minutes late. I'd taken a wrong turn at block 1 and found myself in the physics block ... A fifth year non-exam drama group lounged about some stacked chairs in the main hall. Sixteen of them had managed to turn up. Twenty-five names were on the register. The school hall looked like a youth club; I walked purposefully to the stage.

GAIL: Oh, God, it's him, Dixon.

HOBBY: Got him for tutor and for drama.

GAIL: What's happened to Mrs Hugill?

HOBBY: Left. I hate drama. Only did it for a skive.

GAIL: Yeh and me. It was this or music. Got any cigs?

HOBBY: They wouldn't let me do music, said I was too clumsy. I've got two Woodbines, my granny's.

GAIL: Buy a tab off you at break?

NIXON: Get a chair, I said, in a friendly, sort of youth worker type of tone.

HOBBY: What's he say?

NIXON: Grab a chair, everyone.

GAIL: We're not doing any work, are we, sir?

NIXON: Can you grab a chair . . .

GAIL: I'll give you some crisps if I can tab you . . .

NIXON: Can you all please get a chair and come and sit around the stage in a half-circle.

HOBBY: How long have you been smoking?

GAIL: About four months.

HOBBY: Why don't you buy some bastard cigs then?

GAIL: I am going to do.

HOBBY: When?

GAIL: Tomorrow.

NIXON: Can you get a chair and stop waving them around? I know I just said get a chair but I didn't expect you to swing it around your head.

HOBBY: If I tab you and you don't bring any cigs, I'll drop you . . .

GAIL: I will, honest . . . Honest, I will . . .

NIXON: Get a chair and sit on the BASTARD.

GAIL: What's he say?

HOBBY: Dunno.

NIXON: Will everyone please sit on a chair?

GAIL: Who's he think he is?

HOBBY: Are you going to bio or are you twagging it?

GAIL: Is she here?

HOBBY: Her car's here. It's that red 'un.

GAIL: I'm off downtown then, get a milk shake.

NIXON: When everyone is ready . . . Good . . . I think it would be a good thing for us to start with a very important person in the world of drama. Mr William Shakespeare. And in particular a play that you've probably seen but don't realize it. *Romeo and Juliet*.

> (GAIL *and* HOBBY *groan.*)

Which is a tragedy.

GAIL: And it's the basis for *West Side Story*, and it's about neighbours arguing.

HOBBY: We've done it . . .

NIXON: Oh . . .

HOBBY: We did it with Mrs Hugill.

GAIL: And we did about two tramps who're waiting for somebody and he never turns up.

HOBBY: And that was boring.

GAIL: And we've done *Hamlet*. About a prince who kills his uncle. Haven't we?

HOBBY: Yeh. And two killers who are after somebody and one of 'em's a deaf and dumb waiter.

GAIL: And we've done *Beverly Hills Cops. Beverly Hills Cops Two* . . .

HOBBY: *Neighbours* . . .

GAIL: *Eastenders* . . . 'Hello, Arfur . . .' 'All right, my love.'

HOBBY: Good that . . .

GAIL: What else have we done?

HOBBY: *Indiana Jones*.

GAIL: Yeh. *Jewel of the Nile* . . . We've done all there is in drama . . .

NIXON: At that moment, a giant of a lad, Peter Saxon, stood up. He must have been six feet seven, with tattoos on his arms and a line across his neck which read, 'Cut here.' 'I wanna say something,' he said. 'I've got some drama to tell you . . .' 'Go on then, Peter,' I said, not knowing what to expect . . .

(*He becomes* PETE SAXON.)

Right, I'm Peter Saxon now . . . One day, sir, last year, it was great. Me and Daz Horne decided to run away, to seek our fortune. We was going to go to London. It was a Tuesday, I think. But it could have been a Thursday. No, no, it was a Tuesday, cos we had Mr Cooper for technical drawing. Mr Cooper's soft, sir, you can swear at him and all sorts, we used to call him 'gibbon head', cos he had a bald head and looked like a gibbon. Anyway, me and Daz are in his class and I throws a chair at him, so he goes and hides himself in a store room, so me and Horney lock him in the store room, and then we get a chair and stand on it and look at him through the window in the top of the store room, and I keeps shouting 'gibbon head' to him . . . Anyway, then we twags it and gets a bus to the station. I couldn't stop laughing, sir, honest, just the picture of gibbon head sat in that store room killed me off. Anyway, Horney says that we've got drama with Mrs Hugill before dinner, so we comes back to do our drama lesson. In drama we did 'different visions of hell'. I was a cyclops and Horney was my mam. Anyway, me and Horney got into stacks of trouble. But I liked doing plays when Mrs Hugill was here . . . Sir, as far as I know, sir, Mr Cooper is still locked in the store room . . .

GAIL: He's a liar . . .

NIXON: That was good, Peter. The kids had raw potential, but I had to get them into plays. They were a funny bunch, but I think they liked me, and I liked them. Whitewall wasn't so bad.

GAIL: Sir? Can we do *E.T.*?

HOBBY *and* GAIL: (*Together*) E.T., phone home . . .

(*Music.*)

The staff room.

NIXON: After the first month I was beginning to feel fairly confident. And I also had my eye on Jackie Prime, PE mistress.

PRIME: Jackie Prime was tall, sun-tanned, bouncy and an expert at netball and tennis . . . She was developing dance in the gym and took an interest in all games.

NIXON: Morning.

PRIME: Morning.

NIXON: How did the first eleven get on?

PRIME: Lost sixty-seven nil. St George's team are in a different class . . . and Oggy Moxon, our captain, was sent off for spitting.

NIXON: Who's Oggy Moxon?

PRIME: He's the best player we've got. But he's a handful.

NIXON: I see.

PRIME: Have you tasted the coffee? It's like something brought back from a field trip.

NIXON: It was eight pence and was forced down you by Madge the tea lady.

PRIME: We have our own kettle in the gym. For PE staff only.

PARRY: Morning.

TEACHER A *and* TEACHER B: (*Together*) Morning, Mrs Parry.

PARRY: Morning, Mr Nixon. I hope you're still thinking about *The Mikado*. I wouldn't want your mind to wander on to other things.

NIXON: Don't worry, Mrs Parry, I'll be at rehearsals.

PARRY: Good, Mr Nixon. Good. Did you know Whitewall has a farm?

PRIME: Well, it's not actually a farm, Mrs Parry, we do have a pig.

PARRY: My dear Miss Prime, we have a number of pigs.

PRIME: One's an old sow.

NIXON: And geese?

PARRY: Two geese.

NIXON: I was doing duty around the back of the canteen, I was attacked by the geese ... But I have discovered how to avoid the smokers, simply look the other way.

PRIME: Look, I must go, I've got baths. It's fairly obvious where the kids are going to smoke, and if you want to catch the smokers you can, but if I was you, I wouldn't go behind the sports hall ...

NIXON: Why?

PRIME: That's Oggy Moxon's patch. All the staff leave Oggy well alone.

NIXON: And then she left. She was a breath of fresh air ... A bubble in an otherwise flat brew ... Oh, God, I was becoming infatuated with Jackie Prime.

GAIL: But Jackie Prime didn't see Nixon as anything at all. When she looked, he wasn't there, he was just another teacher and she was being sociable.

JONES: You can't sit there, that's Marcus's seat.

NIXON: What about over here?

JONES: That's someone's seat. Frank Collier's.

NIXON: Oh, right. Is this anyone's paper?

WHITHAM: Yes. It's Deanie's, he's on the loo.

NIXON: I can't share a cheek on the edge of that, can I, Mavis?

JONES: Sorry, Jeff.

NIXON: Even after seven weeks finding a regular seat in the staff room was a nightmare. I was told by Mr Dean that a lot of new staff preferred to stand outside in the rain. Mr Sawyer had been

at Whitewall's for two years and not ever got a seat in the staff
room.

WHITHAM: I do not believe he is doing this. Look at the timetable,
Basford's gone bananas.

NIXON: I longed to be down in the gym and have a cup of tea with
Jackie Prime. But – it was a forlorn fantasy.

WHITHAM: The man does not care, he just doesn't care.

JONES: What's the matter, Maureen?

WHITHAM: I'm on cover for Mick Edwards's remedial English group.
I hate them. I do. I hate that group.

JONES: I know what you mean. I've just had Trisha Foreshore. If
that girl says 'I'm bored, miss' once again I'll ring her soddin'
neck.

WHITHAM: But they hate me, he knows they do. It's not fair.

JONES: Do you know what she says? We're looking at the digestive
system, and she says, 'Miss, the oesophagus is one long tube
running from mouth to anus.' I said, 'Very good, Trisha, how
did you find that out?' She says, 'Miss, I went to the dentist
and he looked in my mouth and he could tell that I'd got
diarrhoea.' I said, 'It's pyorrhoea, girl, pyorrhoea, bleeding
gums . . .' I give up on some of 'em, I really do.

WHITHAM: Remedial English. He knows I've got a doctorate and he
puts me on remedial English.

NIXON: There was another big fight at breaktime. Silly sods.

(*Music.*)
Back of the sports hall.

GAIL: The cock of Whitewall High was Bobby Moxon, known to all
and sundry as –

SALTY: – Oggy Moxon.

GAIL: There was no doubt at all that Oggy was dangerous, all the
teachers gave him a wide berth. He was sixteen going on
twenty-five. Rumour had it that he had lost his virginity when
he was ten and that Miss Prime fancied the pants off him.

HOBBY: When Oggy Moxon said 'shit', you did. When he said it was
Wednesday, it was Wednesday.

GAIL: One Wednesday, I was stood outside one of the mobile

classrooms. Mr Dean had sent me out of the class. I'd told him that I thought Peter the Great was a bossy gett! And he sent me out. I'm stood there with a mood on when Oggy comes past.

(SALTY *becomes* OGGY MOXON.)

OGGY: All right, Gail?

GAIL: Yeh. I knew that he fancied me.

OGGY: What you doing?

GAIL: Waiting for Christmas, what's it look like?

OGGY: I'm having a party in my dad's pub, wanna come? Most of the third year is coming. Should be a good night.

GAIL: Might come then.

OGGY: Might see you there.

GAIL: Might.

OGGY: Wear something that's easy to get off. Your luck might be in.

GAIL: I hate him.

HOBBY: I do.

GAIL: Somebody ought to drop him.

HOBBY: Who? All the staff shit themselves when they have to teach him.

GAIL: Oggy Moxon's speech about being hard: I'm Oggy Moxon ... We said you'd have to use your imaginations. I'm Oggy, I'm as hard as nails, as toe-capped boots I'm hard, as marble in a church, as concrete on your head I'm hard. As calculus I'm hard. As learning Hebrew is hard, then so am I. Even Basford knows I'm rock, his cane wilts like an old sock. And if any teachers in the shitpot school with their degrees and bad breath lay a finger on me, God be my judge, I'll have their hides. And if not me, our Nobby will be up to this knowledge college in a flash. All the female flesh fancy me in my five-o-ones, no uniform for me never. From big Mrs Grimes to pert Miss Prime I see their eyes flick to my button-holed flies. And they know like I that no male on this staff could satisfy them like me, cos I'm hard all the time. Last Christmas dance me and Miss Prime pranced to some bullshit track and my hand slipped down her back, and she told me she thought that I was great, I felt that arse, that schoolboy wank, a tight-buttocked, Rebok-footed, leggy-arse ... I touched that and heard her sigh ... for me. And as I walk my last two terms through these corridors of sickly books and boredom, I see grown men flinch and fear. In cookery one day my hands were all covered with sticky paste, and in haste I asked pretty Miss Bell if she could get for me an hanky from my pockets, of course she would, a student on teaching practice – wanting to help, not knowing my pockets had holes and my underpants were in the wash. 'Oh, no,' she yelped, but in truth got herself a thrill, and has talked of nothing else these last two years. Be warned, when Oggy Moxon is around get out your cigs . . . And lock up your daughters . . .

(*Music.* GAIL *and* HOBBY *pick up a chair each; they are about to put the chairs on the desks at the end of a lesson.* NIXON *puts on his coat. They buttonhole him, they want to talk to him. He hangs around, really wanting to be elsewhere.*)

GAIL: Sir, are teachers rich?

NIXON: (*As if in anguish*) Noooo!

GAIL: What about Mrs Parry, she's got a massive car?

NIXON: She might be, but I'm not.

HOBBY: Are you married, sir?

NIXON: (*Another difficult response*) No. Next question.

(HOBBY *and* GAIL *try to think of another question which will have the effect of keeping* NIXON *talking to them. Meanwhile he picks up his briefcase.*)

GAIL: Sir, is this a school for thickies?

NIXON: Why?

GAIL: Cos when we're going home, all the kids from the posh school, St George's, ask us if we can add up, and they ask us if we've got any table-tennis homework.

HOBBY: Sir, all the kids who go to that school are snobs . . . Their dads drive big cars . . .

GAIL: And they call us 'divvies' . . .

HOBBY: Sir, because they go there they think they're better than us.

GAIL: And, they say our teachers are shit. Oh, sorry, didn't mean to say that.

HOBBY: Mr Basford's sons go there, don't they?

GAIL: Yeh, two twins. 'Twinnies' they're called. They're right brainy . . . Sir, have you got a girlfriend?

NIXON: Not at the moment.

GAIL: Brilliant.

HOBBY: Do you like it at this school, sir?

NIXON: Yeh, it's OK. You lot are awkward, but OK.

HOBBY: Sir, what do you think it's most important for a teacher to
do?

NIXON: Well, I think a teacher should have a good relationship, if
he hasn't got a relationship he can only ever be a teacher, never
a person.

GAIL: What about Mr Basford, he hasn't got a good relationship
with the kids . . .

NIXON: Well, I can't speak for Mr Basford, can I?

HOBBY: Sir, the bell's gone . . .

NIXON: You'd better go and get it then – and go quietly. (*A
pause.*) It was a trip to see *The Rocky Horror Show* that got me
really close to those three, although I had to watch my step
with Gail, she kept putting her hand on my leg during the sexy
bits.

HOBBY: Science fiction . . . Whooooo. Double Feature.

GAIL: Doctor X has built a creature.

(HOBBY *becomes* MR BASFORD.)

NIXON: Mr Basford, you wanted to see me?

BASFORD: Mr Nixon, I understand you took a group of fifteen-
year-olds to see a play featuring transvestites from Transylvania?
I can imagine what educational value that has.

NIXON: A black mark from Basford. Mrs Parry had omitted to tell
me about the joys of doing cover. Usually a student would
appear like the ghost of Caesar and present you with a pink slip,
this would tell you where to go and who to cover for. Mr
Basford was in charge of the cover rota.

BASFORD: Nixon N.I. to cover for Fisher F.I. third-year games . . .
And the best of luck.

The gymnasium.

PRIME: All right, all third-year deadlegs from Mr Fisher's group
shut up, said Miss Jackie Prime. If you want to watch the 1974
World Cup Final on video go to the lecture theatre with Mr

Clarke's group. Those who want to play pirates in the gym get changed, you without kit better see Mr Nixon.

HOBBY: A whole line of kids wearing anoraks came forward. Mr Nixon looked staggered, he'd been left to deal with PE's cast-offs.

GAIL: And amongst the throng was the legendary Barry Wobschall. Barry never did sport. He hated games.

HOBBY: Barry was fifteen but had the manner of an old man. He lived with his grandad and spoke with all the wisdom of someone four times his age. Every day for the past two years he had worked on a milk round.

NIXON: Where's your kit?

RON: Sir, my shorts don't fit me.

NIXON: What about you?

PIGGY: Sir, my mother put my shorts in the wash and they got chewed up because the washer has gone all wrong . . .

NIXON: Oh, yeh.

PIGGY: It's true, sir, honest.

NIXON: What about you, Barry Wobschall, have you got any kit?

BARRY: No, sir.

PIGGY: He never brings any kit, sir.

NIXON: I wasn't asking you, was I, Simon Patterson?

PIGGY: No, sir.

NIXON: What about a note, Barry? Have you brought a note?

BARRY: Sir.

NIXON: Oh, let's have it then.

GAIL: Barry handed him the note. It was small and crumpled. Barry looked in innocence as Nixon opened the piece of paper.

(GAIL *hands* NIXON *a piece of paper.*)

NIXON: (*Reading*) 'Please leave four pints and a yoghurt this Saturday.'

BARRY: It's the only note I could get, sir.

NIXON: I tried to talk Barry Wobschall into changing his options. His sort of humour in a drama class would have been dynamite. But he wouldn't change, he said he preferred doing geog, because it was peaceful and he liked copying maps.

GAIL: On the thirteenth of October Jackie Prime was at the GCSE meeting held at St George's. She was walking around the quadrant. A choir singing.

(*A choir sings.*)

NIXON: It's beautiful.

PRIME: There's been a grammar school here since 1912.

NIXON: It's just a different world. I hear they're opting out.

PRIME: It's very likely. They've got a fantastic drama studio, dance facilities.

NIXON: If they opt out they'll charge fees. It'll be like a private school.

PRIME: They say that they won't, but maybe they will. Only time will tell.

NIXON: Mr Basford's kids come here.

PRIME: You sound surprised . . . And Jackie Prime was off, into St George's gymnasium.

NIXON: It was fantastic. There was something reassuring about St George's that made you want to teach there. Something soothing and academic. The same, I was beginning to think, could not be said of Whitewall.

(*The choir stops.*)

Back of the sports hall. GAIL *as* DENNIS *and* HOBBY *as* OGGY MOXON, *are flicking through a magazine.*

DENNIS: Where did you get it?

OGGY: My dad gets 'em delivered in brown-paper parcels . . .

DENNIS: 'S have a look.

OGGY: It's disgusting . . .

DENNIS: What is, what is?

HOBBY: Oggy had stolen one of his father's dirty magazines, for fifty pence third years could have a quick look. For a quid first years could have a glance.

GAIL: It was break and Oggy and Dennis are sharing a few cigs and a finger through Oggy's dad's magazine.

NIXON: What're you doing, lads?

OGGY: Nothing . . . I'm Oggy.

NIXON: Well, you're obviously doing something.

OGGY: No, we're not.

NIXON: You're not smoking, are you?

DENNIS: No.

OGGY: What if we are?

NIXON: It'll stunt your growth, you know?

OGGY: So what?

NIXON: What have you got there?

OGGY: A book.

NIXON: I know it's a book.

OGGY: It's my dad's so if I was you I'd leave it with us.

NIXON: Well, I think that I'm going to have to report you.

OGGY: Good. You do that.

NIXON: You know what that means, don't you?

OGGY: Yeh, I'll get kicked out of school with any luck. Great. I don't want to be here, anyway.

GAIL: By this time a massive crowd had gathered. Various voices shouted, 'Smack him, Oggy. He's only a drama teacher.'

NIXON: I think you'd better come with me to see Mr Basford.

OGGY: Big deal, he's not going to do anything.

NIXON: Oh, really?

OGGY: Yeh, really.

NIXON: Well, we'll see about that. I might have to deal with you myself.

OGGY: What you gonna do, sir? Pretend I'm a tree?

NIXON: I'm going to have to report you.

OGGY: That's tough of you, why don't you have a go with me now, just me and you?

NIXON: I'm going to have to report you.

OGGY: You do that, sir . . .

NIXON: And I turned and walked away, with kids jeering and shouting in the background. And very faintly I heard Oggy Moxon say . . .

OGGY: You wanker . . .

NIXON: It was my first horrific confrontation. I'd played it all wrong . . . I couldn't deal with Oggy. And if I couldn't, who I thought was fairly streetwise, what about Mrs Grimes, or Julie Sharpe, or those nice quiet supply teachers who never have a wrong word for anyone?

HOBBY: As Nixon walked back to report Oggy, he started to think about getting out of teaching. He started to wish his probationary year away.

NIXON: I wasn't talking to you. I was talking to Paul Drewitt, now will everyone hush down? I shalln't say it again. All right, we'll wait till everyone's quiet before we go home.

PIGGY: Sir, the bell's gone.

NIXON: I know the bell's gone, Simon Patterson, and I'm not bothered, I can stay here, all night!

(GAIL *exits. Music.*)

The drama club.

NIXON: During September I held drama club in the school hall after four o'clock. Salty, Gail and Hobby were regulars, we did all sorts of work. But it didn't really meet with the approval of Doug, the caretaker.

(NIXON *and* HOBBY *play some witch scenes from* Macbeth. GAIL *as* DOUG *the caretaker enters.*)

DOUG: Come on, let's have you, Niko, time to go home. I thought you lot were withdrawing good will? Come on, it's half five, let's have you. Time to go find a space somewhere else.

NIXON: Just five more minutes, Doug?

DOUG: No, come on . . . I've got this floor to buffer. Mrs Parry's got a *Mikado* rehearsal tonight for principals. And I've got the mobiles to do for night class, and then the sports hall, cos five-a-side's on tonight. And somebody's gone crackers in the sixth-form bogs . . .

NIXON: Just give us a few more minutes, Doug . . .

DOUG: A few more minutes? Bloody hell, where would I be if I gave all the staff a few more minutes?

NIXON: Come on, Doug, don't be such an ogre.

DOUG: I'm asking you to leave, that's all.

NIXON: But it's the manner of it . . .

DOUG: I've got to get this buffered, that's all I'm bothered about . . .

NIXON: It's taken me ages to get these interested in doing a play – do us a favour, give me another twenty minutes . . .

DOUG: I can't, Mr Nixon . . . We're short-staffed . . . I've got three
cleaners off and Jim's back's playing him up . . . I'm only doing
my job.

NIXON: I'm only trying to do mine.

DOUG: Look, you don't get paid for this, get yourself off home . . .

NIXON: I bet you wouldn't get Basford out of his office . . .

DOUG: You should have a proper room for this drama thing. I
mean, doing it in the hall, it's a disgrace . . . Sometimes I can't
get a shine on the floor, I have to polish it . . . And that's a
bloody job.

NIXON: If you can tell me, Doug, where there is any morsel of
space for me to do drama I'd be happy to move. Is there . . .
Eh?

DOUG: Well, it's not worth bloody doing.

NIXON: There isn't anywhere . . . I've got the main hall and that's
it.

DOUG: If you ask me they should take it off, the bloody timetable, I
mean, they don't do any writing, make as much noise as they
bloody like, waste of Education Authority's bloody money if
you ask me.

NIXON: You silly old sod, you don't know what you're talking about.

DOUG: That's swearing, nobody swears at me, I don't get paid to be
bloody sworn at. Wait till I tell Mr Basford.

(DOUG *moves upstage. Music.*)

The staff room.

NIXON: Thursday, November the ninth. Staff room. One of my
biggest fears was that I was teaching the wrong book at O level.
I had been doing *Twelfth Night* for ten weeks when I heard a
rumour on the grapevine that the actual set book was *A
Winter's Tale*. Mr Basford put me right on that, he also put me
right on some other things.

(HOBBY *becomes* MR BASFORD.)

BASFORD: I hear that you've had a bit of a run in with Doug. Don't
upset the caretakers, Jeff, they do a great job.

NIXON: I suppose we're all trapped in the same system. Kids. Staff.
Caretakers. How are your lads doing at St George's?

BASFORD: Fine.

NIXON: You live out that way?

BASFORD: Me? No. I live down Greenacre Parade.

NIXON: That's this school's catchment area.

BASFORD: That's right.

NIXON: Why didn't they come to this school?

BASFORD: (*After a pause*) St George's gets people into Oxford.
Thirty per cent get five or more O levels, that's why. Fifteen
per cent get four here at Whitewall. Parents have the right to
choose schools, and I'm choosing.

NIXON: But St George's is ten miles away . . . It must cost a fortune . . .

BASFORD: I'm making sure my kids have the best possible education.

NIXON: And you can afford it. What about kids like Gail Saunders,
can their parents pay for them to travel to St George's? No.
They can't even afford to pay out for a school trip . . .

BASFORD: So what am I supposed to do, make my lads disadvan-
taged because others are? Waken up, Jeff. Parents have a right
to send kids to the school of their choice.

NIXON: And kids have a right to a good education regardless of
whether their parents have the ability or willingness to choose
for them. You know as well as I do that a lot of parents don't
attach a great deal of importance to education, that doesn't
mean that we ditch their kids . . .

BASFORD: Listen, Mr Nixon . . . When you have any family, what
will you want for your kids? Will you want them to do drama,
let's say, in an old hall with no facilities and books that are
Sellotaped together or would you prefer they worked in an
atmosphere where everything was new, and you could have
what you wanted? You think about what you'd really want.

NIXON: But that's not the point. Surely all schools should be the
same, have the same facilities, have the same cash, cash made
readily available. Shouldn't we want the best for all kids, not
just those whose parents can pay to send them to a good school
whether it be fees or bus fare? All kids deserve the right to be
educated to their potential.

BASFORD: And that's the sort of system we have now. A grade-six kid is grade-six potential.

NIXON: That's bullshit and you know it. Examinations are a framework that we fit kids into.

BASFORD: Do not talk to me like that, Mr Nixon.

NIXON: And don't talk to me like that, you bloody fascist . . .

BASFORD: I knew what you were as soon as I saw you.

NIXON: What are you talking about?

BASFORD: You know what I'm talking about, I'm talking about *The Mikado*.

NIXON: What about it . . . ?

BASFORD: Eight years I've been in that society . . .

NIXON: And then he stormed off . . .

WHITHAM: You've had it now, said Maureen Whitham, scale two humanities, as she sat listening and thumbing through the *Times Ed*. Old Basford will make your life a misery, he'll have you on cover from now till eternity. Nobody calls Basford a fascist and gets away with it. The man's dangerous, I'd be careful tackling him. He's done a lot for the school. And after all they're his kids, he can do what he likes . . .

NIXON: I felt that I was wrong, that we shouldn't have a fair system, that we should let bright kids get bright and treat the less able kids like rhubarb, keep them in the dark and shit on 'em. And everywhere I looked I could see the difference between dog piss in Hobby's grandma's garden and garden parties and degrees at St George's. And the truth was that the garden party was what I wanted . . . Whitewall was killing me, sapping me, frustrating me – wearing me down . . . As Christmas approached I fell into a deep depression, I had 200 first-year reports to do, O level marking and the Christmas carol concerts meant that I couldn't get in the hall to teach.

WHITHAM: Hey, Jeff, have you seen the *Times Ed*? Scale two going at St George's. Starts summer. A level theatre studies, drama studio . . . Video equipment . . .

NIXON: No, I'm not into that.

WHITHAM: Oh, you're not planning to stop here, are you? Everybody's trying to get out. They call this place Colditz at the County Hall. Don't be a mug, Jeff, when you see a hole in the

fence go for it. I've got an interview coming up, in local radio
... Here, I'll leave it with you.

HOBBY: Mr Nixon?

GAIL: Sir?

HOBBY: Can I go to matron?

SALTY: Look, come away from the gas taps.

HOBBY: Sir?

SALTY: Just find a space.

GAIL: Sir, she's hit me.

HOBBY: Sir, I haven't.

SALTY: Find a space.

GAIL· Sir, she has.

HOBBY: When will we be back in the hall?

SALTY: Find a space!

GAIL: Are we doing the *Marat–Sade*?

HOBBY: Can I go to matron?

GAIL: Are we doing *Billy Liar*?

HOBBY: Sir, she's taken my pen.

GAIL: Sir, I haven't.

HOBBY: Sir, she has, sir.

GAIL: Sir, I haven't.

HOBBY: Sir, she's taken my book.

GAIL: Sir, I haven't.

HOBBY: Sir, she's taken my partner.

GAIL: Sir, I haven't.

HOBBY: Sir, she's taken my glasses.

GAIL: Sir?

HOBBY: Mr Nixon.

GAIL: Sir?

HOBBY: Niko?

GAIL: Jeff?

HOBBY: Hey.

GAIL: You.

HOBBY: Sir.

NIXON: (*Shouting*) Right! Everybody, hands on heads, and fingers
on lips.

(*Music. Blackout.*)

ACT TWO

Christmas time at Whitewall's.

The broom is stuck upside down in an upstage desk. Trimmings, a star and a piece of crêpe paper adorn the broom, which is now a Christmas tree. SALTY, GAIL *and* HOBBY *take time putting up the tree.*

GAIL: Christmas at Whitewall and love was in the air. All over the school there were Christmas trees and cards and trimmings, and every breaktime we would queue up to snog Martin Roebuck under some mistletoe in the reference section of the library.

HOBBY: Christmas also saw the culmination of Gail's interest in Mr Nixon.

GAIL: I love him . . .

HOBBY: You don't.

GAIL: I do . . . I am infatuated . . .

HOBBY: What's it feel like?

GAIL: Brilliant . . . I was on his table for Christmas dinner . . .

HOBBY: Yeh, but does he love you?

GAIL: Dunno, but I'll find out at the Christmas dance . . .

HOBBY: Why, what are you going to do?

GAIL: Snog him . . .

HOBBY: *Oooooohhhh*, you're not . . .

GAIL: I'll need some Dutch courage but I am . . .

HOBBY: I don't believe it . . .

GAIL: Listen, I've got it all worked out. We go to the off-licence, you go in and buy some cider.

HOBBY: Why me?

GAIL: Then I'll bring some spring onions from home. We'll drink the cider then eat the spring onions.

HOBBY: Spring onions, why?

GAIL: Because Doug and Mr Hatton will be on the door of the

Christmas dance and Mrs Parry says if anyone is suspected of drinking alcohol they won't be allowed in ... And I want to make sure I get in.

HOBBY: Are you sure Mr Nixon is going to the dance?

GAIL: Course he is, I've asked him a dozen times. I've sent him forty cards in the Christmas post.

HOBBY: Must have cost you a fortune?

GAIL: No, my aunty works in a card shop, anyway it's the thought that counts.

HOBBY: So I went into the off-licence, and bought two large bottles of cider.

GAIL: Which we drank through a straw. And then we stuffed ourselves with spring onions.

MR HATTON: Bloody hell. Have you been eating spring onions?

HOBBY: That was Mr Hatton's reaction as we came into the disco.

GAIL: Brilliant, we're in, I told you it'd work, I'm slightly merry but not out of control.

HOBBY: I feel sick. I hate onions.

GAIL: Salty?

SALTY: What?

GAIL: Have you seen Mr Nixon?

SALTY: No, is he coming? Brilliant.

GAIL: Is he here yet?

SALTY: Hey, can you smell onions?

HOBBY: Niko hadn't arrived, he was up in the pub with the rest of the staff, and he was sat very near to Miss Jackie Prime. Meanwhile down at the disco Mr Dean was doing Jimmy Saville impersonations and playing records that were three years out of date ...

DEANIE: Yes, indeedy, this is the sound of the Human League, 'Don't you want me baby' ...

GAIL: Oh shit, look out, Oggy Moxon.

(SALTY *becomes* OGGY.)

OGGY: Got you ...

GAIL: Hey, oh ... great ...

OGGY: Giz a kiss then ...

GAIL: Haven't you got any mistletoe?

OGGY: I don't need mistletoe. Why didn't you come to my party,
You owe me one.

GAIL: Later, eh, maybe later. I dashed away from Oggy, leaving
him wondering what perfume smells like onions.

HOBBY: It is a fact of life that all teachers dance like retards. They
dance like they're all out of a music documentary. It must be
the weight of all that knowledge in their heads which makes
them look like they're in the back seat of an old Ford Cortina.
Mr Dean was a supreme example of bad dancing.

DEANIE: Now then, now then, what have we here? Uncle Ted, a bit
of the old boogie-woogie.

(*He demonstrates extreme bad dancing.*)

HOBBY: Oggy?

(SALTY *becomes* OGGY *and kicks someone in the face.* HOBBY
reacts.)

There'd been some trouble in the toilets, Oggy Moxon had hit
Kev Jones for nothing . . .

GAIL: Kev said that Oggy hit him because he fancied me. Oggy
tried to get me to dance but both times I left him and went to
the toilets.

(*She moves upstage.*)

NIXON: Simon Patterson, very smart. Merry Christmas.

HOBBY: Merry Christmas, sir.

NIXON: Where's Salty?

HOBBY: I think he's dancing. Gail's in the loo. Have you been
drinking, sir?

NIXON: Only a few pints, I'm in my new car.

HOBBY: Yeh, you need a car when you're drinking and driving.

NIXON: The Christmas dance had all the seriousness of a big disco,
and the fifteen- and sixteen-year-olds looked stunning, done up to
the nines, and only Mr Moorcroft, Head of RE, seemed not to be
moved by the gyrating bottoms and boobs . . . At ten thirty, when
things seemed like they were bubbling, Deanie played the last
record, a smoocher, and Gail Saunders appeared in my arms and
suddenly my face was confronted by the strong smell of onion . . .

(SALTY *as* NIXON *and* GAIL *smooch.* HOBBY *as* OGGY
MOXON *hangs around.*)

GAIL: It was fantastic . . .

NIXON: It felt rather awkward, I didn't know how tight to hold Gail or where to put my hands . . .

PARRY: Mrs Parry looked on, she felt a mixture of jealousy and condemnation. But it wasn't unknown for teachers to dance with students, especially at Christmas. After all, as she had said, students were treated like young adults here at Whitewall.

GAIL: Doug, the caretaker cleared the dance floor in a few minutes. And just as I was going to kiss Mr Nixon, he turned his head to wish Doug –

NIXON: (*Turning his head*) – a merry Christmas, Doug.

HOBBY: Oggy Moxon had seen Gail and Niko dancing but he left the hall in silence.

GAIL: Mr Nixon said that he would give me a lift down home. Salty and Hobby decided to walk it home and maybe get a kebab.

NIXON: I got into my car, an A-reg Escort, and Gail jumped in beside me, and before I knew it, into the back jumped Oggy Moxon.

(HOBBY *becomes* OGGY MOXON.)

OGGY: Oh, yeh, what's all this then? Bit of slap and tickle with the drama teacher, Gail. I thought all drama wallahs were puff-balls?

NIXON: Will you get out, Oggy?

OGGY: Will you get out, Oggy? No, I will not.

NIXON: Get out.

OGGY: No, let's go a ride, eh? Drop me down home, will you?

NIXON: Get out.

OGGY: Make me.

NIXON: Get out.

OGGY: Make me.

NIXON: I shalln't say it again.

OGGY: I shalln't say it again. Come on, sir, make me get out.

NIXON: This is my car, I'm not in school hours, now get out.

GAIL: Come on, Oggy. It's not fair.

OGGY: What's not fair? You want me to go so that you can have Mr Nixon all to yourself?

NIXON: I'm going to get Mrs Parry.

OGGY: What the fuck is she going to do about it?

NIXON: Will you get bloody out?

OGGY: You make me.

NIXON: Arrgh . . .

GAIL: Oggy!

> (NIXON *hits* OGGY *in the face. Screaming,* OGGY *pulls himself out of the car.*)

OGGY: You've broke my nose, you bastard.

GAIL: Mr Nixon . . .

OGGY: You bastard . . .

HOBBY: There was blood everywhere.

GAIL: I was screaming, Nixon was shaking.

NIXON: A few members of staff came running from the school.

HOBBY: Oggy staggered away from the car. (*As* OGGY) Our Nobby'll get you, Nixon. Wait till next term, our Nobby'll hammer you. (*Pause.*) And he was off into the dark. It was like a film. Everyone was shouting and trying to calm things. And in the distance you could hear Oggy Moxon shouting, 'I'm gonna do you, Nixon. I'm gonna do you . . .'

GAIL: As we stood, a boy ran past us and jumped into his father's car. And a voice bellowed out . . .

NIXON: Stop running, Simon Patterson!

> (*Blackout. After a pause the lights come up again.*)

New year. The staff room.

PARRY: Morning, Jeff.

NIXON: Morning, Mrs Parry.

WHITHAM: Happy New Year.

PARRY: Happy New Year.

WHITHAM: Had a nice time?

NIXON: Lovely thanks, we went away.

> (*He starts to dismantle the Christmas tree.*)

PARRY: So did we.

WHITHAM: We stayed at home.

PARRY: You'll never guess what?

WHITHAM: Go on.

PARRY: Jackie Prime got married, to Colin Short, Head of PE from St George's, did it over Christmas.

WHITHAM: I didn't know. . . .

PARRY: Neither did I.

NIXON: What was that?

PARRY: For Prime read Short. He's a hunk of a fella, all man . . .

NIXON: Oh . . . Happy New Year . . .

PARRY: You did what, Mr Nixon? said Mrs Parry. Her yellow skirt clashing with her pink blouse.

NIXON: I . . . erm . . . erm . . . headbutted him in the face.

PARRY: If he decides to report this to the police or to his parents I'm afraid you're for the high jump.

GAIL: But Oggy Moxon didn't report the incident to either his dad or the police, but he told Nobby, and Nobby said that he would fix Nixon.

NIXON: During every lesson I had one eye on the main entrance in case Oggy's brother appeared. And I wondered how many staff had said to how many kids 'Bring your dad up' and then wondered all day if they would.

HOBBY: Three or four days went by and nothing happened. Oggy's brother didn't appear and many teachers winked at Mr Nixon as much as to say 'nice one'.

(*Music.*)

Nixon's bedsit.

NIXON: Most of my nights were spent indoors marking, going over the same mistakes and the same right answers. I was turning into a monk. I lived close to the school so I couldn't go to the local pub, it was full of the sixth form, and I didn't know whether to be all mates or to tell the landlord that they were under age. So I stayed in and listened to Janis Ian and Dire Straits, and waited to see if I'd get an interview at St George's . . .

The main hall.

GAIL: During January the shine seemed to go off Nixon.

SALTY: And once we heard that he was applying somewhere else we sort of drifted away for a bit. But we had a laugh. One day he asked us in drama to do a play about corporal punishment in schools, so we, Hobby, me and Gail did this thing about school killers.

HOBBY: Right, in the staff room there's a red phone, like a batphone, and it glows really red when someone's on the other line.

GAIL: And in each classroom under the desk there's a buzzer, so if a teacher gets into some trouble or has a kid who is getting stroppy she can press the buzzer, and the phone rings.

SALTY: Right, in the staff room, just like sat about all day, drinking coffee, and reading ancient books, are these ninjas, Japanese martial arts experts, who are trained to kill kids, with karate chops or sharp stars that they throw. And in the staff room are a number of wires, so that these ninjas –

HOBBY: – when they get the call –

SALTY: – can jump out of the window of the staff room and be at the root of the problem in a few seconds . . .

GAIL: Right, I'm the French assistant, and I'm teaching.

HOBBY: I'm Rachael Steele – and I throw something at the board.

GAIL: (*With a French accent*) Who was that? Who was that who was throwing missiles towards my head? This is very dangerous and could be if someone gets hurt . . . Was it you, Rachael?

HOBBY: What, miss?

GAIL: You know what?

HOBBY: No, I don't, you frog . . .

GAIL: And then suddenly the French assistant presses the buzzer for insolence.

SALTY: The phone rings . . .

HOBBY: The ninjas are in action . . . Out of the staff-room window, coffee all over the place . . .

GAIL: Five seconds later . . . They arrive, kick the door down, tear gas all over the place . . .

HOBBY: The teacher had a mask secreted in her desk.

GAIL: *Merci*, ninja . . .

SALTY: *Bonjour*.

GAIL: The French assistant is back at work . . .

HOBBY: A call is made to Mr and Mrs Steele, would they like to come and collect the remains of their daughter Rachael from the school morgue. She was killed during a French lesson. Thank you . . .

NIXON: It was stories like that, which kept me, Jeff Nixon, alive at Whitewall. And to my surprise the kids in drama got better and better, their imagination knew no bounds . . .

GAIL: You can't teach imagination, can you, sir?

NIXON: I don't know . . .

GAIL: When was the battle of Hastings?

NIXON: Ten sixty-six.

GAIL: What can you do with a brick?

NIXON. Eh?

GAIL: What can you do with a brick? I saw this in a magazine . . .

NIXON: Build a house . . .

GAIL: Yeh, and . . .?

NIXON: Throw it.

GAIL: That shows the violent side of you. You can do unlimited things with a brick. You can drill a hole in it and wear it around your neck . . . You could marry a brick . . .

HOBBY: My cousin married a prick.

GAIL: There's lots of different answers. It says in this magazine that you can exercise your imagination, that's what we do in drama.

HOBBY: And art . . .

GAIL: Yeh, but we don't do it in much else, do we? We're like robots. Who invaded England in 1066? Arm up, Norman the Conqueror. Arm down, computer program complete.

(*Music.*)

Mrs Parry's office.

NIXON: On January the twenty-first Mrs Parry called me to her office. She said it was urgent. Oggy has pressed charges, I knew it.

PARRY: Jeff. Thank God you're here.

NIXON: What's the matter, is it Oggy Moxon?

PARRY: Worse.

NIXON: His brother . . . Nobby . . . He's come to fix me?

PARRY: No. Can you do Coco? Mr Gill, who had the part, slipped a
disc last night building the set. Can you step into the breach,
Jeff? I'd regard it as a great personal favour?

NIXON: What about asking Mr Basford?

PARRY: Derek Basford is never a Coco, Jeff.

NIXON: But I'm in the chorus.

PARRY: You can do that as well. Do it for me, Jeff . . . You can't let
me down, Jeff Nixon.

NIXON: And so it was that Mrs Parry got me to play Coco.

PARRY: Wonderful, wonderful, we rehearse Wednesdays and Sundays
. . . See you Sunday.

GAIL: When Mr Basford heard the news he went barmy with the
cover rota.

NIXON: And for the next three weeks, I was on cover all the time,
French, German, physics, childcare, rural studies, needlework.
(*Music.*)

The Mikado *rehearsals.*

PARRY: Pick your teeth up, Mr Dean . . . Just pick them up and
carry on singing . . . Move left, dear, move left . . . Good . . .
There's no need to slouch in the chorus, Mr Basford. Remember
you are gentlemen of Japan not lepers. Dignity.

NIXON: Three members of the chorus were smoking.

PARRY: Carry on, carry on . . .

NIXON: Mrs Parry's last production, *The Pirates*, lasted eight and a
half hours . . . This looks like it could be longer . . .

DOUG: Face the front . . . Sing out front . . .

PARRY: Stay on stage, don't come out and watch, stay in the wings
. . . It's no good saying 'I was just coming to watch this bit',
stay on stage . . .

NIXON: The stage was a cattle market . . .

PARRY: Carry on, carry on, just do it . . .

NIXON: But for Mrs Parry it was close enough for jazz.

PARRY: Amateurs, Mr Nixon, never work with animals, children
and amateurs.

NIXON: I'm sure it'll be . . . erm . . . great, Mrs Parry.

PARRY: I do hope so, Mr Nixon. This is my fifth *Mikado*, I haven't quite got it right yet ... But we're trying. Do you know your lines yet?

NIXON: Yes.

PARRY: Oh ... Well, marvellous.

NIXON: Would you like me to get up and do my bit?

PARRY: Oh, no, if you know your lines you needn't bother coming till the dress rehearsal, I know you'll be brilliant ... OK, everyone, let's press on. Where's the Mikado, where's Pooh-bah, where's Nanky Poo?

DOUG: They're in the music room playing bridge.

PARRY: Well, tell them that I need them NOW!

DOUG: Oi ... you're bloody on ...

NIXON: During February the mock exams were held in the main hall.

DOUG: Doug, the caretaker, was as smug as a Cheshire cat. Ha ha, you'll not be able to do any drama now, Niko ... Basford's scotched you this time. Seven weeks these desks have got to stay in here ... He could have put these in the gym but Dave Fisher asked him not to ...

NIXON: It's OK, Doug, I'm going to do all my drama classes in the back room of the George and Dragon.

DOUG: I hope you get that job at St George's ... Let them have a basin full of you ...

NIXON: I reckon that I could teach drama anywhere and no one would mind. In the cookery class.

> (*The class scream. They are improvising around* The Marat–Sade. GAIL *tells the audience she is Jean-Paul Marat.*)

HOBBY: In the coal bunker ...

SALTY: In the boiler house ...

GAIL: Canteen ...

HOBBY: Sports-hall showers ...

SALTY: School gates ...

GAIL: Swimming baths ...

HOBBY: Woolworth's ...

SALTY: Simon Patterson's bedroom.

ALL: Stop running, Simon Patterson.

NIXON: What I couldn't fathom is why a school didn't have a space that was solely used for exams. You would have thought that somewhere along the way from the first paper ever sat at Oxford that some boffin would have seen that schools need purpose-built rooms to do exams in. But then what did I know?

PARRY: You knew that you'd got an interview at St George's . . .? Congratulations, said Mrs Parry.

NIXON: She was one of my referees. So joining the G. and S. had its advantages. But rumour had it that Basford wrote all references and I knew he'd be happy to see me go. Drama didn't feature in his scheme of things.

(HOBBY *becomes* MR BASFORD.)

BASFORD: Mr Nixon, can I ask you to keep the noise down? I've got a sixth-form group in the lecture theatre, we can't hear ourselves think.

NIXON: You what, Mr Basford?

BASFORD: It's like an asylum in here.

NIXON: Yeh, great, isn't it? They've really taken to it. We're doing the *Marat–Sade*. It's set in a bath house.

BASFORD: Quiet. Keep them quiet. I said keep the noise down.

NIXON: Hang on, Mr Basford, I wouldn't do that to you.

BASFORD: It's like a flaming riot.

NIXON: They're enjoying themselves.

BASFORD: Enjoying themselves? They sound like they're screaming to get out of your lesson, they can't stand it.

NIXON: I'm sure that there's more sixth formers screaming to get out of yours . . .

BASFORD: Watch your step, Nixon.

NIXON: He was pissed off because I'd got an interview. Apparently, according to Mr Dean, he had applied for the Head at St George's job and had not had his references taken up . . . It had made him a bitter man . . .

(*Music.*)

St George's private school.

MRS COATES: Well, thank you very much, Mr Nixon, it's been a pleasure talking to you. Obviously we have other candidates to see but we should be able to let you know either way before the end of spring term.

MRS CLIFTON: His interview at St George's had gone very well. Mrs Clifton, one of the governors of St George's, thought he would be outstanding. She also thought he would be a marvellous asset to St George's Amateur Players, a society run by Mrs Clifton.

NIXON: St George's was a sanctuary compared with Whitewall. Kids stood up when a teacher went into a class, no one leaped for the door when the bell rang, and their drama studio was pure heaven. I was told that the caretaker at St George's often sat in and watched drama classes, and not a single person had walked through the drama studio ever.

HOBBY: Chalk and cheese.

NIXON: That's the difference. Unbelievable.

GAIL: Colditz, Jeff. The great escape.

(*A choir sings.*)

Tennis courts.

GAIL: One Wednesday when not a lot was happening Mr Basford had organized a tennis competition. Some of the third year were allowed out on to the courts.

SALTY: You mean *court*.

GAIL: Whitewall only had one decent court. The rest were like dirt tracks.

SALTY: Mr Nixon had been invited to take part at the last minute because Mick Edwards had a meeting with the Social Services.

HOBBY: Forty love, game Basford. Hard luck, Mr Dean.

GAIL: Mr Dean got thrashed and so he took his class back to the mobiles to study the unification of Germany. He was a bad loser.

HOBBY: Forty love, game Basford. Bad luck, Mr Fisher, you've got bowlegs. Couldn't stop a pig in a ginnel . . .

GAIL: Mr Basford was once an ace tennis player. Jackie Prime told me that he was a County player in his youth.

SALTY: He had no kit, he looked like Barry Wobschall. Borrowed a pair of pumps from big Pete Saxon and Salty lent him some shorts . . . Somehow, mysteriously, got a bye into the final. And in the final played Mr Basford, who had annihilated Jackie Prime's husband. He was glad about that.

HOBBY: Bad luck. Mr Short.

SALTY: Hey, Shorty, too much bed, not enough sleep. When Nixon came on to the court all the kids were laughing.

(*They laugh.*)

GAIL: Niko looked like somebody from Barnardo's. Nothing fitted him.

HOBBY: Are you sure you know what you're doing, Mr Nixon?

NIXON: All the kids had their faces pushed against the wire of the court.

(*They pull a face, to show this.*)

GAIL: 'Go on, Mr Basford, smash the ball through his head.' That was Oggy Moxon.

HOBBY: Forty love.

GAIL: Smash him, Basford.

HOBBY: Game, Basford.

GAIL: Jackie Prime was smirking the sort of smirk that only PE staff can do.

HOBBY: Game, Basford.

(*They play tennis by tapping a chair and watching a ball.*)

GAIL: 'Come on, Mr Basford, humiliate him,' shouted Oggy, like a wild animal.

SALTY: And he tried to. It was like watching Christians in the Colosseum.

HOBBY: Love all.

SALTY: Fifteen love.

HOBBY: Well done, Mr Nixon. You've won a point. I didn't know you could play.

NIXON: Yeh, what he didn't know, what none of the staff knew, was that I was an under-nineteen tennis international . . . And I thrashed Basford. One six, six love, six love.

GAIL: Mr Basford left the courts in haste. All the kids looked gobsmacked.

NIXON: I could have spared him, but why should I? As I walked from the courts I bumped into Oggy Moxon.

(GAIL *becomes* OGGY MOXON.)

OGGY: Our Nobby's gonna fix you.

NIXON: Great.

OGGY: Hey, I thought you were a fart. Didn't know you could play tennis.

NIXON: Neither did Mr Basford. And you tell your Nobby if he comes up here, I'll shove this down his neck.

OGGY: Right. I'll tell him.

(*Music.*)

HOBBY: With the end of term only six weeks off Niko had this idea of me, Gail and Salty doing a play about school life for the leavers.

SALTY: It was great because Niko had arranged for us to get out of other lessons, cos we didn't have exams.

GAIL: And most teachers were happy to let us go.

SALTY: It was brilliant, like we had the freedom of the city. It's great . . . I'm missing maths to do drama, brilliant . . .

GAIL: Salty was over the moon. He was running around school like a headless chicken. He had written in spray paint on the side of the gym –

SALTY: Mr Basford is a fat Basford.

HOBBY: All the staff thought it was fairly amusing. Basford didn't, he put Salty on a long list of Easter leavers·who had to see Mrs Parry.

PARRY: You don't come to school to fool about, Ian, to waste your time. We treat you like young adults and we expect you to behave accordingly. I don't think that writing swear words on a wall is a mature thing to do. Do you?

SALTY: No, Mrs Parry.

PARRY: Well, why did you do it, Ian?

SALTY: Fed up, Mrs Parry.

PARRY: Fed up of what? What are you fed up of, Ian?

SALTY: Loads of things, Mrs Parry. Having to leave school.

PARRY: Well, we all have to leave school some time, don't we?

SALTY: Yeh, but that's it, Mrs Parry, out there, there's nothing, it's just a load of lies. A load of promises that never happen. I'm sixteen, and I might have wasted my time in school and I've got to bugger off. Maybe I'm not ready for that. I've woken up too late, Mrs Parry. I don't want to be a piece of rhubarb. I want another chance. What's the word I am? I'm a late developer, Mrs Parry, I've got some interest, I've found something I'm interested in – with Mr Nixon. Who is it that says we only have one chance, Mrs Parry? Is it God, cos if it is, it's not the same God my mother talks about . . .

PARRY: Everyone has to grow up, Ian. Leaving school is just a part of growing up.

SALTY: Yeh, but nobody out there cares. If people did care you'd be able to say to me, 'All right Salty, stop on, start again, have another crack' . . . I can't negotiate, Mrs Parry, you can't negotiate . . . Who is it who traps us both? Politicians . . . them men on the telly with funny haircuts, them men who talk about choice and equality and fairness . . . Why don't any of them live on our estate? Why don't I see any of them down the welfare hall or at the Bingo? They're not bothered about us. Do you believe what they say, Mrs Parry? It's all a load of lies. They don't care, and what's worse, you know, is that they're not bothered that they don't care. Then I turned and left her room.

PARRY: Ian, Salty, come here immediately . . .

(Music.)

The staff room.

WHITHAM: Congratulations. You did it.

JONES: Well done, Jeff.

WHITHAM: When do you start?

NIXON: September.

JONES: Another success for the escape committee.

WHITHAM: We'll have a drink after *The Mikado*, said Maureen Whitham, who was playing Sing Sing. I've got my job in local radio, make it a double celebration.

NIXON: I was obviously very pleased. The kids said that I would change, going to a snob school. But it was an unbelievable feeling. And for some reason Jackie Short, née Prime, kissed me. I felt like a great weight had been lifted from my shoulders, I could breathe once more, I was free. Thank God I was free . . .

JONES: Hey, I've got another interview, it's my seventeenth this month.

WHITHAM: Orrrrr ...

NIXON: The opening night of *The Mikado* was extra–or–dinary.

(*Blackout. After a pause, the lights come up again.*)

PARRY: Thank you, thank you.

(GAIL *presents her with a bouquet.*)

Thank you, thank you all. I'd like if I may to thank everyone concerned. I'd like to thank Gerald, my husband, for being so patient, and also Daphne and Clarence, my two wonderful children, and of course Doug, the caretaker, without whom this production would not have been possible. And also all the backstage team ... Come on, fellas, let's have you out here ...

NIXON: It was the shortest production of *The Mikado* in history, fifty-five minutes. Forty-six pages of the libretto had been skipped over. But it was still a success.

PARRY: And I'd like to thank Simon and Peter for numbering the chairs.

NIXON: The thank yous went on for an hour.

PARRY: And Joyce, Hilda and Frances who did the little buns and cakes, and how lovely they were as well.

NIXON: The cast stood there wilting.

PARRY: And Martin and Chris for cutting the squares of cinemoid which made all those lovely colours. And to Desmond and Sue who helped park the cars. Thanks to you all.

GAIL: On the last night of *The Mikado* Mrs Parry threw a party in the sixth-form common room. Everyone chatted and drank Pomagne from paper cups. Basford was there. (*As* BASFORD) So I suppose it's congratulations, Mr Nixon?

NIXON: Sorry?

BASFORD: Congratulations. You must feel very pleased with yourself?

NIXON: Not really.

BASFORD: You were a very good Coco, it was quite a swansong.

NIXON: Thanks very much, Derek.

BASFORD: I'm sure you'll have a great time over at St George's. It's what you want, isn't it? They're quite into drama over there.

The twins are thinking of drama as an option. This is not a
school for drama, never has been, never will be.

NIXON: I'll miss the kids.

BASFORD: Not for long. You just have a thought for us, still stuck
here. Mind you, every cloud has a silver lining, as they say. Mrs
Parry has just asked me if I'd like to play Nathan Detroit in
next term's *Guys and Dolls*.

NIXON: And are you?

BASFORD: My dear boy, the part was made for me.

HOBBY: All the kids were really sad when Nixon left, and me and
Salty and Gail all cried.

GAIL: We never saw Niko again. Somebody told us that he was
having a good time at St George's, and that all the posh kids
loved him. When we left school I got a job typing, and I did
some dance. I was also in the chorus of *Guys and Dolls*.

HOBBY: And I got this job with my uncle. And Oggy Moxon ... it
was like on a farm, hard work, but good fun.

SALTY: I didn't know what I did. I could think anything up. I
wanted to write songs for Wham! and be a millionaire, but Mr
Nixon said it was too far-fetched ... But I'd like to ...

(*A school bell rings. End of school. The lights change.* SALTY,
GAIL *and* HOBBY *are lost. They move around the stage
slowly, and pick up their bags. Silence.*)

GAIL: Oh, well ... that's it then.

HOBBY: The end.

SALTY: Mr Nixon, can I just say before we go, sir, don't leave,
sir. The kids here need teachers like you. Don't go to that snob
school, sir.

GAIL: Sir, if you stay, we'll come back and bug you. We'll let you
know how we're getting on. I'll come and cut your hair if you
like ... I'm doing a scheme at the hairdresser's, it's twenty-five
quid but my mam says it's better than nothing. Just.

SALTY: Sir, I'm doing a scheme, painting and decorating, should be
a laugh, I'm crap at art. Might end up on an advert ... Be a
star then, sir ...

GAIL: Don't leave, sir ...

HOBBY: I'm doing french polishing, gonna hate it.

SALTY: If you stay and do another drama play, we'll be in it . . .

HOBBY: Best thing I've ever done at school this . . . It's the only thing I'll remember . . .

SALTY: We could have a laugh, start a group up.

GAIL: And rehearse at nights . . .

SALTY: Hey, we could do all sorts . . . *Marat–Sade*.

GAIL: Comedies.

HOBBY: Tragedies.

GAIL: Westerns.

SALTY: Kung fu . . .

GAIL: Sir, romances . . .

HOBBY: Sex plays . . .

SALTY: Sir . . . I've got it . . . Why don't you do *The Mikado* . . . ?

GAIL: *Mikado*. Sir, you said that was shit.

HOBBY: Anyway . . . See you, sir . . . See you, Mrs Hudson . . .

SALTY: Yeh. Thanks, sir . . .

GAIL: Yeh.

HOBBY: Yeh, thanks.

SALTY: Yeh.

GAIL: Thanks a lot.

SALTY: See you . . .

HOBBY: Tara . . .

GAIL: Yeh.

> (*They walk away. They freeze.* 'Gentleman of Japan' *from* The Mikado *plays. Blackout.*)

UP 'N' UNDER

To the Rugby League fans of Hull

AUTHOR'S NOTE

The whole idea behind writing this play was to present a theme for the theatre in Hull. However, the story of the bet and the achievement of the men who accept the bet is universal . . . thus the sundry references to the London Marathon as the absolute metaphor of amateur sport.

The staging needs to be fast and slick. The rugby sections that are apparent take into account that the dancer and not the poet is the father of the theatre. Thus this is an attempt to create a popular piece of drama that is all action – at the time of writing the most popular videos available on the mass market are the *Rocky* videos. This is an attempt to stage *Rocky* . . . and where else? In Yorkshire, of course.

J.G.
1984

CHARACTERS

ARTHUR HOYLE Ex-player, owns a painting and decorating business

PHIL HOPLEY English teacher, an ex-Loughborough player

FRANK ROWLEY Local butcher

TONY BURTOFT Apprentice miner (striking)

STEVE EDWARDS Garage mechanic

REG WELSH Gambler and manager of the Cobblers' Arms

HAZEL SCOTT Athlete and club-owner

The play may be presented without an interval if preferred.

Up 'n' Under was given its world première by the Hull Truck Theatre Company at the Edinburgh Festival on 10 August 1984, with the following cast:

ARTHUR HOYLE	Peter Geeves
PHIL HOPLEY	Richard May
FRANK ROWLEY	Richard Ridings
TONY BURTOFT	Chris Walker
STEVE EDWARDS	Andrew Dunn
REG WELSH	Andrew Dunn
HAZEL SCOTT	Jane Clifford

Directed by John Godber

This production toured England and Scotland from September to December 1984, making a brief appearance at Hull Truck's home base, the Spring Street Theatre, Hull, and the Donmar Warehouse, London.

Up 'n' Under transferred to the Fortune Theatre, London, on 26 March 1985, with the following cast:

ARTHUR HOYLE	Stewart Howson
PHIL HOPLEY	Richard James Lewis
FRANK ROWLEY	Jonathan Linsley
TONY BURTOFT	Chris Walker
STEVE EDWARDS	Andrew Dunn
REG WELSH	Andrew Dunn
HAZEL SCOTT	Sarah Harper

Directed by John Godber

ACT ONE

Enter FRANK, HAZEL, TONY *and* PHIL. *They stand along the back.* FRANK *takes a rugby shirt from the hooks and passes it across to* HAZEL. *She catches it and places it carefully over the sit-ups rack.* FRANK *takes up the speech.*

FRANK: Here on the very playing fields of Castleford your eyes will gaze in awe at splendid sights unseen . . . Your mind will jump and question the wisdom of our tale . . . But we care not. So, let battle cries be heard across our fair isle, from Hull . . . to Liverpool. Let trumpets sound and brass bands play their Hovis tunes.

(HAZEL *throws the ball, which she has by now picked up from the bench, to* FRANK, *then retreats back to her position upstage centre.*)

For here, upon this very stage, we see amateur Rugby League, a game born of rebellion, born of divide in 1895. For the working class of the north, for the working class. All around, pub teams throng the bars, club teams meet in lowly courts, amateurs all. Yet even as I speak a game commences in this battling competition; the Crooked Billet from Rochdale play the Cobblers' Arms from Castleford, unbeaten gods of amateur rugby sevens, unbeaten many seasons with greatness thrust upon them. Yet many know this to be true, still, one man takes the stage – our hero: Arthur Hoyle, a very lowly figure, yet the stature of a lion, a painter and decorator by trade. His quest will be, within our two-hour traffic, to challenge the might of the Cobblers, to throw down the gauntlet and hope to break the myth that is the Cobblers' Arms . . . His journey may be long and weary, and though you must travel with him, you never can assist, no matter how you pine to; your role is but to sit, and watch. Yet soft, for as you gaze upon our breezeblock 'O', Reg Welsh appears, manager of the Cobblers, and trainer of their team; a very big fish on this our dish of amateur Rugby League. Here before your very eyes, two rivals meet: Reg and Arth.

(REG *and* ARTHUR *enter.*)

REG: Arthur.

ARTHUR: Reg.

FRANK: And they will bet in lofty sums. But mark this, Arthur's coffers are very low, his mouth is very loose, and oft this and his brain are as separate as two mighty continents. My masters, is he mad or what is he? He is apt to make daft bets . . . to idle threats and boasts. From me enough, I let them play their stuff. So let our story unfold, as two great rivals pledge their gold . . .

REG: Arthur . . .

ARTHUR: Reg . . .

REG: How are you, sunshine?

ARTHUR: Not bad . . .

REG: How's the wife?

ARTHUR: Still living in the same house.

REG: Like that, is it, Arthur?

ARTHUR: You know Doreen, Reg, she'd argue with fog.

REG: Takes after you, Arthur.

ARTHUR: Dunno.

REG: No.

ARTHUR: No, I've changed, Reg . . . I was a hothead, you know that as well as anybody . . . I've cooled down.

REG: Good to hear that, Arth.

ARTHUR: Well, old age and poverty helps, doesn't it?

REG: Dunno about the poverty.

ARTHUR: No, right.

REG: You did some daft things in your day, Arthur lad.

ARTHUR: I know.

REG: Can you remember when you poked the linesman in the eye at Warrington?

ARTHUR: I can.

REG: And when you head-butted the referee at St Helens?

ARTHUR: Yeah.

REG: Eh, and when you burnt down the goal posts at 'Unslett?

ARTHUR: Oh, for disagreeing with that offside decision.

REG: Didn't see that one, read about it in the paper.

ARTHUR: Good times, Reg.

REG: Yes.

ARTHUR: Good times.

REG: I must say, Arthur . . . it's good to see you settled.

ARTHUR: Oh, yeah . . .

REG: The way you were going I never thought you'd make thirty.

ARTHUR: No.

REG: You could still have been playing.

ARTHUR: If it hadn't been for you, Reg.

REG: Now don't be like that, Arth.

ARTHUR: But it's true, you were on the board that got me banned, you know that as much as anybody.

REG: Let's not get into all that . . .

ARTHUR: You brought it up.

REG: No matter what I say to you I'll not convince you that it wasn't only me who pushed to have you banned . . . no matter what I say . . .

ARTHUR: That's the way I saw it, anyway . . .
    (*A beat.*)

REG: Cigar?

ARTHUR: Don't smoke.

REG: Still fit?

ARTHUR: Still trying.

REG: Good to hear it.

ARTHUR: We can't all live a life of leisure, can we, Reg?

REG: But I've worked for it, Arthur sunshine . . . worked for it . . . making money is all about having money, investing money.

ARTHUR: Yeah . . .

REG: You must have a bob or two?

ARTHUR: I've got a bob or two.

REG: I thought so.

ARTHUR: And that's all I've got.

REG: What do you think to my lads this year?

ARTHUR: All right.

REG: Come on, Arthur, ... they're more than all right, they're magnificent ... The Magnificent Seven, that's what I call them.

ARTHUR: They've got their problems, Reg.

REG: What do you mean?

ARTHUR: They're good on the ball ...

REG: Yeah ...

ARTHUR: Bad in defence.

REG: Give over ... their defence is clam-tight.

ARTHUR: No, is it, heck.

REG: It is.

ARTHUR: Well, you take it from me.

REG: The Cobblers'll beat any side you want to name.

ARTHUR: They're not that good, Reg ... listen to me, I'm telling you.

REG: I thought you might have learnt some sense as times go on ... pity you haven't ... same old Arthur.

ARTHUR: Same old Reg ... full of shit.

REG: Oh, you're not worth talking to.

ARTHUR: The truth hurts.

REG: You make me laugh ... a feller with half an eye could see how good they are.

ARTHUR: In that case I must be going blind.

REG: Look at that ... free and economic distribution ... fast hands ... unbeatable ... completely unbeatable.

ARTHUR: No.

REG: They are.

ARTHUR: Reg, they're not.

REG: I'm not arguing with you ... you know I'm right.

ARTHUR: I could train a team to beat 'em.

REG: Talk sense.

ARTHUR: I am talking sense.

REG: Doesn't sound like much sense to me.

ARTHUR: I could get a team together to beat the Cobblers.

REG: Have you had some beer?

ARTHUR: No.

REG: Can you hear what you're saying?

ARTHUR: I know what I'm saying and I mean it . . . I've thought it for years.

REG: Arthur, you're talking out of your arsehole.

ARTHUR: Steady.

REG: You are talking utter crap and you know it.

ARTHUR: No, I'm not. I could get a team to beat 'em.

REG: Don't be such a pillock.

ARTHUR: I said, steady with the language, Reg.

REG: Well, you're talking such rubbish, man.

ARTHUR: I'm not talking rubbish, I'm talking facts . . . there's a way to beat these, no problem.

REG: There's no way you're gonna get an amateur club to beat these, no way.

ARTHUR: Rubbish.

REG: No way.

ARTHUR: Rubbish.

REG: No way, Arthur . . .

ARTHUR: I could do it . . . I could train any team in the North to beat these.

REG: OK then, put your money where your mouth is.

ARTHUR: Eh . . . ?

REG: Put your money where your mouth is.

ARTHUR: Ar . . . dunno . . .

REG: See what I mean? You're the one who's full of shit.

ARTHUR: All right, then, I bet you . . .

REG: That you can train a given team to beat my lads?

ARTHUR: Yeah, I bet you, Reg.

REG: How much? Four grand . . . five thousand . . . Ten thousand, Arthur? Let's make it a decent bet, shall we?

ARTHUR: I bet my mortgage . . .

REG: What about Doreen?

ARTHUR: I bet my house . . .

REG: Keep it sensible.

ARTHUR: I bet my house that I can get a team to beat them set of nancy poofters, Reg Welsh . . . that's the bet, shake on it.

REG: You'll lose . . .

ARTHUR: We'll see . . .

REG: I mean it.

ARTHUR: Any team in the North, come on, name a club side . . . I'll
train 'em.

REG: We'll meet in the next sevens.

ARTHUR: When is it?

REG: Five weeks' time.

ARTHUR: That's great . . . name my name.

REG: No turning back . . .

ARTHUR: You've got my word.

REG: It's a bet?

ARTHUR: Come on, name the team I've got to train.

REG: I'll make arrangements for us to meet in the draw.

ARTHUR: I'll leave the dirty work to you.

REG: I'll pull a few influential strings.

ARTHUR: What's the team, Reg?

REG: I name the Wheatsheaf from near Hull.

ARTHUR: Nice one . . . now name a team.

REG: I name the Wheatsheaf, Arthur.

ARTHUR: The Wheatsheaf Arms?

REG: That's the one.

ARTHUR: You're joking.

REG: The bet's on.

ARTHUR: Bloody hell . . .

REG: Five weeks then, Arthur . . . I look forward to the game . . .

(REG *exits*.)

ARTHUR: The Wheatsheaf?

HAZEL: Now, hear this news of the Wheatsheaf . . . The Wheatsheaf
pub . . . infamous in rugby circles. Yet in all their history they
have never won a single game, and what's the same, they never
have seven men. As you saw, Arthur's head was loose, he
wished he'd shut his gob. You know right well the bet is unfair,
but to pull out now would be disaster. The path he treads is
narrow and long . . . the job is on . . . to train this team into the
likes of which has ne'er been seen.

(HAZEL *exits*.)

Lights come up on FRANK, TONY *and* PHIL, *who are sitting despondently in their dressing room.*

FRANK: Give 'em another five minutes . . . then . . . home.

PHIL: There is a brighter side to it, historically speaking.

TONY: What?

PHIL: The long-running tradition of the Wheatsheaf team losing, because of lack of players.

TONY: I wonder what's happened to Steve and Tommy?

FRANK: Steve'll be messing about with his car, putting new headlights on it . . . or cleaning the engine down with Palmolive.

TONY: It's a smart car he's got . . . goes like a bomb.

FRANK: It ought to go like a bomb and blow his bloody head off.

PHIL: Sick jokes . . .

FRANK: Thank you, doctor.

TONY: Well, anyway, this is my last game.

PHIL: And me . . . the last time I'm going to look a prat.

TONY: If we can't get seven then that's it for me. Anyway, you don't look a prat.

    (PHIL *notices* TONY *has no socks.*)

PHIL: Where's your socks?

TONY: Forgotten 'em.

PHIL: Brilliant!

TONY: I can't afford to be going out and buying sock after sock.

PHIL: That's brilliant, that is, there's only three of us, and you two look pathetic. You could at least make an effort.

FRANK: We have made an effort, we've turned up.

PHIL: You're not playing in them, are you?

FRANK: What?

PHIL: Jesus sandals.

FRANK: Why not?

TONY: What if somebody stamps on your toe?

FRANK: I'll crucify 'em.

TONY: Sandals, that's just the pits, that is.

FRANK: I'm playing in these and you lot can knackers.

PHIL: Oh, I mean, this is just pathetic . . . we can't play with three . . .

TONY: Maybe we could ask to borrow a couple on loan for half an hour.

FRANK: Yeah, a couple of props from the Cobblers?

TONY: If we run about really fast maybe they'll think there's
more.

FRANK: Yeah . . .

TONY: I was joking.

FRANK: It's a bit desperate, really.

PHIL: Did either of you train this week?

TONY: What was that?

PHIL: Train . . . you know, training . . .

FRANK: Is that a foreign . . . ?

PHIL: Try saying it . . . it's dead easy . . . Training . . .

FRANK: Is it French?

TONY: Tra – Track . . .

PHIL: No . . . training . . .

TONY: Pain . . . paining . . .

PHIL: Nearly.

TONY: No, I can't say it.

FRANK: I can't do it . . . The last time I trained, Queen Victoria had
just died.

TONY: Last time I trained she'd just been born.

PHIL: The last time I trained the earth was a gaseous mass.

TONY: Weird . . .

(STEVE *appears.*)
Steve . . . yo . . .

FRANK: Yo . . . Steve . . .

PHIL: Yo . . .

STEVE: Yo . . . here we go, here we go, here we go . . .

PHIL: Where's the others?

TONY: Where've you been?

STEVE: Got lost in Goole . . . found this great pub . . . Theakston's
Old Peculiar on draft . . .

TONY: Nice one.

PHIL: Where's Tommy and Jack?

STEVE: Tommy can't come and Jack's wife says he's gone fishing.

PHIL: Brilliant!

FRANK: Why can't Tommy make it?

STEVE: I think him and their lass have had a bit of an argument. I

could hear her shouting as I walked down the garden so I
thought I'd leave it.

PHIL: Oh, brilliant thinking, Steve . . . if you'd've called for him he
might have come.

TONY: If you say brilliant again I'll die.

PHIL: Brilliant.

STEVE: We're not going to play with just four, are we?

FRANK: Are you joking? We were playing with three.

STEVE: Let's leave it and get in the beer tent.

FRANK: Get changed, it'll be a laugh.

STEVE: Who for?

TONY: Upton Social Club and about a hundred and fifty spectators.

FRANK: Look at it like this, if we lose it's only fifteen minutes then
straight into the beer tent.

STEVE: Hey, I don't like all this positive talk.

TONY: Like what?

STEVE: Like *if* we lose . . . I'm more used to *when* we lose.

PHIL: At least it's not raining . . .

TONY: There's a bad wind, though . . .

STEVE: There's a bad wind in here. Is it you?

TONY: Is it, heck.

FRANK: It's that Theakston's.

(STEVE *is looking in his bag.*)

STEVE: Oh, shite, man . . . I've left me shirt . . .

PHIL: Oh, thanks . . . that's . . .

TONY: Bloody brilliant . . .

FRANK: I've got a spare one . . .

(*He dips into his bag and produces a massive shirt.*)

Here, get that on . . .

STEVE: Oh, I can't wear that, Frank . . . I'll look like a balloon.

TONY: Get it on . . . bit of wind and you'll be laughing.

PHIL: Put a shirt on, Steve, I feel sick.

STEVE: Shut your moustache, will you?

FRANK: Come here, let me play a tune on your ribs.

(STEVE *puts the shirt on.*)

STEVE: Look at this.

PHIL: Man at Top Shop?

TONY: Wham! Jitterbug.

FRANK: Man at Oxfam.

TONY: Who does the shirt belong to, Frank? Your lass?

    (*A beat.*)

PHIL: Oh, sore point.

FRANK: That's the only bloody thing she left when she went.

STEVE: Have you got a mortgage for it?

FRANK: I've got some good memories of that shirt . . . we used to go camping in it.

PHIL: Right, are we ready? Steve, ready?

    (STEVE *has the shirt on but is looking for his jockstrap in his bag.*)

STEVE: That's not mine.

TONY: Well, it's not mine.

PHIL: Come on, let's start to think about the game.

TONY: Rugby is a game played by men with odd-shaped balls.

FRANK: Oh, oh . . . every one a winner. For me rugby is a game of two halves.

TONY: Give blood: play rugby.

FRANK: Give orange: play squash.

    (TONY *groans.*)

    Hey, not bad, I just made that up.

PHIL: Right, listen . . . are we going to play or not?

STEVE: No.

TONY: Might as well.

FRANK: We can ask to put one man in the scrum.

STEVE: We're not going to do the war chant, are we?

    (*They perform a hideous war chant.*)

PHIL: Are we, hell, let's just get out there . . . and get it bloody over with.

STEVE: Let's get in that bloody beer tent.

    (*They all run downstage and find a space. The weather is quite cold and they react accordingly.* STEVE *will tuck his hands right down his shorts.* TONY *has picked up the ball.*)

TONY: Tony Burtoft. Apprentice miner. Age twenty-two. Weight 190 pounds. Height six foot one. Position centre. Hobbies: racing whippets.

(*The ball is thrown.*)

FRANK: Frank Rowley. Butcher. Age thirty-two. Weight 215 pounds. Height six foot one. Position prop. Hobbies: anything to do with my hands.

(*The ball is thrown.*)

STEVE: Steve Edwards. Car mechanic. Age twenty-five. Weight 180 pounds. Height six foot one. Position loose forward. Hobbies: drinking.

(*The ball is thrown.*)

PHIL: Phil Hopley. Teacher. Age twenty-nine. Weight 160 pounds. Height five foot eight. Position stand-off. Hobbies: reading, Scrabble, hunting around antique fairs on a Sunday. (*Pause.*) Right, here we go . . . if anyone gets the ball, this time . . . pass!

ALL: Oh, yeah . . .

(*The players go upstage and freeze.* HAZEL *enters.*)

HAZEL: I' faith, good sirs, the fools the Wheatsheaf played
And lost well bad.
The largest defeat they'd ever had.
The petal-soft warriors sickened by the score,
Will in time vow to play no more.
Take heed of how they've lost a game,
I' faith, good sirs, who can they blame?
Only themselves . . .
Thus Arthur's quest is harder still,
Made so by our author's quill.
How can they play with motive gone?
Can Arthur coax them?
Now watch on . . .

(*The players come out of their freeze.* PHIL *leaves the ball upstage.*)

PHIL: That is it this time and I mean it.

STEVE: And me.

PHIL: You? You never did a bloody thing.

STEVE: Why, what did you do?

PHIL: At least I moved.

TONY: Did you? I must have blinked.

PHIL: Why don't you tackle, Steve?

STEVE: Why don't you pass?

PHIL: I did pass.

STEVE: Not to me.

PHIL: I can't pass to you unless you move on to the ball ... and don't stand there like a dickhead.

FRANK: I think I'll have a nice big piece of T-bone when I get home.

TONY: I bet we'd beat 'em at darts.

STEVE: Dominoes.

FRANK: Drinking.

> (FRANK *laughs.* ARTHUR *enters upstage and crouches down to the players.*)

ARTHUR: All right, fellers?

TONY *and* STEVE: All right.

ARTHUR: Arthur ... Arthur Hoyle ... nice to meet you.

PHIL: Don't tell me you're a scout for the British touring party.

FRANK: Don't you mean ENSA?

ARTHUR: No ... I thought you had a bit of bad luck in that game ...

> (*They all burst out laughing.*)

STEVE: Hey, come on, man, fifty-four nil in fifteen minutes, that's more than a bit of bad luck.

TONY: That's a tragedy.

ARTHUR: You can laugh but I thought you displayed some fine talent, some promise.

TONY: Has he got a white stick?

FRANK: Has he got a brain?

ARTHUR: OK, there were only four of you ... but even so.

PHIL: Yeah, well, thanks for the thoughts.

ARTHUR: Do you have a trainer?

STEVE: Do worms have legs?

FRANK: We did ... but he's gone fishing.

ARTHUR: Look ... I don't know how you'd feel about this, but I'd be willing to train you ... help you out ... I used to play a bit.

PHIL: No ... er ...

ARTHUR: I tell you what we could do if you like ... Give me a trial ... Five weeks' trial ... How about that? Just up to the next sevens.

PHIL: No, thanks, mate ...

STEVE: Hang on, Phil. How do we know that you're any good?

ARTHUR: That's why I'm suggesting that you take me on for a five-week trial.

FRANK: Well, it's not for me, I've had enough.

ARTHUR: Come on, fellers, you don't mean to tell me that you're willing to pack in playing Rugby as easy as that?

FRANK: Yeah, that's exactly what I mean.

STEVE: We can't even muster seven players.

ARTHUR: That's where I come in ... use my influence ... pull a few strings ...

FRANK: No ... we're over the bloody hill.

ARTHUR: (*Aside*) I'll rot in hell for the lies I tell. (*To the players*) Rubbish, over the hill ... Look at Brian Bevan.

FRANK: It's too much like hard work.

STEVE: Yeah ... thanks anyway.

ARTHUR: Oh, come on, lads ... give us a break.

TONY: What's in it for you?

ARTHUR: Love of the game, that's all.

PHIL: I don't know ...

ARTHUR: Listen, come to training at Walton sports field. Tuesday, right? Think about it.

PHIL: Yeah, we will.

STEVE: I'm gonna think about that beer tent.

FRANK: Mmmm, nice idea ...

(STEVE, PHIL *and* FRANK *stand to leave.*)

STEVE: See you, Arthur, nice to meet yer ...

(*They start to walk off.*)

ARTHUR: Think about Tuesday, lads.

(*They give an uninterested 'yeah'.* TONY *remains. A beat.*)
Good lads.

TONY: Not bad.

ARTHUR: Lost interest?

TONY: Yeah ... Winning's easy, innit? Losing's hard.

ARTHUR: Don't tell me. How long have you been playing?

(*He throws the ball to* TONY.)

TONY: Oh, a ball! Started at school.

ARTHUR: Haven't you got any proper kit?

TONY: Nobody's bothered . . . We used to pay subs but that's died off. Did you see Frank's sandals? He's daft. Apparently he was a right animal . . . but their lass left home and he lost interest.

ARTHUR: Self-respect?

TONY: What?

ARTHUR: Don't matter. What about the others?

TONY: Phil's a decent player when he gets the right ball . . . He's a play-maker . . . he played at college or summat in Leicester . . . summat.

ARTHUR: Loughborough?

TONY: Yeah, I think that's it. Rugby Union.

ARTHUR: Aye, it would be . . . whisper it.

TONY: Yeah.

   (*A beat.*)

   Did you play?

ARTHUR: Hey, I'm not that old.

TONY: Er . . .

ARTHUR: Hooker . . . Wakey Trinity.

TONY: Whooohhh!

ARTHUR: I only played a couple of first-team games.

TONY: Got the build for a hooker.

ARTHUR: Yeah . . . What's happened to the other three?

TONY: Hardly ever turn up.

ARTHUR: Haven't you got any influence?

TONY: No way.

ARTHUR: You could have a word with them, couldn't you? Get them to train . . .

TONY: I can try, but I can't promise.

ARTHUR: I'll give you a couple of quid.

TONY: What?

ARTHUR: If you have a word.

TONY: Yeah, can do.

ARTHUR: Look, here's a fiver . . . just have a word with 'em, get 'em out there on Tuesday.

TONY: What's it all about, this?

ARTHUR: I love the game, that's all, let's just say that.

TONY: You can say what you like for a fiver.

ARTHUR: You'll train, won't you?

TONY: Yeah.

ARTHUR: What do you think to the Cobblers' Arms?
      (*Music.*)

TONY: Brilliant.

ARTHUR: Do you think so?

TONY: There's not a team in the north to touch 'em ... unbeatable ...

ARTHUR: Oh, I don't know. How would you feel about playing against 'em?

TONY: They're in a different league, man, it'd be like playing against tanks.
      (*Lose music.*)

ARTHUR: Anyway, it's only a thought. We can dream, can't we?

TONY: Dream we can.

ARTHUR: Do what you will, you know, Tuesday?

TONY: Yeah, right, I'll get off, then ... see you ...

ARTHUR: Tuesday.
      (TONY *exits.*)
      Our lass'll kill me.
      (*Blackout.*)
      She'll kill me.

REG *enters behind* ARTHUR.

REG: I'm not a wicked man, though many say I am a bastard. I'm a fair man, I like to see fair play. Old Arthur's sweating, I can smell his piglike stench from here. Silly sod to bet his house in such a way, and as you saw I tried to speak in sensible terms and halt his foolish gob. I wouldn't take a house, not from an ordinary bloke. I wouldn't let him choke by Doreen's hand. Here's what I'll do: I'll conjure a note, and on it I've wrote: 'It's a determined man who's bet all he's got.' I'll take three grand off you in this bet, Arthur, pal. Don't want to see a proud man out of house and home.

ARTHUR: Three grand, Reg.

REG: In cash, I like cash. What the hell would I do with your hovel, anyway?

ARTHUR: Yeah, right, thanks, Reg.

REG: How's the training going, Arthur?

ARTHUR: Great.

REG: Yeah?

ARTHUR: Couldn't be better.

REG: Lads eager, are they?

ARTHUR: Yeah ... As soon as I put the prospect to them they almost bit my hand off.

REG: Really?

ARTHUR: Have you made inquiries about the draw?

REG: You leave that to me. I'm even thinking of giving you a bye to the final. Make it more of a prestige game for your lads. Don't want to leave 'em with nothing.

ARTHUR: Yeah ... right ...

REG: Just make sure that you've got a team ... otherwise it could be embarrassing.

> (*Light out on* REG.)

ARTHUR *takes off his anorak through the ensuing speech. He wears a rugby shirt under his coat. A rugby ball is thrown on to him. He looks around for the players to appear.*

ARTHUR: Tuesday night I waited and waited ... Walton sports field was a desert of green, with not a player to be seen at all ...

> (HAZEL *enters and sits on a bench.*)

HAZEL: My Lords, on Walton's fields he stood in storms and hail,
And blowing gales the like of which would crack your cheeks,
Which you have heard from tales.
Every hour he stood alone the stronger grew his cause,
More determined was his soaking gait.
But still his part was to wait ... and wait ...
His thoughts lay with success,
He knew he dare not fail ...
And as he stood drenched on yon fair fields ...
The rest were supping ale ...

> (*Downstage are* FRANK *and* PHIL, *with a drink of beer. They have had a few.*)

PHIL: Oh, funny ... honestly funny ... some of the things they come out with, honestly funny.

FRANK: Yeah?

PHIL: Oh, yeah.

FRANK: Like what?

PHIL: Oh, all sorts ... I mean, stories in the staff room, funny.

FRANK: Yeah, yeah ... like what?

PHIL: Like this kid writes, William the Conqueror's first name was Norman.

   (*This meets with death.*)

FRANK: (*Taking a drink*) Oh, yeah.

PHIL: (*Undaunted*) Funny ... and this lad says ... No, I can't tell you, it's sick.

FRANK: Tell us, Phil man.

PHIL: No, it'll upset you, it's sick ... you're a man of sensibilities, you're a sensitive man, Frank.

FRANK: I cut dead meat up ... I'd hardly call that sensitive.

PHIL: So ... I've got this class ... a couple of years ago ... and this has just come to me ... we're talking about the Ripper ...

FRANK: Yeah ... yeah ...

PHIL: A slow-learning group ... reading and writing problems ...

FRANK: Like me ...

PHIL: And we're trying to diagnose what to do with the Yorkshire Ripper.

FRANK: Yeah, go on ...

PHIL: And this little lad says, 'Sir?'

FRANK: Yeah ...

PHIL: 'Sir, I know what we could do with the Yorkshire Ripper.' I says, 'Great, go on, Stuart ... what would you do?' Then he says, 'I'd send him to America.'

FRANK: (*Begins to laugh.*) Norman the Conqueror ...

   (FRANK *and* PHIL *begin to cackle and then the cackling subsides. They both sigh ... drink their beer. Blackout.*)

ARTHUR: And I'm waiting and waiting.

   (*Lights up on* FRANK *and* PHIL.)

PHIL: What do you think to this Arthur bloke?

FRANK: He's got a painting and decorating firm, I've seen his van.
   Decent player in his day.

PHIL: Could be handy, could that. I want my living room Artexing.

FRANK: What do you reckon about *this* lot?

PHIL: I don't know.

FRANK: He's keen.

PHIL: If he's out on Walton sports field by himself he is keen. He'll
   be arrested for loitering.

FRANK: Wonder who turned up?

PHIL: I could guess.

FRANK: Not Steve.

PHIL: No chance . . . he'll be trying to pick something up.

FRANK: He ought to pick something up, incurable.

PHIL: Tony'll turn out.

FRANK: Yeah. Mate I was talking to yesterday reckons this Arthur's
   a weird bloke . . . says his brain's in a box somewhere.

PHIL: Yeah?

FRANK: Hard case.

PHIL: Just let him start with me.

FRANK: And me.

PHIL: I'll tell him where to get off. Listen, you couldn't see your
   way to letting me have another batch of them T-bones, could
   you? You know those you got off the back of a warehouse?

FRANK: Yeah, come and pick them up . . . and bring a few mags
   with you.

PHIL: You dirty sod.

FRANK: Where do you get them from?

PHIL: All over the place, you never know when they're gonna show
   up. The other day we were reading *Women in Love*, this fifth-
   year lad whips out this porno book. 'Look at this, sir,' he says.
   'This is women in love.' I'd never seen anything like it . . . I
   gave him a dressing down, made him feel embarrassed and
   confiscated the magazine, told him I was going to burn it.

FRANK: And did you?

PHIL: Did I, hell . . . I kept it . . . it was a classic . . . I'll bring it
   down.

FRANK: If you would.

(*A beat.*)

Another drink?

PHIL: How many's this?

FRANK: This is six . . .

PHIL: Yeah, go on, then, I haven't got far to walk.

FRANK: No?

PHIL: No, only to the car.

(*He drinks and hands* FRANK *his glass.*)

Cheers.

(*Blackout.*)

HAZEL: Yet still alone, and with his thoughts only, he sat there, bald and wet, and yet the wind and rain had ceased and all the air was clear . . . He turned his mind to lofty thoughts of subjects he held dear.

(*Light on* ARTHUR.)

ARTHUR: This never happens in *Rocky* . . . I love *Rocky*, me. I've seen them all, *Rocky One, Two* and *Three*. I like *Rocky Two* the best – you know, where Adrienne's dying in hospital and Rocky's there with his trainer, and she just moves her fingers and says, 'Win, Rocky, win.' Oh, I was just stood in the cinema, shouting. I felt a right fart, and when I looked around everybody else was shouting and all.

(*Light out on* ARTHUR.)

HAZEL: And so the time has come and on this stage, good sirs, needs must I play my part, and meet our hero face to face. The sands of time run fast . . . five weeks is but a blink in the history of our globe. Arthur's quest is waning and Reg has his team in training.

(HAZEL *drops into a press-up position and begins to perform press-ups with ease.*)

ARTHUR: Not bad.

HAZEL: Eh?

ARTHUR: Pretty impressive.

HAZEL: If you're a flasher, I'm not interested.

ARTHUR: You what?

HAZEL: If you're one of those little men who hangs about flashing his wares, I'm not interested.

ARTHUR: I'm not a flasher . . . I'm training . . .

HAZEL: Training . . . uh?

ARTHUR: My lads are on a five-mile run . . . (*Aside*) I'll rot in hell for the lies I tell.

HAZEL: And you're the first one back?

ARTHUR: Sharp . . . very sharp . . .

HAZEL: Oh, trainer, eh? I didn't realize.

ARTHUR: Been jogging, have you?

HAZEL: Yeah. Light jog . . . I've just had a heavy session.

ARTHUR: Husband at home, then, is he?

HAZEL: Don't come the crudity with me, fatty, you're barking up the wrong tree.

ARTHUR: Oh, I stand corrected.

HAZEL: Weights . . . I train with weights.

ARTHUR: A couple of bags of sugar on the end of a broom handle?

HAZEL: Oh, I can see that you're fit . . . every curve in your physique screams out . . . fitness. How often do you train – once a year?

ARTHUR: Ha ha . . . very funny . . .

HAZEL: You men make me laugh.

ARTHUR: That's hard . . . I bet . . . seeing you . . .

HAZEL: I see them like you down at the club, a game of squash, a sauna, twenty cigs, and a heart attack . . . Rugby players are the worst. Training session and then seven pints of Guinness. Fitness . . . you don't know what fitness is.

ARTHUR: Here, catch.

> (ARTHUR *throws the ball quite hard but she catches it easily. Through this speech they continue to pass the ball.*)

Where's this club, then?

HAZEL: Above the supermarket.

ARTHUR: Oh, yeah . . .

HAZEL: Showers . . . sauna . . . solarium, loose weights . . . getting some Nautilus at Christmas.

ARTHUR: How much is it, then?

HAZEL: Interested, are you?

ARTHUR: Only making conversation.

HAZEL: You could have a free trial.

ARTHUR: Who owns it?

HAZEL: A woman called Hazel Scott.

ARTHUR: Dave Scott's wife . . . the international scrum half?

HAZEL: That's right . . . we separated two years ago . . . Give me a ring if you're interested . . . we're in the *Yellow Pages* . . . I'll show you what training is . . .

ARTHUR: I doubt it . . .

HAZEL: If I was you, I'd start to worry about your team . . . I think they must have got lost . . .

ARTHUR: Now I can see why your husband left you.

HAZEL: I left him.

> (HAZEL *exits, taking the ball with her. She reaches a side of the stage and does a perfect reverse pass.* ARTHUR *catches it . . . and follows her off.*)

ARTHUR: Not bad . . . hey, listen . . .

> (*The lights go down.*)

STEVE *comes on, wearing a pair of overalls. He lies down and is looking under a car.* PHIL *follows, wearing a tracksuit, and then* FRANK, *in his butcher's togs. Their speeches overlap, and their actions are done to the audience.*

STEVE: I think that what you've got is a fracture on a brake pipe . . . fluid's escaping, and you need new shock absorbers on both the front sides. Apart from that, and a dicky front light, the car's fine.

PHIL: The kestrel is, of course, not only a real feature in Casper's life, but it also serves as a symbol of the freedom that Casper will never have himself until he manages to escape from the environment that he currently finds himself caged in.

FRANK: I can't really let you have that for less than two pound. It's the best rump steak, you see . . . I've got to make a living. Tell you what . . . give us one ninety.

> (ARTHUR *enters upstage.*)

ARTHUR: Oi!

ALL: Sorry, what did you say . . . sir? Lad? Love?

ARTHUR: Oi, it's me . . .

(*They all look around for* ARTHUR, *who has invaded their very privacy.*)

ALL: What?

ARTHUR: What happened?

ALL: What?

ARTHUR: What happened on Tuesday, lads, eh?

ALL: Not here, I'm busy.

ARTHUR: I said . . . what bloody happened?

ALL: (*whispering*) Go away.

ARTHUR: No.

ALL: Look, this is embarrassing . . . sorry . . . sir/class/love . . .

ARTHUR: Come tomorrow . . . Walton fields . . .

ALL: Go away . . .

ARTHUR: Tomorrow?

ALL: All right . . .

ARTHUR: See you tomorrow, then . . .

(ARTHUR *goes. General cover lights.*)

PHIL: Now soon to sing their songs of old,
   Their battle chants of war,
   So let music play and voices swell
   And sunken hearts rise from dark hell.

   (STEVE, FRANK *and* PHIL *take off their outer clothes, revealing training gear, tracksuits, etc.*)

   Hey, Frank . . . 'She was poor but she was honest.' (*Sings*):
   She was poor but she was honest,
   Victim of a rich man's whim.

ALL: First he fucked her, then he left her,
   And she had a child by him.
   It's the same the whole world over,
   It's the poor what gets the blame.
   It's the rich what gets the pleasure
   And it's all the bloody same.

   (TONY *enters, in training gear.*)

STEVE: Hey up . . . Club song . . . 'Blackbird' . . .

FRANK: Which version . . . clean or filthy . . .?

TONY: Filthy . . .

PHIL: You lot are worse than the kids at school.

TONY: We are kids.

STEVE: Some of us.

TONY: Ooohh, getting all defensive, just because you shave ... don't come all macho ...

STEVE: Oh, big word for an apprentice miner, int it?

TONY: Here's another big word.

STEVE: What?

TONY: Eat shit, you skinny gett!

FRANK: I love the humour.

STEVE: 'Blackbird' ... Club song by Steve Edwards ... Mr Hopley, sir ...

PHIL: Is it one of your own compositions, lad?

STEVE: Yes, sir ... It's taken me years of creative turmoil and anguish ...

PHIL: Right, let's hear it, lad, if it's any good you can put it in your sixteen-plus English file.

STEVE: Once a boy was no good,
took a girl into a wood.

FRANK: Bye bye, blackbird.

STEVE: Laid her down upon the grass,
Pinched her tits and slapped her arse.

ALL: Bye bye, Blackbird.

STEVE: Took her where nobody else could find her,
To a place where he could really grind her,
Rolled her over on her front,
Shoved his ...

ALL: Yo ...

STEVE: Right up her ...

ALL: Ears ... Blackbird, bye bye.

PHIL: Give me the other version, any day.

STEVE: Boring.

FRANK: Three out of ten.

TONY: One out of twenty from the Russian judge.

PHIL: (*In a French accent*) Luxembourg ... *nul points* ...

TONY: Get this one going ... ba da da ... ba da da ...

(*They do a rendition of the Flying Pickets' 'Spring in the Air'.
It is a common impersonation of the Flying Pickets. As they*

sing, ARTHUR *enters with a number of rugby balls under his arms. He throws the balls to the lads.*)

ARTHUR: Catch. What have we got here, *Opportunity Knocks?*

FRANK: Just having a song.

ARTHUR: If you want to sing, you're in the wrong game.

PHIL: Just a laugh.

ARTHUR: Just . . . let's have a word . . . I don't want to waste time. Tonight we'll work on general fitness . . . cardiovascularity.

STEVE: I think my tea's ready.

TONY: Shurrup.

STEVE: Don't start.

ARTHUR: Ball-handling . . . and the speed of moving the ball from the . . . play the ball . . .

PHIL: We know all this . . .

ARTHUR: I'm assuming you know nothing.

TONY: He doesn't.

PHIL: Piss off.

TONY: Touchy.

ARTHUR: I want to know if you've ever had any set moves, from penalties . . . or from scrumming . . .

PHIL: What about other players?

ARTHUR: That's my worry . . . I'll be playing hooker for a start.

STEVE: Can you hook?

ARTHUR: You'll have to wait and see.

TONY: What time'll we finish?

ARTHUR: Why?

STEVE: He's got to be in bed.

FRANK: With their lass.

TONY: I don't want to be late.

FRANK: Nor me.

ARTHUR: Look, let's just make a start . . . Right . . . let's have a run.

FRANK: A what?

ARTHUR: Start off with three miles . . . just to get warm.

STEVE: Warm?

FRANK: No . . . I'm not running about . . . I've been on my feet all day at work . . . I'll have a game of touch and pass . . .

ARTHUR: It's only a short run, Frank.

FRANK: I don't want to overdo it, I want to be able to walk tomorrow.

PHIL: Come on, Frank . . . take it steady . . .

ARTHUR: Look, it's not a race . . . it's just a matter of finishing . . . Don't you watch the London Marathon?

FRANK: Watch, yeah . . .

TONY: Let's get summat done . . . I'm gonna miss *Top of the Pops* at this rate.

FRANK: Oh, come on, then.

> (*They all stand in a line across the stage. Those not talking make a heavy breathing and plodding noise . . . sub-Berkoff.*)

STEVE: Out we went . . . over the crisp grass of Walton fields . . . Down the slope which led to the main road . . .

PHIL: Through the gate . . . and on to the pavement . . .

TONY: The change of running surface . . . jarred . . .

STEVE: Arthur led . . .

FRANK: And we like warriors followed bunched behind him . . .

STEVE: The night was drawing in . . .

ARTHUR: It wasn't dark but . . . it would be in the hour . . .

PHIL: Car sidelights were beginning to ease their way effortlessly towards us . . .

TONY: Sodium street lights sparkled to life . . .

STEVE: As we hit a hump-backed bridge . . . the weariness . . . the fatigue . . .

PHIL: The complete and utter lack of fitness was beginning to register in us all . . .

STEVE: My legs felt heavy . . . calves aching . . . a hard pounding drumming reverberating up my back . . .

TONY: The bridge brow was in sight and then the descent . . .

FRANK: Twenty yards of easy running . . .

ARTHUR: I didn't realize that three miles was so long . . .

FRANK: Saliva dripping from my mouth like a hungry dog . . . and I was aware of the effort of moving my frame . . .

STEVE: The dread of meeting pedestrians loomed . . .

PHIL: And mannequins . . . grinning, smirking their smug sickly expressions . . .

STEVE: Their form is constant . . .

FRANK: They never change . . . age leaves them untouched . . .

TONY: Our tracks rumbled along the tarmac . . .

PHIL: The sight of people . . . and the impulse to make more effort to push harder . . .

ARTHUR: Fifty-five minutes . . . for three miles a slow pace . . . but a lot of meat in the pack . . . we returned with the light fading . . .

(*They are all exhausted and collapse where they are.*)

Get your breath . . . All right, Frank . . .?

FRANK: Just about . . . feel a bit sick . . .

ARTHUR: Deep breaths, Frank, son.

FRANK: I'm OK.

STEVE: Nice one, Frankie.

FRANK: I bet I can't move tomorrow.

ARTHUR: You will . . . same again tomorrow.

PHIL: What next, Arthur?

FRANK: That'll do for me.

PHIL: Not bad for a start . . . I'm about as fit as D. H. Lawrence.

ARTHUR: I think he's dead.

PHIL: That's what I mean.

STEVE: Nice and easy session . . . pass me the Guinness drip, will you?

TONY: Enjoyed it.

STEVE: I have.

PHIL: You're not a bad bloke, are you, Arthur?

ARTHUR: Aren't I?

PHIL: No, you're all right, mate, all right . . . I had my doubts . . . but you're an honest man . . . I can smell a crook, but you're OK.

ARTHUR: Thanks.

PHIL: I mean it.

TONY: Yeah . . . and me . . .

FRANK: Do you know what our training amounted to in the past? We'd meet in the Wheatsheaf . . . have about six pints, pick thirteen men . . .

STEVE: If thirteen ever turned up.

FRANK: Then it was back to my place to watch the videos.

ARTHUR: I love *Rocky* . . . *One*, *Two* and *Three*.

PHIL: Pulp crap.

ARTHUR: Oh, Barry friggin' Norman now, are we?

STEVE: Hey, we had some laughs. Can you remember that time when Jack's cousin said that he wanted a game . . . turned up, played and got his ear-lobe bit off . . .

FRANK: He played well.

PHIL: We only lost thirty–nil that game.

ARTHUR: No more losing talk . . . think positive. I want to succeed.

TONY: I know what'll succeed: a budgie with no teeth.

PHIL: That's the sort of comment this team doesn't need.

STEVE: Let's not get into it tonight, eh?

FRANK: Yeah.

STEVE: Can you remember when I broke my hand?

TONY: You didn't do that playing rugby.

PHIL: That's true.

STEVE: I'll tell you what I did do. I shat into my shorts once.

> (*Blackout. They freeze.* ARTHUR *stands behind them in over-head light.*)

ARTHUR: Ar . . . you're good lads, honest, no edge to you . . . you love needling each other. The only thing you have in common is the game . . . I feel a right prat, you've taken to me, and you don't know why I'm doing all this. In any case, I don't think about it much . . . only at nights . . . I lay awake . . .

> (*Lights up.*)

STEVE: Get away, man . . . I don't believe you.

PHIL: It's true, and she married his brother-in-law's nephew.

FRANK: What did Jack say?

PHIL: What would you say?

STEVE: She looks like a really nice lass and all.

ARTHUR: I tell you what . . . let's get down to the Wheatsheaf and have a pint, shall we?

TONY: Sounds like a good idea.

STEVE: That's the sort of training I like, Arthur.

PHIL: What about the fitness?

ARTHUR: Look at it like this . . . it's a celebration . . . all I want to do is to show my gratitude to you lot for turning out for training.

FRANK: You had to twist our arms a bit, though.

PHIL: I nearly had a fit when you came into school, the kids went wild . . .

ARTHUR: I think it's the head . . .

PHIL: Probably . . .

ARTHUR: Well, what do you say, then? A swift five down the Wheatsheaf Arms? I'll get the first round in.

STEVE: I'll drink to that.

FRANK: And me.

A change of lighting. The players set up the gymnasium with the following equipment: lat machine, exercise bike, bench press, hack squat, sit-ups bench, step-up bench.

HAZEL: And so to play a major part within this vasty 'O'. Arthur trained with just one jog, his players' skills, well, naff, he could have laughed but took them for a drink of sack. Now remember how on Walton fields came the offer of a club. It was training that would win the day, not supping in the pub. Thus Hazel takes the boards once more, training in her gym, all plush and modern and well equipped; well, fit athletes train, and gross obese men slim. But soft . . .

> (*The players chuckle with glee.*)

For as we speak, the tissue-paper gladiators approach, led by their hero our coach. How will they fare with yon weights? The training will be tough. I see a question on yon fair face, sirs, are they man enough?

> (HAZEL *proceeds to the sit-ups bench and begins exercising. The players have frozen at the back of the stage.*)

TONY: Hey, not bad.

FRANK: Nice work.

PHIL: Arthur, who's that?

ARTHUR: Ar, right. Hazel, can I introduce you to the team?

HAZEL: Yeah.

ARTHUR: This is Tony, Phil, Frank.

HAZEL: Hello. Come to have a go at getting fit, have you?

TONY: Yeah.

HAZEL: How are the ten-mile runs?

FRANK· What?

ARTHUR: Great, thanks.

HAZEL: It's going to be hard slog . . . over the next twelve sessions.

TONY: Yeah.

PHIL: Be gentle with us.

HAZEL: (*to the audience*) I took them around each machine, explaining its function and explaining some common fallacies about weight-training. I could see at a glance that they were sceptical, to say the least.

> (PHIL *is on the exercise bike.*)

PHIL: (*Whispering*) She's not training us, is she?

ARTHUR: In a word?

PHIL: In a word.

ARTHUR: Yes.

FRANK: Great stuff.

PHIL: You're joking.

TONY: He is.

ARTHUR: I'm not.

PHIL: She's a woman.

ARTHUR: I thought you were educated.

PHIL: I am.

ARTHUR: She's probably twice as fit as you.

TONY: No way.

ARTHUR: Just give it a go.

FRANK: I'm not bothered . . . It's a good idea.

PHIL: I'll just feel uncomfortable.

ARTHUR: She's used to training men.

TONY: Tell us another.

ARTHUR: It's her gym . . . she got body-builders 'n' all sorts of athletes coming here and she trains 'em.

PHIL: I still say it's a bit much.

> (HAZEL *goes up to* PHIL.)

HAZEL: That's for women.

> (*Embarrassed reaction from* PHIL. *The others laugh.*)

PHIL: Obviously.

> (STEVE *enters, late.*)

STEVE: Oh, yes, what is this . . . luxury a-gogo?

ARTHUR: Hazel, this is Steve.

STEVE: Hazel . . . nice to meet you.

HAZEL: Hello.

STEVE: Do you have a nut in every bite?

HAZEL: Humorous as well, isn't he?

STEVE: Not funny but fast.

HAZEL: OK then, warm up on the bike . . . let's make a start . . . We'll start with a circuit . . . Arthur, legs . . . Frank, sit-ups . . . Tony lats . . . Phil bench . . . we're looking . . .

ARTHUR: I feel like I've shit my pants.

HAZEL: I'm waiting.

ARTHUR: Sorry.

HAZEL: We're looking for quick ten reps, make sure that the movement is strict, do not cheat . . . if it's too light, don't worry, it'll serve as a warm-up exercise, and go.

STEVE: Hey, look at this . . . I love it . . . this is about my standard.

> (*Each man begins to exercise. The weights clunk about.* HAZEL *watches.* STEVE *fools.*)

HAZEL: Concentrate on the movements.

STEVE: Anybody want anything bringing from the shops? 'Riding along on a push-bike, honey . . .' Ho ah ho ah . . .

> (*He starts to make hand signals . . . and banks the bike.*)

Get out of the way.

HAZEL: Come on, cut it out.

STEVE: Get out of the way.

HAZEL: Very funny, now pack it in.

> (HAZEL *has a look around the gym and sees all the lads on the machines, performing the exercises pathetically. She is very displeased.*)

All right, change.

> (*They all change.* ARTHUR *bangs the leg machine.*)

Don't bang the weights.

> (*The lads move to a different machine.* HAZEL *gives them the go-ahead. They begin work on the machines. The effect is comic (and much improvising of the comic elements of the machines, should be allowed).* HAZEL *goes around to the various machines and encourages the lads to perform correctly.* TONY *is performing a neck-press with the weight to his head.*)

TONY: This one hurts your head.

(HAZEL *encourages* FRANK *on the hack-squat.*)

FRANK: It's not very good for my piles.

(HAZEL *gets them to change machines. A lighting change.*)

HAZEL: (*Sitting on the bike*) I worked them slowly to begin with. I could see that they were desperately out of shape . . .

(*All the lads perform one exercise.*)

. . . and, to give them their due, they played their part. We trained for a full week, split system, and Arthur would work at the back of the gym on ball skills.

(*The lads perform two repeats of the exercise.*)

As we got into week three it was time to push them. (*To the players*) By the time we're finished you'll be doing thirty reps each.

ALL: Thirty?

(*The players become more motivated and begin to count to themselves. HAZEL is still encouraging their work. They count to thirty and as they count the volume increases, so by the time they reach thirty they are completely shouting. Blackout.*)

ACT TWO

The players are still counting. HAZEL *walks around, encouraging them.*

HAZEL: Come on, pull!

STEVE: Get off.

HAZEL: No, pull . . . good . . .

      (TONY *is on lats.*)

    Pull . . .

TONY: I can't . . . pull . . .

HAZEL: Force it . . . pull . . . just your back . . . good . . .

      (ARTHUR *is doing step-ups on the bench.*)

    How many, Arthur?

ARTHUR: Twenty.

HAZEL: Another . . . ten.

ARTHUR: No, I'm knackered . . . I want a rest . . .

HAZEL: Another ten . . . come on . . . I'll count you . . . one . . . two
    . . . three . . . four . . . five . . . six . . .

ARTHUR: I'm gonna spew.

HAZEL: Two more . . . one . . . two . . . good . . .

ARTHUR: Oh, shit . . .

      (ARTHUR *dashes offstage to be sick.*)

HAZEL: Listen, lads . . . listen . . . a minute . . . Phil, Tony. You've
    really got to go for it now, you've really got to push it . . . push
    to the limits of the pain barrier . . . otherwise the training's point-
    less.

FRANK: It's no good, I've had enough.

HAZEL: You've got to go more, Frank . . . hit the wall and straight
    out the other side . . . that's what it's about, fellers.

STEVE: Can we just have a minute?

HAZEL: OK, a timed minute . . . starting now . . .

      (*They all relax.* HAZEL *times them.*)

PHIL: Do you get something sexual out of all this?

HAZEL: Don't talk shit . . . forty seconds . . .

PHIL: You're a sadist . . . aren't you? Go on, admit it.

HAZEL: Thirty seconds . . .

TONY: This is harder than pit work.

STEVE: You're never there in any case.

TONY: I am when we're working.

HAZEL: Fifteen . . .

FRANK: Where's Arthur?

HAZEL: Being sick . . . time, lads . . . a minute . . . back you get . . .

PHIL: No, hang on . . . have another minute.

HAZEL: No, come on.

TONY: Wait on a bit, Hazel.

HAZEL: You said a minute.

PHIL: Not a literal minute, a minute as in five minutes.

HAZEL: Get back on these exercises, all of you.

STEVE: No . . . have a minute, man, for God's sake . . .

FRANK: In a tick . . .

HAZEL: Now.

PHIL: We've been doing all the work . . . it's easy to shout at people,
     I should know, I'm a teacher.

HAZEL: OK . . . if you want to take that attitude, fair enough.

FRANK: Thanks.

PHIL: We'll train again in five or ten . . .

HAZEL: When your muscles have grown cold?

TONY: Sarcasm . . .

STEVE: The lowest form of . . .

HAZEL: That's OK by me, it's your money, I suppose.

TONY: Eh?

    (*A beat.*)

STEVE: You what?

PHIL: What is?

HAZEL: All this training going to waste . . . it's a waste of your
     money.

TONY: Have we got to pay for all this?

HAZEL: No . . . this is free . . . the bet, I mean . . .

PHIL: What are you on about?

STEVE: What bet?

HAZEL: You're not that thick . . . come on . . .

PHIL: What's all this about a bet?

HAZEL: OK, forget it . . . Let's get back to work.

FRANK: No . . . hang on, I smell something a bit fishy.

STEVE: I think it's Tony.

TONY: Bollocks, you.

PHIL: Is this summat to do with Arthur?

HAZEL: I really don't know.

TONY: Come on, leave it . . . it's got nothing to do with us.

(ARTHUR *enters.*)

ARTHUR: Jesus Christ . . . I've just thrown half my insides up . . .
    What's got nothing to do with you, Tony?

TONY: This bet.

ARTHUR: No . . . right . . . Come on, let's push on.

PHIL: I want to know about this bet, Arthur.

FRANK: Yeah, how does it affect us?

ARTHUR: Who told you?

HAZEL: I thought they knew.

ARTHUR: They do now.

STEVE: What is it . . . top secret or something?

ARTHUR: Right . . . I suppose I'd better tell you.

HAZEL: I think you'd better . . . before we go any further.

ARTHUR: Sit down, lads, this might hurt.

FRANK: Us or you?

ARTHUR: Both.

(*They all sit down.*)

So I told them about the bet . . . and they were quite amiable
about it. Steve offered to put some money against them winning.

STEVE: I'll have twenty quid against us, Arth.

ARTHUR: We haven't got a chance, they said . . . they were right.

TONY: We haven't got a chance.

ARTHUR: They didn't like Reg Welsh, that was clear.

STEVE: He's a bastard . . . and a crook . . . take that from me . . . I did his
    car once . . . he never paid me . . . sent two of his thugs around.

ARTHUR: That's the way Reg works.

FRANK: It makes no difference anyway . . . if we enter we might not

get drawn against the Cobblers in any case . . . we'll still
probably go out in the first round.

ARTHUR: I had to tell them that it'd all been set up, that Reg had
arranged for us to have a bye . . . so we'd meet in the final . . .
that went down like a fart at a wedding.

TONY: You what?

STEVE: It's set up?

ARTHUR: That's what I said.

PHIL: Why us?

TONY: Yeah.

FRANK: We've never bloody won a game.

STEVE: No . . . never will.

PHIL: Oh, yeah . . . I'm beginning to see it all . . . you and Reg
Welsh must have had a good laugh about us . . . eh? Is that it?
The Wheatsheaf . . . the joke side . . . the side who play with
four men . . . is that it?

TONY: Right . . . I'm not flogging my heart out for you to win three
thousand . . . not to be made the laughing stock . . . for the likes
of Reg Welsh.

ARTHUR: What have you got to lose . . .? It's my money . . .

FRANK: It's your money, but it's our pride . . . We've had enough
gibes shoved down our throats without being set up against the
best side in Yorkshire . . . We want to win for a change.

ARTHUR: This is your chance.

PHIL: Rubbish, that's utter rubbish and you know it. I'm off . . .
Come on, Steve.

STEVE: I'm coming.

ARTHUR: Listen . . .

TONY: No . . . you've got yourself in this shit . . . you get yourself
out of it . . . don't get us involved.

FRANK: So Reg Welsh thinks we're a joke team, does he?

ARTHUR: Listen, Frank . . .

FRANK: Well, that's fine by me. We are a bloody joke team . . . The
game's off . . . You tell him . . . see if he finds it funny . . .

(FRANK *leaves upstage, singing 'Swing low, sweet chariot'. All*
the rest collect their belongings and leave. HAZEL *and*
ARTHUR *are left*.)

HAZEL: Sorry.

ARTHUR: Ar . . .

HAZEL: I er . . .

ARTHUR: Doesn't matter.

HAZEL: I thought they knew.

ARTHUR: They had to know, I suppose.

HAZEL: Why didn't you tell them?

ARTHUR: I wouldn't have got them this far . . . The mention of the Cobblers and legs turn to water.

HAZEL: Can you blame them?

ARTHUR: No.

HAZEL: Well, then . . . do you want a drink?

ARTHUR: No . . . I feel physically and morally sick.

HAZEL: Have another word with them.

ARTHUR: No.

HAZEL: Why?

ARTHUR: Funny.

HAZEL: What?

ARTHUR: I suppose Reg was right . . . said I'd seen too many *Rocky* films . . . where the underdog always wins.

HAZEL: It's nice to think about . . . nice ideal . . .

ARTHUR: That's all it is . . . an ideal.

HAZEL: We need that sort of thing . . . to escape to.

ARTHUR: Life's a bastard when you stop to think about it.

HAZEL: Nobody wins.

ARTHUR: Ar, well . . . that's my bank savings down the friggin' shoot.

HAZEL: He'll take the money, then?

ARTHUR: Every last penny . . . plus the fact that I'll be the laughing stock . . .

HAZEL: So that's my part of the bargain wrapped up too, I suppose.

ARTHUR: 'Fraid so.

HAZEL: Another icon shattered.

ARTHUR: You what?

HAZEL: Broken dream.

ARTHUR: Ar . . .

HAZEL: Oh, well . . .

ARTHUR: I'd like to be able to blame somebody . . . but I can't.

HAZEL: What are you going to do?

ARTHUR: Ever heard of suicide?

HAZEL: Don't be stupid.

ARTHUR: I think I'll just stay here for a bit . . . if that's all right with you.

HAZEL: Stay as long as you like . . . I'm going to nip down to the bank.

ARTHUR: Me too.

    (HAZEL *exits*.)

Have you ever been out of your mind,

And a scream of some kind

Would be something obscene?

I feel like that now the day's at a close.

I knew that it wouldn't work out, I suppose.

And so as they all say . . . to you, adieu and farewell . . .

. . . and for the lies that I've told?

I'll go rot in hell.

    (*He gets up slowly and leaves.*)

TONY *comes into the gym and begins to train.* STEVE *enters and gets on the bike.* FRANK *and* PHIL *follow and start their exercises.*

PHIL: Oi, fat bald bastard!

ARTHUR: Eh?

PHIL: Get training, it's on . . .

ARTHUR: It's not.

TONY: It is.

STEVE: So get moving.

FRANK: Come on, Arthur, move it.

PHIL: If we win we split the cash . . . If we lose . . . it's all yours.

ARTHUR: It's a deal . . . and listen, lads . . . thanks.

    (*A spotlight picks out* HAZEL.)

HAZEL: The harder they trained the more single-minded they became, for the next three weeks they worked . . . and strained and pained and planed the gained muscular power . . . into shape, resilient and every hour . . . they could, they knew they should, devote their time to the cause of winning. To the front page clause: 'The Wheatsheaf beat the Cobblers out of Castleford.' It was a tabloid dream, from a team that have schemed to pass and switch the ball, to play all fair and give the ground a swift turn of stud . . . They would if they could, give the ball some air . . . to turn defence to blunders with overlaps and scissor moves and lofty up 'n' unders of a genre not seen for years. Above all else, determined not to lose . . . they chose to fight, though as you've seen upon this stage they've had the right for flight . . . to withdraw . . . let brass bands be heard and battle cries of awe ring from Hull to Featherstone . . . And let our heroes know that they are not alone . . . in their struggle to be kings on a paper throne . . . Five weeks now gone . . . The Wheatsheaf mean to see their form . . . We see them now . . . Still before the storm . . .

Lights up. The players are slowly finishing their exercises. They are tired and drop to a resting place. HAZEL *walks around and gives them a towel. They sit still and sweating . . . quiet . . . breathing heavily . . . They remain silent. Then:*

PHIL: Hey!

ARTHUR: What?

PHIL: Do you want to hear a poem I've written about the game?

TONY: No.

PHIL: It's good, listen . . . It's a rip-off from Shakespeare.

STEVE: Ronny Shakespeare used to do the washing for my Mam.

PHIL: Prologue *Romeo and Juliet* . . . it's taken from.

FRANK: Very good . . .

PHIL: Listen, you philistines . . . you'll get this . . . it's good:
    Two clubs each unlike in dignity,
    In fair Castleford where we'll lay our scene,
    A stupid bet, a bigotry . . .
    A grim determination to win a match so keen . . .
    What do you reckon?

TONY: Brilliant . . .

PHIL: 'Bigotry' doesn't really work . . . but I couldn't think of another word.

STEVE: How about pillock?

PHIL: No . . . it doesn't even work as a half-rhyme.

TONY: Bloody hell!

ARTHUR: Yeah.

FRANK: Knackered.

STEVE: I feel drained.

HAZEL: You've done well . . . should be pleased with yourselves . . .
I'll put the showers on . . .

    (HAZEL *exits*.)

TONY: No shower for me . . . straight down home.

STEVE: Early to bed . . .

PHIL: Yeah.

ARTHUR: No . . . not for me.

FRANK: Why not?

ARTHUR: I can't sleep unless I've had a drink.

PHIL: You're in a bad way.

ARTHUR: If I don't have a couple of pints I just lay looking at the
lampshade.

STEVE: I'll join you for a pint in the Sheaf, Arth.

ARTHUR: Right . . . a couple of pints, fish and chips . . . then up the
wooden hill to Bedfordshire.

FRANK: Sounds like Tupper of the Track.

ARTHUR: Working-class hero.

FRANK: True enough.

ARTHUR: Born with a silver knife in his back.

STEVE: I feel right nervous.

TONY: I don't feel too bad . . . I will do tomorrow . . . I'll shit
myself.

STEVE: Take some extra shorts, then.

    (*A beat*.)

PHIL: Arthur?

ARTHUR: What?

PHIL: At the risk of sounding pedantic . . .

ALL: Whoooo!

TONY: Get a big sign, 'Sage at work.'

PHIL: All right, point taken.

STEVE: Brilliant.

TONY: Oh, yeah, brilliant . . . brilliant . . .

4 **Five Plays**

ARTHUR: Go on . . .

PHIL: I don't suppose you've overlooked the fact that we've still got only five players?

ARTHUR: In the 1914 Rourke's Drift test Britain only had ten men . . . and still beat a side of thirteen.

PHIL: That's little comfort.

ARTHUR: Don't worry.

FRANK: Have you got it in hand . . . as they say?

ARTHUR: I've made some arrangements . . . Right, I'm down the showers and into the Wheatsheaf for a skinful.

PHIL: Who's taking Steve and Frankie tomorrow?

ARTHUR: Me . . . I'll pick you up about half ten, Frankie?

FRANK: Yeah.

ARTHUR: I'll make arrangements later, Steve.

STEVE: Hang on, I'm coming . . . See you in Castleford, lads.

ALL: Right oh . . .

FRANK: Castleford here we come . . .

STEVE: Frankie goes to Castleford . . . eh, hear that?

TONY: Piss off.

STEVE: Tony's good at one-liners.

    (STEVE *and* ARTHUR *leave,* STEVE *singing 'Relax'*.)

TONY: I don't think all this health food's been good for me.

PHIL: How come?

TONY: I'm on the toilet all the time.

FRANK: It's good that, clear you out.

TONY: I don't know about that . . . I feel like one long tube from mouth to arse.

PHIL: Oesophagus.

TONY: Oh, ar . . .

    (*A beat.*)

PHIL: How do you feel, Frank?

FRANK: OK.

PHIL: Did you have a glance at those mags?

FRANK: Oh, yeah . . . very nice, very tasteful . . . yeah . . .

PHIL: Educational, aren't they?

FRANK: Yeah.

PHIL: I've got a couple of videos that might be worth a nod.

FRANK: Oh, right ... tomorrow night, maybe ... after the game?

PHIL: Let's see how it goes.

TONY: How do you think we'll do?

PHIL: Dunno.

FRANK: I must admit that I think we look quite good.

TONY: Depends who Arthur's bringing in.

PHIL: I've got a feeling that that might be another of Arthur's little foibles.

FRANK: Yeah ... you might be right.

TONY: Oh ... If we lose, he's knackered.

PHIL: That's the price of gambling.

TONY: Funny how you just do things, don't you? Make a decision to do something and then do it. That marathon ... they do it just to say they've done it.

PHIL: Creativity, isn't it?

TONY: Is it?

PHIL: Well, what would you have been doing if you hadn't been training?

TONY: Arsing about, I suppose.

PHIL: Right ... it's all part of the creative impulse ... I tell the kids at school ... creativity takes on many forms ... They can't see it.

FRANK: Well, it's part of the health thing, isn't it? Life's like a tightrope ... I read this in a book somewhere ... never really forgotten it ... life's a tightrope ... we all travel in one direction, and if we don't surround ourselves with things to do ... to help balance us ... we fall off ... something like that, anyway.

PHIL: I think I know what you mean.

TONY: Do you think we ought to help Arthur out if we lose?

FRANK: In what way?

TONY: With the money.

PHIL: We're not going to lose ... no way am I having a woman make my back and legs and arms ache for five weeks to lose ... no way ... Shower, Frank?

FRANK: No.

PHIL: Tony?

TONY: Can do.

PHIL: See you there.

TONY: See you.

(HAZEL *enters, carrying fresh towels.*)

PHIL: See you tomorrow, Hazel . . . You'll be there, won't you?

HAZEL: Oh, don't worry . . . I wouldn't miss it for the world.

PHIL *and* TONY: See you.

(TONY *and* PHIL *exit.*)

HAZEL: Aren't you going for a drink, Frank?

FRANK: No.

HAZEL: Oh.

FRANK: I don't feel like it, to be honest.

HAZEL: That's a shame.

FRANK: I feel all melancholy.

HAZEL: Oh, what's brought that on?

FRANK: This game.

HAZEL: Oh.

FRANK: When I was younger I used to play regularly . . . Tina would bring the kids to watch.

HAZEL: Aren't they coming tomorrow?

FRANK: No.

HAZEL: Oh.

FRANK: We . . . er . . . we split up, you see.

HAZEL: Oh, I'm sorry.

FRANK: Took the kids . . . I hardly see them now. They used to love to come and watch . . . Carl and Peter . . . two good props in the making . . . Their mother'll be making them as soft as pudding.

HAZEL: That's mothers for you.

FRANK: Do you have any kids?

HAZEL: No.

FRANK: All this serious training, the lads as a team . . . brought it all back to me.

HAZEL: Yeah?

FRANK: I wasn't bothered when we were losing . . . it didn't matter then, but we're in with a chance now . . . I want them to be

proud of me, do you know that? I want them to be proud of me
. . . and she's making them as soft as shit.

HAZEL: Go home, Frank.

FRANK: Yeah.

HAZEL: Save all the hatred for the field.

FRANK: You know what, Hazel?

HAZEL: No, what?

FRANK: Well, the lads and me were talking and we think that you're
all right for a woman.

HAZEL: Well that's very big of 'em, Frank . . . very big of 'em.

FRANK: I think that I will have that drink after all. Are you coming?
(*A beat.*)

HAZEL: Well, if I'm going to be one of the lads, I think I'd
better.

*Lights cover to blue wash. All the gym equipment has been removed save
the two benches, which are placed side by side mid-stage. Brass music.*
ARTHUR *stays centre stage.* HAZEL *is downstage in a spotlight.*

HAZEL: So a steady drink for one and all, and then home to bed as
the hour moved on apace. Our heroes bid each other adieu, and
with confidence in their hearts they knew they stood a chance, a
chance to win, to regain lost pride. They knew that fate was on
their side.

ARTHUR: I know it sounds funny but that night I prayed, I don't
know why, I'm agnostic. Then I looked at my bank book,
placed it under Doreen's underwear in the bottom drawer, then I
went to sleep.

(*Lights fade on* ARTHUR. PHIL *enters, with a hot-water
bottle, wearing a dressing-gown.*)

HAZEL: Though Arthur slept in slumberland, in Phil's three-
bedroomed semi his mind was filled with nightmarish thoughts
and sleep he hadn't any.

PHIL: It's a very funny thing, when I was playing at Loughborough
I never got nervous, I never had a thought about the game but
tonight I'm like a bag of nerves . . . I've been to the toilet . . .
back here to bed . . . I'm going to the toilet again in a minute
. . . I'm sweating, sweat's dripping down my brow, even my

palms are wet . . . I'll have to hope that I can, well . . . drift off
to sleep.

   (*Lights change to a red wash covering the stage.*)
And there I was, playing at Wembley in the Challenge Cup
Final, playing for Fulham against the mighty Featherstone.
There was hundreds and hundreds of bloated red faces looking
down on me. I was on the wing and hundreds of yards away
from the rest of the team. Featherstone looked massive. I gazed
up and caught flashes of their kneecaps. They ran through to
score, I glimpsed sight of hairs on the palms of their hands. We
were losing. We needed a try. There was five minutes to play.
There was an incident off the ball. 'Gerroff me, you fat pig.' I
saw a gap, big as an ocean opening up in front of me. 'Pass the
ball . . . pass the ball!' And then it came out of a blur, the ball.
God, I was nervous. I saw it coming towards me . . . daren't
take my eye off it . . . I caught it and I ran. But I didn't move
. . . I looked up . . . and the whole of Featherstone were coming
towards me . . . men, women, children . . . miners, shop assist-
ants, garage-owners . . . all on the field after me . . . so I ran . . .
but the faster I ran the slower I went. I looked around for
someone to pass to . . . but they were all having lunch . . . sat
down having lunch in the middle of Wembley Stadium . . . 'Go
on, Phil,' they said. 'Go on . . . run mate, run' . . . and I was on
the Underground, going down the Piccadilly Station, running
and they were all running after me. Then a policeman stopped
me and I tried to explain but he wanted my name and where I
lived. I hit him . . . and ran. It was like running in a dream . . .
jumping over buildings and landing at different places . . . but
wherever I landed they were still there, coming around the
corner. I ran up an alleyway . . . I was cornered . . . I looked
around at them . . . trapped, so I ran . . . I ran towards them
. . . I just closed my eyes and ran . . .

A bluish-coloured wash covers the stage, quite dimly. ARTHUR, TONY,
FRANK *and* STEVE *move about in the lights, growling and making large
movements. They are the Cobblers team. They arrange the benches so
they're like they were at the beginning of Act One. The players sit down.*

On the backs of their shirts they have COBBLERS' ARMS *emblazoned.*
They wear full rugby regalia – the players will play the parts of both
teams. Lights up.

ARTHUR: Somebody's gonna get smacked.

TONY: Yeah.

FRANK: I'm gonna kill somebody.

TONY: Yeah, kill!

STEVE: Hurt their bodies.

ARTHUR: Somebody's gonna get their necks broke and their bodies
      hurt.

TONY: Yeah . . . and hurt.

FRANK: What are we?

ALL: Mean.

FRANK: What do we want?

ALL: We want to win.

FRANK: What will we do?

ALL: We'll kill to win.

FRANK: Who are we gonna kill?

ALL: The Wheatsheaf wallies.

FRANK: Why?

ALL: Coz we hate the bastards.

ARTHUR: (*Shaking his fist*) Somebody's gonna get some of this!

TONY: Keep the ball tight . . . until we've made the overlap.

STEVE: Don't switch it, then . . .

ARTHUR: Run straight at 'em . . . Run till you can see the whites of
      their eyes, and when you can see the whites . . . stick an arm
      straight in 'em.

FRANK: Right, here we go.

ARTHUR: Put the willies up 'em.

> (*They sing a warlike chant, with a slapping of thighs and a*
> *banging of feet on the floor. This gets louder and louder, ending*
> *in screams and growls. Blackout.*)

Lights up to reveal the same players, but very quiet (in total contrast)
and sitting down. They have just heard what the Cobblers have done.

STEVE: Hear that?

TONY: Yeah.

STEVE: Jesus Christ, I'm shitting it.

ARTHUR: Ar . . .

FRANK: I think they mean business.

TONY: Do they know that we've had a bye on purpose?

ARTHUR: Yeah.

TONY: They are not going to be too happy about that, are they?

ARTHUR: No.

STEVE: Have they got seven men?

FRANK: And two subs . . . I watched them play the first round.

TONY: Yeah, the subs are like whippets.

STEVE: They would be.

ARTHUR: Remember what I've said all along . . . don't let your nerves get the better of you. Stick to the plans.

TONY: Where's Phil?

> (PHIL *enters, walking as if he's got the shits – which he has.*)

PHIL: Have you seen the size of that lot?

STEVE: Where've you been, man?

PHIL: Toilet.

TONY: Trying to escape.

PHIL: I'm loose.

FRANK: We'll all be loose by the time we've finished this.

PHIL: They have got some big lads.

ARTHUR: Yeah . . . and they've brought a couple of ringers in.

TONY: He wants his money, doesn't he?

ARTHUR: He's not gonna get it, though . . . over my dead body.

STEVE: Hey, steady on, Arthur, I'll play but I'm not going that far.

TONY: How long is there?

ARTHUR: Five minutes.

FRANK: Let them go out first.

PHIL: They're out . . . I could hear them chanting when I was on the toilet . . . the seat was vibrating.

STEVE: What's the weather like?

PHIL: Not bad . . . good for running.

ARTHUR: Keep it wide . . . don't let them keep it tight.

TONY: Wide . . . right.

STEVE: Oh, before I forget, Arthur . . . nice one on the kit.

FRANK: Oh, yeah . . . good stuff, mate.

TONY: Yeah.

ARTHUR: I know this is the wrong time to say this, lads ... but I had to fork out a fiver each for the hire of the kit ... if at some time in the not too distant future ...

PHIL: Did I have a dream last night?

STEVE: And me ... I was playing at Wembley.

(PHIL *looks at him.*)

FRANK: I know what you mean, I was playing all last night.

ARTHUR: Remember the set moves when you get a call ... move it, right?

ALL: Right.

STEVE: Arthur, I suppose these ringers you were talking about were just figments of your imagination, they're not going to appear, are they?

(*A beat.*)

ARTHUR: Ar, well ... it's a very long and complicated story.

(*A beat.*)

ALL: Aye, it would be.

(HAZEL *enters, wearing the same kit. Music plays. All the players look together as a team at* ARTHUR.)

STEVE: You're not serious?

FRANK: Is this the arrangement? I mean, she might get hurt.

HAZEL: Well, what did you expect?

PHIL: Does she know the moves? I mean, I'm not being rotten, Hazel, just ... well, you know?

ARTHUR: Where do you think I got the idea from?

FRANK: He is not thick.

STEVE: No, we are.

TONY: Well, if you play as good as you train ... it's OK by me.

STEVE: And me.

PHIL: And me.

HAZEL: Right, thanks, team.

TONY: I feel a bit emotional.

FRANK: Let's get out there.

ARTHUR: Yeah.

TONY: Having a woman playing ... I love it, aarrhhh!

PHIL: It will probably throw 'em.

STEVE: It's thrown me.

ARTHUR: Well, let's just say . . . all the best.

FRANK: All the best, Arth.

TONY: Good luck.

ARTHUR: And you.

PHIL: It's ridiculous thing to do, Arthur . . . but thanks.

HAZEL: If you don't live life to the full, what's the point?

PHIL: Here we go, then.

> (*They all prepare. There is a sudden air of complete seriousness.
> They shake and concentrate . . . and then . . . out into the stage
> space they run . . . They jump up and down in the stage space
> . . . ARTHUR steps forward . . . and shakes hands with 'Frank'
> of the Cobblers.*)

ARTHUR: Hope it'll be a good game.

'FRANK': You're going to die.

ARTHUR: Don't be like that.

'FRANK': You're in a box.

HAZEL: Which way are we playing, Arthur?

ARTHUR: Our kick off.

TONY: What's their captain like?

ARTHUR: I think he must have trouble at home.

STEVE: How come?

ARTHUR: He's not a happy man.

PHIL: Oh.

ARTHUR: I don't think that they like us very much.

STEVE: Funny, that . . . they look a friendly bunch.

TONY: Has anybody seen *Flesh-eating Zombies*?

FRANK: I know what you're saying.

PHIL: I don't like the look of mine.

ARTHUR: Man-for-man marking.

TONY: I'll have yours, then.

PHIL: Right, fill out the space . . . all the area.

> (*The players move into the space.*)

STEVE: They are massive.

PHIL: I bet they can't run.

STEVE: Half of 'em can't talk.

> (*He mimics a gross beast.*)

HAZEL: They've got legs like tree trunks and shoulders like they'd swallowed two dustbins . . . They hate us . . . you can see it.

FRANK: Why do the opposition always look so big?

TONY: I bet they've only got four teeth between 'em.

PHIL: Watch for the funny switch . . . up on 'em quick.

TONY: Once the first tackle's been made I'll be OK.

STEVE: I'm like a jellyfish.

HAZEL: How do you think I feel?
    (*A beat.*)

FRANK: Straight on 'em, a man each . . .

ARTHUR: Anybody ever seen *Zulu*?

TONY: He's off . . .

STEVE: You ought to be on *Film '84*.

ARTHUR: It reminds me of *Zulu* . . . Rourke's Drift . . . we're the British . . . they're the . . .

PHIL: Warriors . . . millions of 'em, all stood on the cliffs, I've seen it.

FRANK: Looks like it . . . and all . . .

PHIL: Yeah . . . they all got killed.

ARTHUR: They got V Cs, though.

TONY: I'll be Michael Caine.

STEVE: Aren't we having a team photo, Arthur?

ARTHUR: We'll have it later.

STEVE: In hospital?
    (*A whistle is blown.*)

HAZEL: Arthur kicked off a large rambling grubber kick along the ground . . . The sound of leather on leather was sickening, even from the kick off . . .

TONY: Nobbler Knowles . . .

PHIL: For the Cobblers caught the ball . . .

STEVE: Their most feared forward . . .
    (ARTHUR *during this time has held off a ball.* FRANK *positions himself so that the back of his shirt shows the Cobblers' insignia – he is therefore now Nobbler Knowles. 'FRANK' takes the ball at pace, and despite desperate tackles from the Wheatsheaf players he scores a try downstage centre. He turns round and becomes* FRANK *again. Dejection among the Wheatsheaf side. They retrieve the ball.*)

PHIL: Steve . . . tackle!

STEVE: Tackle that?

PHIL: Yeah.

STEVE: I didn't see you making much effort.

PHIL: I was covering.

STEVE: I was covering.

TONY: Your eyes, eh?

HAZEL: Good start, lads.

FRANK: What about the conversion?

PHIL: They'll not bother . . . They know that they've won.

ARTHUR: Right, come on . . . let's see nobody chickening out, right?

> (ARTHUR, HAZEL, PHIL *and* STEVE *move sideways across the stage, covering the Cobblers.*)

Our kick.

HAZEL: Arthur kicked a nice long one, which bounced inside their twenty-two metres line.

STEVE: For God's sake, watch that big 'un.

> (ARTHUR *passes the ball to* 'FRANK' (NOBBLER), *who runs and is challenged by* STEVE *and* PHIL, *but manages to pass to* 'TONY' (STABBER), *who tries to get around* ARTHUR *and does, but is caught by the shirt by* HAZEL. *She tries to push him back, but he runs to score another try for the Cobblers.*)

HAZEL: Sorry, lads . . . I had him.

TONY: Eight–nil . . . in two minutes.

STEVE: It's all over, lads.

TONY: You said it.

STEVE: All over.

TONY: Oh, shite.

ARTHUR: Come on . . . get it together . . . they're only flesh and blood . . . Think about the game . . . Come on . . .! (*Shouting*) Long kick, Phil. (*Whispering*) Short one.

'TONY': Watch out for the long one.

> (ARTHUR *rolls the ball onstage*. PHIL *runs forward and picks up the ball*. 'TONY' (STABBER) *is over him and won't let him play the ball.*)

Play the ball.

PHIL: In a tick.

'TONY': Play the ball.

PHIL: Let me get up, then.

'TONY': Play the ball.

PHIL: Hang on.

'TONY': Play it!

PHIL: All right . . . no need to get physical.

> (*A push from* 'TONY'.)

Steady on . . . it's only a game.

'TONY': Come on, then, short-arse.

> (*Another push from* 'TONY'.)

PHIL: Look, will you pack that in?

STEVE: Send him to the back of the class, Phil.

'TONY': Play the ball.

> (PHIL *plays the ball to* HAZEL, *who passes to* ARTHUR, *who
> passes to* STEVE. STEVE *is hit by* 'FRANK' (NOBBLER) *in
> the cobblers and falls in agony to the floor. He writhes about
> for a while.*)

STEVE: Oh!

PHIL: Come on, Steve, play the ball.

'FRANK': Play the ball.

STEVE: On . . . oh . . . oh . . . my goolies . . . I'm ruined . . . I'm
finished . . .

'FRANK': Play the ball.

ARTHUR: Count 'em.

PHIL: He's only got one.

HAZEL: Fourth tackle coming up.

> (STEVE *gets up.* TONY *comes to watch him.* 'FRANK' *becomes*
> FRANK. STEVE *plays the ball to* HAZEL, *who plays a blind-
> side ball to* FRANK, *who takes it and growls his way to centre
> stage.*)

Go on, Frank.

STEVE: Leg it, Frankie.

> (FRANK *begins to move but is brought down by* 'TONY'
> (STABBER). 'TONY' *stands over* FRANK *in the same manner
> as before.*)

'TONY': Play the ball.

FRANK: Hang on a minute, man.

'TONY': Play the ball.

FRANK: Hang on.

'TONY': Play it!

> (*In slow motion* FRANK *grabs* 'TONY' *by the shirt, brings his head back and nuts him full in the face. The reaction is given from the rest of the players who make the sound effects.* 'TONY' *goes down and bounces off the floor.*)

PHIL: Nice, Frank . . .

FRANK: (*to referee*) I think he's got something in his eye, Ref.

> (FRANK *plays the ball to* HAZEL, *to* ARTHUR, *to* STEVE *(who is still struggling after the kick in the goolies)*.)

STEVE: Not to me . . . I can't move.

> (STEVE *passes the ball to* PHIL)

PHIL: I found some space on the left, even if it meant running around the back of our line. I put my head down and ran.

ARTHUR: Go on, Phil.

HAZEL: Nice, Phil.

FRANK: Lovely man . . . go on, yer . . .

PHIL: A man to beat . . .

> ('TONY' *tackles but* PHIL *breaks free. He scores in the corner. He and the rest of the team are elated.*)

A try . . . a try in the corner!

STEVE: I don't believe it.

TONY: Whooh!

> (*Shouts of delight all round.*)

FRANK: Brilliant!

ARTHUR: Great solo effort, lads . . . great solo effort . . . well played, lads.

PHIL: (*Breathless*) Thanks.

HAZEL: Eight–four.

ARTHUR: Come on, we can beat these.

HAZEL: One flukey try.

ARTHUR: We can hammer this lot.

PHIL: Hey, look at 'em, they don't believe it.

> (PHIL *makes a V-sign at the audience.*)

TONY: Come on, keep it going.

> (HAZEL *stands centre stage. The rest of the players are at the*

back of the stage. HAZEL *picks up the ball. The rest prepare to work a move.*)

HAZEL: You could see that they didn't like it . . . It was eight–four, with three minutes of the first half left to play. Their kick to us a long one right down to the touch in goal area . . . I picked it up and they were on us like growling bears.

STEVE: Hazel!

HAZEL: I saw Steve coming inside, calling out . . .

STEVE: Here . . . give it . . .

(STEVE *receives the ball and begins to run downstage left.* TONY *comes from upstage left and takes the ball on a scissor movement.* TONY *has the ball centre stage and delivers a reverse pass to* PHIL, *who gives a quick ball to* FRANK, *who finds* ARTHUR. ARTHUR *takes the ball on downstage and performs a dummy downstage right, and moves centre stage. This movement must be done at speed in order to get the slow-motion effect later.*) ARTHUR *is stood centre stage.*)

ARTHUR: And I'm there in the clear with about ten yards to go . . . and there it is, another try . . . beneath the sticks a captain's try . . . yes, what a marvellous equalizing try from Billy Boston.

(ARTHUR *dives. The players celebrate and lift* ARTHUR *aloft.*)

TONY: Half-time.

PHIL: Eight all.

ALL: Eight all eight all eight all eight all.

(ARTHUR *drops his shorts, baring his bum to the Cobblers.*)

STEVE: Up yours, Reg Welsh.

(*A change of colour wash to blue for voice-over action replay.*)

VOICE-OVER: (*in an Eddie Waring accent*) Now let's just have a look at that try once again . . . let's see how it all started, Alex . . . Cobblers kick long and it's collected by Scott . . . formerly of Hunslett . . . and moved swiftly . . . out to Steve Edwards, who's a little slow for a big fellow really, Alex . . . to Burtoft who does well, and then this man Hopley, formerly of London . . . and the England Colts . . . and a fine runner with the ball to Rowley, looking tired and drawn . . . and a captain's try, Alex, for Arthur Hoyle, formerly of Wakefield . . . so as we go into the break it's even stevens . . .

(*Throughout the recent commentary the players have been rerunning the whole of the last try sequence. If the players are of a standard and the space permits, then sundry other moves can well be improvised. At the completion of the rerun the players sit down, breathless, in the middle of the field. It is indeed half-time.*)

STEVE: Eight all.

PHIL: It would have been ten–eight if we'd have bothered with the conversion.

TONY: Forget that . . . we can score tries . . . just keep the ball away from them big 'uns.

STEVE: Anybody got any beer?

FRANK: I've got a feeling that they're gonna get nasty this next half.

PHIL: Yeah, watch that number eight.

FRANK: I'll have him.

HAZEL: Poke his eyes out . . . he scratched me.

ARTHUR: Hazel . . . you're doing well.

TONY: Yeah . . . not bad.

PHIL: They're trying to keep it tight.

ARTHUR: Keep the tackling up, man and ball . . . I think we've thrown 'em.

PHIL: We're doing all right.

STEVE: We're doing brilliant.

ARTHUR: Keep it on this half these ten minutes . . . think about it . . . when you go in go in and mean it . . . look for the blind side moves . . . let's see some flair . . . see some ball play . . .

TONY: I'll tell you what . . . the crowd are loving this . . . I can hear Gayle shouting a mile away.

STEVE: Can I have my share of the brass now, Arth?

ARTHUR: Don't speak too soon.

PHIL: Look at 'em . . . bringing two subs on . . . ringers.

ARTHUR: Bastards.

FRANK: Do you know 'em?

ARTHUR: One of them was a Warrington winger.

TONY: Wonder what they're saying . . .

(*Blackout. Gruff, fierce voices of the Cobblers team are heard.*)

'FRANK': Get that bald head and smash it.

'ARTHUR': Yeah.

'PHIL': Throw the ball about to the wings more.

'STEVE': Try and stretch 'em.

'FRANK': Yeah, stretch 'em.

'TONY': Start putting it together . . . They've come at us . . . Let's start getting back at them.

'ARTHUR': Above all make every tackle hurt . . . Let them know that they've been in a game.

'FRANK': And hurt 'em.

(*Lights back on the Wheatsheaf team.*)

PHIL: Right, we're ready.

ARTHUR: Hey, I've just had a thought.

FRANK: What?

ARTHUR: Wait here . . . shan't be a minute.

(ARTHUR *exits.*)

STEVE: Where's he going?

TONY: Probably had a brainwave.

HAZEL: I've got a feeling that this is going to be a long ten minutes.

PHIL: Listen, Hazel, when you get a break, when you see a gap, go for it . . . you're being predictable.

HAZEL: Right.

(ARTHUR *returns with six gumshields.*)

ARTHUR: Here . . . wear these . . . I'd forgotten about 'em . . . If it's going to get rough . . . it might save a few teeth for someone.

(*They all fit their gumshields. All the players go out on to the pitch. They attempt to talk to each other, but no one can understand what the others are saying. In response to every remark there is a misunderstanding nod. The image should be funny . . . until . . .*)

STEVE: I'm not wearing this, Arthur.

FRANK: Nor me.

ARTHUR: Stick it down your sock in that case.

(*Some stick them down their socks. Some merely throw them to the side.*)

So at eight all we had a chance.

PHIL: But the Cobblers were no duck eggs . . .

FRANK: They came back at us with open rugby . . .

STEVE: And by one minute into the second half . . .

TONY: They had scored two remarkable tries . . .

FRANK: Which they converted.

HAZEL: The score was twenty points to eight.

ARTHUR: We started to swing the ball about . . .

FRANK: Gave it some air . . .

TONY: Every opening we saw we went for with close support . . .

PHIL: With overlaps . . . and quick switching of the ball . . .

STEVE: Tony scored . . . under the posts . . .

HAZEL: Arthur converted and the score was twenty–fourteen.

ARTHUR: Scrum down.

> (*The front row is down.* HAZEL *has the ball. They prepare to go into the scrum position. As they go down there is much growling and biting of ears.*)

FRANK: Come here, I'll bite your neck off.

> (HAZEL *puts the ball into the scrummage.* ARTHUR *hooks.* HAZEL *takes the ball and works a scissors with* PHIL, *who runs into the front row. He is brought down with a sickening thud. He gets up and pushes the tackler in the chest. There ensues a series of pushing involving all the players. The word they use is 'Yeah': hence 'Yeah', 'Yeah', 'Come on', 'Yeah', until a rather nasty scene of fighting breaks out.* ARTHUR *has eventually to be held back by the rest of the players as he threatens the audience.*)

ARTHUR: Right, hit me . . . just hit me, let's see what that'll prove . . . yeah, you chickens . . . I'd take you all on . . . all of you . . .

PHIL: Leave it, Arthur.

ARTHUR: Don't like it, do you? Come on, play the ball, we've got these . . .

TONY: I got the ball inside their twenty-two . . .

HAZEL: And quick as a flash . . .

FRANK: Tony had scored a drop kick.

> (*They all cheer.*)

STEVE: One point for that . . . pathetic rules . . .

HAZEL: Twenty points to fifteen.

ARTHUR: How long left, Ref?

PHIL: Two minutes.

FRANK: Don't let them in our half.

STEVE: For those two minutes the Cobblers threw everything they had at us . . . It was man-to-man tackling all the way, now.

(*Three players are the Cobblers and three the Wheatsheaf. Throughout this it's a tackle on a man each. As they pass the ball from the play-the-ball* STEVE *intercepts and waves the ball at the audience.*)

STEVE: I got the ball from a Cobblers' mistake . . .

(STEVE *gets the ball and weaves in and out of the rest of the players.* HAZEL *stays upstage and* STEVE *passes the ball to her. The rest of the team are standing downstage right in pairs ready to catch* STEVE. STEVE *gives and gets the ball from* HAZEL. *He runs towards the four Cobblers players and jumps into their arms. He makes two attempts to play the ball over the line. On the third he succeeds, and is held aloft by the four, who are now the Wheatsheaf team. Exaltation abounds.*)

A try . . . a try . . . right in the corner . . .

PHIL: Why didn't you go under the sticks?

STEVE: A try . . . in the corner . . .

(*They all congratulate* STEVE.)

TONY: It was a long kick . . . I took it . . . but the angle was too acute . . .

(TONY *mimes the ball going towards the posts. In the event it misses, and the players illustrate their dismay.*)

Bastard . . . sorry, lads.

HAZEL: Twenty—nineteen.

ARTHUR: One minute left.

FRANK: Watch the time-wasting, Ref.

PHIL: Watch the kick . . .

(*The players are all standing upstage.* FRANK *has the ball behind his back. The line-up across the stage reads:* FRANK, PHIL, ARTHUR, TONY, STEVE, HAZEL.)

STEVE: As soon as you get it, attack . . .

ARTHUR: Fifty seconds . . .

TONY: Get it kicked, man . . . Ref, that's time-wasting . . .

ARTHUR: They kicked . . . it was long . . . but I expected that . . .

(FRANK *tosses the ball from behind his back to* PHIL *during the next sequence of dialogue. The ball goes all the way down the line to* HAZEL, *who passes back inside to* STEVE. PHIL *has dropped backstage.* TONY, ARTHUR *and* FRANK *have become the Cobblers, centre stage.*)

PHIL: I stayed back and set off on a long run . . .

FRANK: Close support was needed . . .

STEVE: Up and under!

(STEVE *has the ball. He hoists the ball with a boot.* HAZEL *takes it from behind his back.* PHIL *runs and is hoisted into the air by Cobblers ('*FRANK*', '*TONY*' and '*ARTHUR*').* HAZEL *tosses the ball to* PHIL *and '*FRANK*' (*NOBBLER*) hits him in the mouth. They all fall to the ground.* HAZEL *blows the whistle. All are on the floor.* PHIL *holds his mouth.*)

ALL: Penalty, Ref!

STEVE: I'll take it.

HAZEL: Let me take it.

TONY: I'll take it.

FRANK: Let Phil take it.

STEVE: Let Tony have a go.

ARTHUR: I'll take it.

FRANK: Don't miss.

HAZEL: Twenty seconds left . . . This would be the last kick of the game . . .

ARTHUR: I could kick this in my slippers.

PHIL: Take your time . . .

TONY: Don't hook it . . .

ARTHUR: I know it's a straightforward kick . . .

HAZEL: Arthur carefully placed the ball . . .

TONY: Considered its oval shape . . .

PHIL: Wiped the mud from his boot . . .

STEVE: Stood slowly upright . . .

FRANK: Stepped back majestically . . .

PHIL: Raised his head . . .

STEVE: And struck the ball beautifully . . .

HAZEL: We all looked up to see the ball soar . . . into the air . . .

PHIL: High, very high . . .

STEVE: We watched the ball . . .

TONY: As it . . . ?

ARTHUR: Struck the post . . .

FRANK: And bounced back towards us . . .

(*All the* PLAYERS *mouth 'Fucking hell' as they see defeat. A whistle is blown.*)

TONY: Full time.

ARTHUR: Shit . . . shit . . . shit . . .

(ARTHUR *falls to the floor: 'Jesus Christ.' The other players are stunned. There is a moment's silence.*)

Don't anybody talk to me.

TONY: What're you going to do, Arthur?

ARTHUR: Kill myself.

(*The rest of the team sit about.*)

PHIL: I'm off.

TONY: Where?

PHIL: Get changed.

(*Both go and stand upstage centre, with their backs to the audience, holding hands as the Cobblers.*)

STEVE: Whoooh, eh? Twenty-bloody-nineteen . . .

FRANK: We had 'em worried, though . . .

'PHIL' *and* 'TONY': Well played, Cobblers!

(STEVE *and* FRANK *get a bench each and sit on it. The lights fade to interior.*)

HAZEL: I didn't know what to do or what to say . . . They seemed to have nothing left . . . nothing left to give . . . We all crept silently back to the dressing room and sat.

(ARTHUR *is still left onstage, crying, but the location has changed to the dressing room. The players sit and remain silent for a long, long time. They begin to take off their shoes, socks, shirts, etc.*)

TONY: Rocky didn't cry, Arthur.

ARTHUR: I know.

TONY: Yeah.

ARTHUR: *Rocky*'s a bleeding film.

TONY: I know.

FRANK: Oh, well.

(*A number of cans of beer are intermittently pulled open.*)

STEVE: Well, we can't all be Rocky Balboa, but . . . ?

PHIL: At least we tried.

FRANK: 'Pack up all my cares and woe,
     Here I go, singing low . . .'

ARTHUR: We didn't finish the marathon, though, did we?

FRANK: 'Bye bye, blackbird . . .'

ARTHUR: Sorry, lads . . . I've let you down.

STEVE: Don't worry, Arthur . . . we'll beat 'em next time.

ARTHUR: You what?

FRANK: 'Where somebody waits for me . . .'

STEVE: Next time we play 'em . . . The bastards, I got a right crack
     on my ear.

FRANK: 'Sugar's sweet, so is she . . .'

ARTHUR: No . . . there's no next time.

FRANK: 'Bye bye, blackbird . . .'

TONY: What about the five weeks' trial?

PHIL: Yeah, you've passed . . . coach for life.

HAZEL: Another challenge, Arthur.

ARTHUR: No.

PHIL: Listen, you stay with us . . . you and us lot . . . we're a good
     team.

FRANK: 'No one here can love or understand me,
     Oh what hard-luck stories they all hand me . . .'

PHIL: A great team.

STEVE: One lousy point.

FRANK: There's worse things happen in the world.

ARTHUR: As my dad always said, there's always another day.

PHIL: Very true.

ARTHUR: I suppose that . . . oh no.

FRANK: Go on.

STEVE: Suppose what?

ARTHUR: I've got this daft idea that we go over to Reg Welsh . . .
     right? Double or nothing . . .

PHIL: And they field no ringers?

ARTHUR: Exactly.

TONY: That's six grand . . . Shit . . . This could go on for ever.

FRANK: But next time we'll win.

STEVE: I'm in for that . . . Let's show these bastards.

PHIL: I thought that this was your last game?

STEVE: It was.

FRANK: Just one point.

ARTHUR: What?

FRANK: We find a kicker.

HAZEL: I can goal kick.

TONY: Why didn't you say owt?

HAZEL: Nobody asked me.

ARTHUR: So . . .

STEVE: So what?

ARTHUR: Is it on?

STEVE: You bet.

HAZEL: (*Together with* STEVE) I'm in.

TONY: It's on.

PHIL: (*Together with* TONY) Let's kill 'em.

ARTHUR: What if Reg won't accept the bet?

ALL: Oh, yeah . . .

> (FRANK *begins to sing once more. Slowly they all begin to join in the song of 'Bye bye, blackbird'.* ARTHUR *is the last one to join in. As they reach the end of the second verse they are transformed.* Rocky *theme music plays, and slowly they all stand. Each character is introduced over a loudspeaker and the name of the actor given, like at the end of* Dallas *or a similar soap opera. As the credits are given the actors play selected parts of the play:* TONY'S *try,* STEVE'S *try,* HAZEL'S *exercises,* FRANK'S *head butt.* PHIL *is the last one, with a smack in the mouth. All the players raise a hand to the audience, give a knowing smile that* Up 'n' Under Two *is coming and take their bows.*)

SEPTEMBER IN THE RAIN

CHARACTERS

JACK
LIZ

September in the Rain was first presented professionally by the Hull Truck Theatre Company in 1984 with the following cast:

JACK   John Godber
LIZ   Jane Clifford

Directed by John Godber

ACT ONE

As the audience enters the theatre JACK *and* LIZ *are sitting among their luggage or are getting their luggage together. Ken Dodd sings. A slide of Blackpool is projected on the backcloth.* LIZ *takes some deep breaths. They are waiting for their bus to arrive. They are in their late sixties. They are wrapped up but are not wearing raincoats.*

LIZ: (*To audience*) Oh. Oh, I love the sea air. Clears my head. Do you know I've allus liked Blackpool air, it's thicker in some way, there's more texture to it, you can feel it doing you good. Sommat about it refreshes me. Look at it, even in September it's smashing, even when everything's grey it warms me to be here. I could live here. I've said to Jack many a time, 'We ought to have bought a boarding house at Blackpool, made a go of it, Jack.' He's never been keen. Nowt can move him when he puts his mind to it. Too late to start to make changes now. Mind you, Blackpool's changed. It has. We've just had a last walk down Central Drive and all that's changed, and there wasn't the fancy front on Tussaud's when we first came. Or as many amusements on the Golden Mile, was there, Jack?

JACK: No.

LIZ: We've only been here for a few days, been stopping at a guest house up north, past the Cenotaph, hope that's not an omen. It's quieter up there away from the bingo and the slots. We like it quiet now. It's a nice run to Blackpool, you know? Only takes an hour and a half on the M62. We're from Yorkshire, aren't we, Jack?

JACK: Ar.

LIZ: We used to come here every year.

JACK: Ar, we did, ar.

LIZ: We came to Blackpool for years. Things happen that fast I

can't allus place them in the right year, if you know what I
mean.

JACK: I know what you mean.

LIZ: Jack's allus said that when he goes, they can scatter his ashes all
over Blackpool sands.

JACK: Bloody hell, Liz.

LIZ: He's not been hisself since he had a bit of a do with his heart.

JACK: Bloody hell.

LIZ: That's why we've come ont bus, can't drive and be safe now
really. But it's a lovely run with Wallace Arnold, they've got
hundreds of buses, you can see them all pulling in. People from
all over the place still flock to Blackpool. Hey, you mun't call
Blackpool, not while me and Jack's about. You can't lick
Blackpool for my money.

JACK: No.

LIZ: I allus liked coming ont bus, Jack liked to come int car. Liked
to be able to stop where he wanted. First time we came away
int car, ee, it wa' a laugh. We'd got this Ford Anglia, ain't we,
Jack? Green it was, green and white.

JACK: Ford Popular. It was green and cream.

LIZ: Was it cream?

JACK: Ten, twenty-seven, WY.

LIZ: I'll never forget that registration number.

JACK: Six hundred and fifty-eight pound cash I paid for it.

LIZ: I wanted to put that money down on a deposit for a house.
But you know Jack, if you tell him to do sommat he just goes
and does the bloody opposite.

JACK: I don't.

LIZ: When we came here on honeymoon we stopped at the Metropole. Then we didn't come away for two years because Jack had
hurt hissen at pit. When we came int car we came in September.

JACK: Leger week. St Leger at Doncaster. Pit holidays.

LIZ: This is before we had our Ian or our Pamela.

JACK: It's before we even thought about having our Ian, little sod.

LIZ: Jack, swearing.

JACK: It's even before M62 is this.

LIZ: What a journey, can you remember it? From Upton through

Wakefield to Bradford, Skipton, Clitheroe. We usually stopped at Clitheroe.

JACK: Jimmy bloody Clitheroe. Allus reminded me of Jimmy Clitheroe.

LIZ: Our Ian used to look for the 'soap dodgers' in Bradford. Ee, it wa' funny. And there was a big hold-up at Preston. I've known us be stuck at Preston for two hours.

JACK: We used to set off at six int morning.

LIZ: I didn't like being ont road.

JACK: We set off that early one year we got to Blackpool and they were still eating their breakfasts.

LIZ: First time we came int car we had a bump.

JACK: Ar, we did.

LIZ: Ee, where did we stop that year, Jack?

JACK: We stopped at Beatie Fish's on St Chad's Road.

LIZ: We did not.

JACK: We did, though.

LIZ: We stopped at Mavis's.

JACK: Oh, ar, we did, ar.

LIZ: It was a lovely boarding house. Not as homely as Beatie's.

JACK: We had some happy times at Mavis's.

LIZ: There were some funny buggers in that first year. Sam and Mary?

JACK: Aye, and me and you.

LIZ: We were late setting off.

JACK: I was ready.

LIZ: I wanted to go ont bus, didn't I?

JACK: Ar, awkward as a broken clog.

LIZ: I packed that morning for some reason.

JACK: We wa' listening to forecast on wireless.

LIZ: Not that you were listening. You were stuck in the bloody toilet, as usual.

JACK: I'd just gone to t' bathroom for a shave.

LIZ: You were singing. I wa' on my hands and knees trying to lock the bloody case up.

Through the last sequence of lines they have transported us back in time.

LIZ *is trying to squeeze a suitcase together.* JACK *is standing upstage shaving.*

LIZ: How long are you gonna be? He's allus last minute. Don't bloody answer, Jack. I know I should've packed yesterday. Time is it? I haven't got time to get myself ready yet.

JACK: I can hear you.

LIZ: I wish we'd never bought that bloody car.

JACK: I can hear you.

LIZ: What you doing?

JACK: I'm getting a bloody shave.

LIZ: You should've got one last night.

JACK: I didn't need one.

LIZ: When there's work to be done he's as scarce as rocking-horse shit.

JACK: I can hear you, Liz.

LIZ: I thought you'd gone down the bloody drain. It's allus last bloody minute.

JACK: (*Singing*) The leaves of brown came tumbling down, re-member . . .

LIZ: Jack.

JACK: . . . in September in the rain.

LIZ: Hurry up!

JACK: The sun went out just like a dying ember.

LIZ: It's every time he gets in that bathroom.

JACK: That September in the rain.

LIZ: Put a bloody sock in it.

JACK: To every word of love I heard you whisper.

LIZ: You'll make it rain if you sing like that. Shurrup!
    (*Silence.*)
    And hurry up. It's a quarter to seven. I thought we were getting off early in case anything happened to this bloody car. What about Preston bottleneck? I've got you a Sealeg here in case you feel badly.

JACK: My desert is waiting, dear come there with me,
    I'm longing to teach you love's sweet melody.

LIZ: Jack!

JACK: I'll sing a dream song for you . . .

LIZ: Come on now!

JACK: Painting a picture for two . . .

LIZ: If you're not down here soon I'm not going.

JACK: Blue heaven and you and I . . .

LIZ: Right, that's it. I'm not bloody going. Bugger you.

    (*Blackout.*)

JACK *is helping to close one of the cases.* LIZ *is still closing hers.*

LIZ: I've put yer best shirt in, in case we go anywhere special, and a couple of cardigans. And yer checked shirt and yer short-sleeved shirt. I've not put yer suit in, I've put them old trousers so that you can lounge about in 'em, and them new hankies. Is there owt else you can think of?

JACK: No.

LIZ: Well, we're ready, then.

JACK: Right.

LIZ: That's it, then.

JACK: We're ready then. I want to set off before there gets much traffic ont road. Come on, then.

LIZ: I'll just have to check house.

JACK: What for?

LIZ: I want to leave it tidy.

JACK: Why?

LIZ: I want to.

JACK: There's gonna be no bugger here.

LIZ: I want to leave it tidy then it's clean to come back to.

JACK: That's bloody stupid.

LIZ: Have you done upstairs?

JACK: No.

LIZ: Go and clean toilet. I don't want that mucky while I'm away.

JACK: This is bloody barmy, this is.

LIZ: Have you switched the water off?

JACK: Yeh.

LIZ: I'll leave a key next door with Mrs Witton. Then our Betty can come up on Friday and put us a fire in, warm the water up so that we can wash as soon as we get back, Saturday. Looks like there'll be some washing and all.

JACK: We haven't even set off yet.

LIZ: I've got to make arrangements.

JACK: Shall I take these to t' car?

LIZ: I suppose so. I do t' other.

JACK: I'll take 'em, then.

LIZ: I don't know why we ever had to get a car?

JACK: It's a bit nippy with looks of it.

LIZ: I'd've sooner gone ont bus.

JACK: You can go ont bus. I'll drop you off.

LIZ: Bloody car. It's been nowt but trouble since we got it.

JACK: We've only had it a week.

LIZ: We could have gone ont bus, like we did ont honeymoon.

JACK: You'll not get me going on t' bus again, I'll tell thee that much.

LIZ: Better ont bus.

JACK: Aye, it bloody wa'. I smoked about twenty of other people's cigs, when we went ont bus, that much smoke about, and that was even before we'd bloody set off. There's no smoke int car, we can stop when we want, stretch your legs a bit, have a picnic. It'll not take us two minutes int car. Besides, I felt sick ont bus.

LIZ: I feel sick int car.

JACK: I don't know how you work that out, Liz. You've only been in it once so far.

LIZ: I can't stand that smell. It smells of newness.

JACK: What's tha want it to smell of, oldness? It is new.

LIZ: It's too low down for my liking.

JACK: How d'you mean?

LIZ: It's too near the road.

JACK: You'll be right. Just have another Sealeg. I'll take these.

LIZ: Be careful with my straw basket, it's got a flask in it. Leave it where we can get to it. It's got sandwiches in. It was a funny thing about that Popular, the newness made me feel sick, and it shook me about a lot. But I suppose it was better. Jack, tell 'em about the time we went with Chippy Baggley from Cudworth. Go on, tell 'em.

JACK: No, I'm not. Chippy's this bloke who owns a local bus firm, and we'd booked one of his coaches for a trip. We're all stood, young couples, waiting for his coach to turn up. Saturday morning, half seven. At the end of this street I saw the pit paddy, that's bus we went to t' pit on. 'Look out,' I said. 'Blackpool bus's here.' Everybody looked around and laughed. Then the bus came and pulled up at the side of us. Chippy wa' drivin'. 'Blackpool?' 'Yeh.' 'Get on.' Forty of us sat sideways all the way to Blackpool with bits of coal rolling about all over the floor. That's when I started to think about gettin' a car.

(*Blackout*.)

LIZ: Have you put my coat in?

JACK: Yeh.

LIZ: I've locked everything up, so we're ready.

JACK: Where've you put the keys?

LIZ: House keys?

JACK: No. Car keys.

LIZ: You had 'em last

JACK: You had them.

LIZ: I've not had 'em.

JACK: You have. You went to change your cardigan in the boot.

LIZ: They'll be in the lock then. I left them in the lock.

JACK: No, they're not.

LIZ: Oh, I put them on the top of that bag.

JACK: Which bag?

LIZ: Blue one.

JACK: Where is it?

LIZ: I told you to put it in the boot.

JACK: That's bloody stupid.

LIZ: What is?

JACK: Fancy leaving the keys in the bloody boot.

LIZ: I didn't think. I just put them down.

JACK: I've shut the boot up, haven't I?

LIZ: Who're you shouting at?

JACK: I'm shouting at you.

LIZ: Well, don't shout at me. It's not my fault.

JACK: Whose bloody fault is it, then?

LIZ: That bloody car. Nowt but trouble.

JACK: It's nowt to do wi' t' car. It's you, woman.

LIZ: If we'd packed last night . . .

JACK: Tell us another.

LIZ: I wouldn't be in a rush, would I?

JACK: I don't know, and I don't care. All I'm bothered about is how to get the sodding keys out the boot.

LIZ: You're gunna do it, are you? You're gunna spoil t' holiday.

JACK: *I'm* gunna spoil it. Bloody hell, Liz.

LIZ: It's a great start, I must say.

JACK: Great.

LIZ: In fact, that is it, this time. I'm not going. I'm not. I don't see why I should be blamed for something I haven't done. I'm not going. You spoil every-bloody-thing, shouting at this time of the morning, throwing your weight about. You'll waken Mrs Witton up with yer shouting. I'm stopping here. I'll go down to me mam's. I get blamed for bloody everything. You know what me nerves are like.

JACK: Stop here then. I'll go by my bloody self.

(*Blackout.*)

In the blackout both JACK *and* LIZ *have sat on chairs which were arranged during* JACK's *story of Chippy Baggley. This is now the Ford Popular. Both are sitting in it and both are singing.*

LIZ *and* JACK: You make me feel so young.

You make me feel like spring has sprung,

Bells to be rung,

And a wonderful song to be sung.

And when I'm feeling old and grey.

I hope I feel the way I do today.

You make me feel so young.

LIZ: It's not so bad after all, int car. Is it?

JACK: No?

LIZ: Wanna sweet?

JACK: Sort are they?

LIZ: Barley sugars. I got them in case of travel sickness.

JACK: Yeh, I'll have one.

LIZ: Do you feel sick?

JACK: No, but I'll have one. Ta.

LIZ: It looks a bit cloudy.

JACK: I hope it brightens up.

LIZ: We should've gone away in July.

JACK: No holidays in July.

LIZ: Mind you, I've known it be nice in September.

JACK: When?

LIZ: Well, me mam had a fortnight at Mablethorpe and it wa' quite good for 'um. And when she came home she looked really brown.

JACK: That'd be rust.

LIZ: It only rained once.

JACK: Monday to Friday.

LIZ: If you talk like that you'll but speck on the weather.

JACK: Right.

LIZ: Have you got the thing?

JACK: What thing?

LIZ: Boarding-house thing.

JACK: Inside coat pocket.

LIZ: I wonder what it'll be like?

JACK: Woman sounded all right ont phone.

LIZ: Oh, yeh?

JACK: What's it called, again?

LIZ: 'Beverley Guest House', Woodfield Road.

JACK: It's near football ground.

LIZ: My mam said we should have gone to Beatie Fish's. She says it's daft going to a new place, when you've been well looked after.

JACK: Sommat to do.

LIZ: I hope it's clean.

JACK: You can allus give it a quick tidy up if it's not up to scratch.

LIZ: I hope they haven't got any cats.

JACK: They haven't.

LIZ: How d'you know?

JACK: I asked.

LIZ: Oh.

JACK: Felt a right silly sod and all asking if she'd got any cats.

LIZ: Look at that!

JACK: What?

LIZ: That sign. There. Lancashire sign.

JACK: Bloody hell. I thought you'd seen a ghost.

LIZ: Last few breaths of Yorkshire air.

JACK: Tha what?

LIZ: When I wa' a kid we used to have last few breaths of Yorkshire air before we saw Lancashire sign. Fill us lungs with good air. Come on, breathe deep.

>   (JACK *and* LIZ *begin to take deep breaths as if they are passing the border between Yorkshire and Lancashire.*)

Nearly there now, aren't we?

JACK: Are we, hell.

LIZ: Wanna another barley?

JACK: Yeh.

LIZ: Hey, look . . . wave at 'em.

JACK: Who?

LIZ: Them Scouts are waving at us. Wave at 'em. Hey up, are you going to Blackpool?

JACK: They can't hear you.

LIZ: They're from Barnsley. Wave, Jack.

>   (JACK *gives a curt wave to the Scouts.*)

JACK: Oh, look at it, getting darker.

LIZ: Are we gonna stop in a bit? I'm starvin'.

JACK: Next lay-by.

LIZ: Is it spitting of rain?

JACK: It's as black as t' fire back over Chorley.

LIZ: It's startin'.

JACK: Cats and dogs.

LIZ: It's not forgetting to come down.

JACK: Bloody weather.

LIZ: We pulled up to try and let the rain abate but it didn't. We stopped at the spot where our Ian was sick about ten years later. I don't know about you, but whenever we took our Ian in the car he was always sick at the same place, no matter how many tablets we gave him.

JACK: I thought of writing to the Sealeg firm to claim some money back, but I never did.

LIZ: By the time we reached Preston it was still throwing it down and we were part of the longest traffic jam I'd ever seen.

JACK: That's Preston bottleneck.

LIZ: I remember being scared because our Popular was sandwiched behind a big van and a lorry.

JACK: I was a bit worried because I was well down on petrol, and all the slow moving meant the radiator was overheating, but I never told her.

LIZ: No, he didn't.

JACK: I kept calm. Bloody hell, come on!

LIZ: We wouldn't've been like this if we'd've come ont bus.

JACK: Shurrup.

LIZ: Would we? Is there anyway you can turn road? Is there another way?

JACK: No.

LIZ: Why is it all steaming up?

JACK: Where?

LIZ: In here.

JACK: It's coz it's hot.

LIZ: Is that smoke coming from our car, Jack?

JACK: No.

LIZ: Why are you whistling? Is there sommat up wi' t' car?.

JACK: No.

LIZ: He always whistled when sommat went wrong wi' t' car.

JACK: Nowt's up wi' t' car.

LIZ: I don't like being squashed between two lorries.

JACK: It's right.

LIZ: Aren't you a bit close?

JACK: No.

LIZ: Oh.

JACK: Right?

LIZ: I think you are, you know.

JACK: Who's driving?

LIZ: I know, Jack, but . . .

JACK: Just . . . shurrup.

LIZ: Pull away, Jack.

JACK: Shurrup.

LIZ: Pull away or I'm gerring out.

JACK: Liz.

LIZ: Just back up and don't be stupid.

JACK: Bloody hell, woman.

LIZ: Pull back.

JACK: Right.

> (*Both actors make as if they are reversing a car. There is a sickening thump and both actors are thrown forward. There is a moment's silence.*)

Get out.

> (LIZ *mimes getting out of the car, walks upstage to inspect the damage.*)

LIZ: The back lights and the boot were all dinted, and the lorry's lights were smashed. Ten twenty-seven WY was all squashed up. The lorry driver jumps out of the cabin. He was furious. He gave me such a look. 'Charming.' He marched to the driver's side window and banged on the door. 'Oi oi up, what's tha doing? Are you bloody low, reversing in a sodding jam? Get out, I want a word with thee. Get out.' When Jack got out of the car I disappeared through the other door out of the way.

> (JACK *slowly gets out of the car.*)

JACK: 'S up?

LIZ: Tha' run into me.

JACK: Sos.

LIZ: Hey up.

JACK: Look, piss off. He kept saying, 'I've got your number, I'll be in touch with you.' But he never was. I had a minute, composed myself and got back in the car.

> (LIZ *has walked back to her place in the car and is sitting quite quietly.*)

LIZ: What did you say to him, Jack?

JACK: Just said sorry and that.

LIZ: Oh.

JACK: He could see it wa' an accident.

LIZ: Oh, that's all right, then.

JACK: I'll have another barley.

LIZ: We were another three-quarter of an hour in that jam. But it did mean that the rain had stopped and the sun began to come through really strongly. We used to look to see if people travelling in the opposite direction had suntans or not. If they looked pale and white then it was more likely that we would have the sun for a week.

JACK: When we had our Pam and Ian we'd have competitions to see who could spot the Tower first.

LIZ: Jack usually won. But our Ian did well one year.

JACK: It's theer, Dad, it's theer, I can see Tower.

LIZ: He spotted the Tower three miles outside Skipton, sixty miles from Blackpool.

JACK: It looked glorious when we arrived, all the boarding houses shone out white. The Beverley Guest House was on the sunny side of the street.

LIZ: People were walking around in vests and shirt sleeves. It would be a glorious week.

JACK: We parked the car. I was glad it made it. And walked across the road.

LIZ: We stopped outside, had a look through the window, and rang the bell.

JACK: There were 'No Vacancy' signs at the windows.

LIZ: It must be good, Jack. 'No Vacancies.'

JACK: Ar. There were no vacancies wherever you looked.

LIZ: Mavis came to the door.

JACK: A tall blonde heavy woman, with rosy cheeks and a pleasant disposition.

LIZ: Hello, have you just arrived. Munroes?

JACK: Yeh.

LIZ: I thought you'd never get here.

JACK: Bad jam at Preston.

LIZ: I know, it's wicked in't it?

JACK: Is t' room ready?

LIZ: Yes, I'll get your key. It's right at the back, turn left at the first stairs and then up two little steps. It's the one near the toilet, out of the way. Easy to find.

JACK: Easy to find? It took me half an hour to get the cases round the corner of the stairs.

LIZ: Mavis kept me talking. She was a nice woman, gushy, overflowing but nice in small doses. Her husband had left her but she was making a go of the place with her partner, Gordon, a tall balding man from Lytham St Annes, who, as we later discovered, was sharing Mavis's room at nights.

JACK: Our room was tiny. I was gonna complain.

LIZ: It would have been bigger had Jack been smaller.

JACK: The roof slanted down over the sink.

LIZ: So he could have a wash, Jack had to bend double.

JACK: It wa' no bloody laughing matter washing the sand out of my feet when I'd been on the sands.

LIZ: The room smelt a bit fusty. And the wardrobe only had one coat hanger. Mind you, I'd brought seven of my own. I'd been caught out by that before.

JACK: Before tea we went for a walk down to the Coliseum. We saw Stanley Aklam.

LIZ: They were stopping in a grubby little place down Lytham Road.

JACK: That'd suit Stanley. Whenever he went away he never took his slippers off, or his vest.

LIZ: It was a smashing spread, that first tea, all the tablecloth thickly starched and the cutlery shining, the doilies were really nice and there was a fair choice of buns.

JACK: We had them little triangles of brown bread.

LIZ: It was lovely.

JACK: I could've shoved them up my nostril.

LIZ: We're big bread eaters.

JACK: The ham was that thin you could see through it ... I was gunna complain. I say, love, can I have a word ... ?

LIZ: Don't, Jack ...

JACK: Can we have another pot of tea, love, please?

LIZ: 'Call me Mavis,' she said. I didn't like that.

JACK: You never said owt.

LIZ: I don't tell you everything.

JACK: We had to share a table with Sam.

LIZ: And Mary.

JACK: The noise was soft and polite.

LIZ: A bit like a wake.

JACK: All the different tables were trying to look at each other. But trying not to be seen by anyone.

LIZ: Sam and Mary were different. They were fixtures in the Beverley Guest House.

JACK: Smashing couple.

LIZ: They were in their fifties.

JACK: Be long gone now, worms'll've had 'em.

LIZ: Sam had no teeth and said very little. Mary, it seemed, had Sam's teeth and said a lot. 'Is it your first time here? We've been here for twenty-five, is it, no, I tell a lie, twenty-two years on the trot. We came before Mavis had it. It wa' lovely then. Mavis allus saves the front bedroom for us. Oh, are you near the toilet? Well, it's handy but it's a nuisance middle o' t' night, flush flush. Are you from Yorkshire?'

JACK: Ar.

LIZ: We're from Bolton!

JACK: Used to have a good team.

LIZ: Mary spent most of that evening telling us her life story. Why they'd got no kids, how she met Sam. She spared no detail. What she did for a living.

JACK: What does Sam do?

LIZ: There was an awful silence. Mary looked at Sam. It was embarrassing.

JACK: I've put my foot in it here. Only asked a simple bloody question. Bugger 'em. I had my eye on a butterfly bun. It seemed like a good time to beat Mary to it. She'd eaten most of them.

LIZ: He works ont sewage!

JACK: Oh ar.

LIZ: He worked for t' council and all.

JACK: Yeh.

LIZ: He's got some right stories to tell.

JACK: I bet he bloody has.

LIZ: I've seen some mess in my time.

JACK: Sam said.

LIZ: Sam came to life, telling us stories about going to the toilet, and what he'd done and seen. Jack couldn't stop laughing.

JACK: Once went to this 'ouse in Bolton, Jack, terrace house, when I worked ont council, it were. They'd got a blockage somewhere. Int terrace houses manhole wa' int middle o' street. I sidles up to t' door. 'Shit van here.' 'Bit awkward, because my wife's on.' 'No trouble, I'll just nip your manhole cover off.' Well, I'm not joking, Jack, when I say this, you could have eaten your dinner off that manhole. It was spotless. I couldn't understand it. Anyway, bloke came out to see what the problem was, and his son came out, and the missis next door, and we're all stood there looking down this manhole ... Nothing ... Spotless ... Then slowly this water trickled past, and then this turd ... it was as long an' thick as my arm. We all watched it float past and then we all looked at the husband ... that was his wife. He blushed and looked at me and said, 'Aye she can shit some stuff, our lass.'

LIZ: We went to bed that night with Jack still chuckling over Sam's stories.

JACK: I don't know ...

LIZ: I hardly slept a wink ... and the toilet was flush flush as Mary had said.

JACK: That was our first and last time in that room.

LIZ: Look at this bloody room.

JACK: What's up wi' it?

LIZ: It's a bugger.

JACK: You sleep int lav.

LIZ: I said to ask for a big room.

JACK: I did.

LIZ: I can't stop in here. It smells fusty.

JACK: Go home then.

LIZ: I can't stop in here. There's no air.

JACK: Shurrup, bloody hell.

LIZ: You never listen to me, do you? I said, make sure it's a big room.

JACK: I've had to listen to you all the sodding way here.

LIZ: You never bloody talk.

JACK: We're on to that now, are we?

LIZ: You've only said a dozen words all t' way here.

JACK: So?

LIZ: You never do owt nice ... you're not normal. You never hold my hand or owt.

JACK: It's from one thing to t' bloody next wi' yer.

LIZ: I wish we'd not come.

JACK: I bloody do and all.

LIZ: You spoil every sodding thing.

JACK: Do I?

LIZ: Yeh.

JACK: I'll give yer a bloody woncer in a minute.

LIZ: I'm not sleeping in here.

JACK: Sleep in lav then.

LIZ: My nerves are bloody shocking again with you.

JACK: Why don't you just shurrup?

LIZ: Shan't shurrup.

JACK: We're on bloody holiday agen, are we?

LIZ: Go on, shout, let every bugger hear you throwing your weight about.

JACK: I shall call you sommat in a minute.

LIZ: Yes, you bloody start it ...

JACK: Just shut it ...

LIZ: You shit.

JACK: And you ...

LIZ: Mavis popped up to see if everything was all right. She said, did we like the room.

JACK: I said, yes, but it's small. She said she thought we'd prefer it.

(Lights.)

LIZ: The next morning was absolutely gorgeous. Jack got up early and went down for a paper.

JACK: Even at half-past seven you could see that it was going to be a scorcher.

LIZ: We had our breakfast and got down on the sands. Just at the end of Woodfield Road are steps, which were handy.

JACK: We got a couple of deckchairs from the slob who was dealing with 'em. Thanks, pal.

LIZ: He was nice and bronze.

JACK: Don't start it.

LIZ: Can you put them up, Jack?

JACK: Ar.

LIZ: He's never really been any good with his hands.

JACK: I can shovel.

LIZ: We looked for a spot on the sands. I wanted to be near the wall in the soft sand, so we were out of the breeze. You allus get that breeze at Blackpool, no matter how sunny it is, don't you?

JACK: What about here?

LIZ: No . . . sand's damp.

JACK: Over there?

LIZ: No.

JACK: There's space there?

LIZ: I wanna be int soft sand.

JACK: Why?

LIZ: Then I can bury me feet. Look over here . . .

JACK: We sat between two families of about ten each.

LIZ: Five, don't exaggerate.

JACK: I like to have privacy, I don't like being near people. I can't relax, not with others about.

LIZ: You can't have the sands to yourself, Jack.

JACK: Wish I could.

LIZ: It irritates him. It's the same when we're at home. If there's anyone outside playing with a ball, he's up at the window seeing who it is.

There is a lighting change and both of them are sitting in their respective deckchairs. JACK *may be reading a book.*

LIZ: Aren't you putting your trunks on, Jack?

JACK: No.

LIZ: Put 'em on.

JACK: I don't want.

LIZ: Get 'em put on.

JACK: No, I'm right.

LIZ: Get some sun on your legs.

JACK: I'll roll my trousers up.

LIZ: Tek yer shirt off.

JACK: Why?

LIZ: It'll look like you're enjoying it.

JACK: I'm leaving my shirt on.

LIZ: Everybody else's got their shirts off. Look! Get your stuff off, Jack, let some sun get at your body.

JACK: I'm all right.

LIZ: Stanley Aklam's got his vest off. He's sat over there.

JACK: Looks like he's swallowed a coat-hanger.

LIZ: They're all stripped off bar you.

JACK: They make me feel sick to look at 'em.

LIZ: They're all right.

JACK: If t' cruelty man came round he'd have a field day.

(LIZ *produces a pair of trunks.*)

LIZ: Here, get these on.

JACK: I'm putting nowt on.

LIZ: Nip back to t' Beverley and get 'um on.

JACK: No.

LIZ: Come on, stand up. I'll hold the towel round you.

JACK: Give over.

LIZ: Come on, Jack, get bloody up, get some sun on yer.

JACK: No, I'm right.

LIZ: Look, get behind this towel.

JACK: No.

LIZ: I can't understand you. You never enjoy yersen.

JACK: I am enjoying mysen.

LIZ: You look bloody sweltered. Tek yer shoes off.

JACK: Look I'm right.

LIZ: Tek 'em off.

JACK: No.

LIZ: You're only bloke on Blackpool sands wi' his shoes on.

JACK: You know I don't like sand between my toes.

LIZ: You allus spoil it.

JACK: I'm spoiling nowt. I'm sat here trying to sodding read.

LIZ: Go on, shout.

JACK: I'm not shouting.

LIZ: You could have bloody fooled me.

JACK: You can shite . . . I'm staying as I am.

LIZ: Right!

JACK: Right what?

LIZ: If that's what you're gonna be like all the holiday, I'm going.

JACK: Good.

LIZ: I am.

JACK: Where?

LIZ: I'm not sitting here with you looking like a bloody Eskimo.

JACK: Go, then.

LIZ: I am . . . you spoil bloody everything.

JACK: I'm not teking my bloody shoes off so you can shit.

LIZ: And you.

> (LIZ *exits*.)

JACK: Bloody woman. Do this, Jack, do that, bloody hell. I'm fed up 'on her. Tek your shoes off, she can shite. No I'm not bloody having it, I'm not. Shit to her.

> (LIZ *enters, looking at* JACK.)

LIZ: Hello.

JACK: Are you back?

LIZ: I'm going int sea.

JACK: Oh ar.

LIZ: I'm going for a paddle, Jack. Are you coming?

JACK: Aye, I can do.

LIZ: You're not keeping your shoes on, are you?

JACK: No, I'm gonna tek em off.

LIZ: I asked a woman who was sat near to keep an eye on the stuff, while we went for a paddle. You could do that at Blackpool then, you could trust people.

The lights go out. When they come on JACK *and* LIZ *are standing in the sea. They are in a bright spotlight.* JACK *has his shoes off and trousers rolled to the knee.*

LIZ: What sea is it, Jack? North?

JACK: Irish.

LIZ: Cold, int it?

JACK: 'S right.

LIZ: Are you enjoying it, Jack?

JACK: 'S all right.

LIZ: You're enjoying it, aren't you?

JACK: Yeh, it's all right.

LIZ: Go on, admit it.

JACK: All right, I'm enjoying it.

LIZ: I knew.

JACK: 'S all right.

LIZ: You're just awkward.

JACK: Ar.

LIZ: We can have a walk ont pier after, buy my mam sommat.

JACK: It's bloody filthy, this water.

LIZ: Is it?

JACK: Them's sewage pipes.

LIZ: Wonder if Sam had owt to do with it?

JACK: Wouldn't be surprised.

LIZ: Ugh . . . what's that?

JACK: Where?

LIZ: I nearly stood on it.

JACK: 'S only a jellyfish.

LIZ: Ugh.

JACK: What's up?

LIZ: Oh, look at it!

JACK: Wain't hurt yer.

LIZ: Do they sting?

JACK: Ar, but it's nowt.

LIZ: I'm getting out.

JACK: Why?

LIZ: I don't like it.

JACK: It's bloody nowt.

LIZ: Int it?

JACK: I dare eat it.

LIZ: Let's go over here.

JACK: There'll be others.

LIZ: We stood in that water many a time, an't we, Jack?

JACK: Ar.

LIZ: When our Ian was a baby we stood with him . . .

JACK: And our Pam.

LIZ: Our Ian used to lay in about six inches of water and pretend he
    was swimming, daft sod.

JACK: He had sand on his chest, down his trunks and all over.

LIZ: They used to dig a castle wall to stop the tide coming in.

JACK: Never stopped it, though.

LIZ: Our Ian used to love that.

JACK: I was a dab hand at building motorboats int sand.

LIZ: Aye, he wa'.

JACK: I built one, one year, it was best I'd ever built. Then this family walked past, and they stood all over it. Some people don't care tuppence.

LIZ: Our Ian wasn't bothered.

JACK: I was. It was the best motorboat Blackpool had ever seen.

LIZ: I like it here, Jack.

JACK: Ar.

LIZ: Just me and you.

JACK: What about these others?

LIZ: Bugger 'em.

JACK: Hey up?

LIZ: I don't know what to buy our Betty.

JACK: Don't buy her owt then.

LIZ: Can't do that. She bought me sommat.

JACK: Oh, ar.

LIZ: Look at all t' sea?

JACK: Ar.

LIZ: Makes me feel as if it could sweep me up, a big wave just come and sweep me up.

JACK: Ar.

LIZ: Makes me feel right small, Jack.

JACK: Thy is small.

LIZ: Dun't it make you feel sommat?

JACK: Wet.

LIZ: If we have kids we'll bring 'em here, paddle wi' 'em. Jump 'em over these waves. Let's jump these waves, Jack.

JACK: Gi' up.

LIZ: Come on.

JACK: No.

LIZ: Come on, you're enjoying it.

JACK: Oh, bloody hell.

The two of them begin to jump over waves. JACK *looks as if he is enjoying it. They are not holding hands, they do it on their own.* LIZ *holds her skirt up to jump. They jump.*

This is a big 'un.

LIZ: It's great.

JACK: Ohhh!

LIZ: 'S up?

JACK: Oh, bloody hell . . .

LIZ: Jack, what's up?

JACK: My foot . . .

LIZ: Eh?

JACK: I've been stung. Let me get out . . . I've been stung.

LIZ: Jack?

JACK: Bleeding jellyfish!

 (Blackout.)

JACK *goes upstage and puts on his shoes and socks.* LIZ *remains downstage. A spotlight picks her out. She is in a queue for an ice-cream. She establishes this by looking front and back.*

LIZ: Have you seen the length of this queue? That's the trouble when you want an ice-cream, you have to queue for hours to get one. Jack went back to the deckchairs sulking, trying to blame me for what happened. You can guarantee if something is going to happen to someone, it'll happen to Jack. I think I'll get a '99' cornet with a flake in it. Jack'll not want one. He can do without, for being awkward. He usually had a cornet with red sauce on it. Blood on it, he'd say. He can do without.

Some of the women, honestly, they look a right sight in bathing costumes, they're not bothered, are they? All the bodies in this queue smell of suntan lotion. Some people buy that stuff that tans whether the sun's out or not. That's bloody daft. Some of the men look quite nice. I suppose I was attracted to them really, standing close up and talking. Mind you they were a bit skinny. You could see their ribs.

'I know, int it a long queue?'

'No, only a week.'

'With my husband.'

'He's just been stung by a jellyfish.'

'No . . . I'm not . . . ?'

Some blokes'll say owt. I didn't tell Jack, he'd've dislocated their heads for 'em.

I must have been stood there half an hour. There were all these mothers and fathers with their kids. I started to think, I started to think about having children. I tried to picture Jack holding a son or daughter. I tried to imagine him holding a dog, but I couldn't bring the pictures into mind. I started to wonder, like you do, whether I was capable of having children, whether I was normal, whether Jack was normal. I had this lousy sickening feel in the pit of my stomach that I wouldn't be able to have children. I don't know if you've ever gone through that stage? But . . . I was surrounded by fathers and mothers and young men and I suddenly felt that they were looking at me, as if they could see that I couldn't have kids, as if it was obvious to everyone else except me. I've never really talked about this before . . . and I started to think . . . do I want Jack's kids . . . do I really? What about this bloke I've just been talking to . . . he looks nice . . . kind . . . what about him in the ice-cream van . . . he looks like a film star? I felt really sick, no, really sick . . . I could never know then that our Ian would grow up to be bigger than Jack . . . yeh, bigger than Jack . . . and successful at what he does, or that our Pam would look like our Betty . . . It's a funny carry on.

'What?'

'Oh, sorry, can I have a "99" cornet with a flake and one with blood on?'

   (*Blackout.*)

LIZ *remains static.* JACK *brings her her shoes, which she puts on. They are on the pier.*

JACK: You can say what you like, I don't like being near people. They get me down. I know that they've got to come away but when it's my holiday I'd sooner they stayed at home. You can't move for 'em. Everything becomes a bloody long drawn-out job.

LIZ: That afternoon we had a walk on the Central Pier.

JACK: That's all changed and all.

LIZ: I used to like looking through the wood as you walked, looking at the sands and water below. There was a bloke with a monkey who wanted to take Jack's picture.

JACK: Get lost.

LIZ: Have it taken, Jack. It'll be a laugh.

JACK: I'll break t' camera.

LIZ: Stand still, Jack. Let him get that monkey on you.

JACK: Is it house trained, this bloody monkey?

LIZ: Smile, Jack.

(JACK *freezes as* LIZ *surveys the tableau.*)

It'll look good, will that.

JACK: I bet it will.

LIZ: Only one problem.

JACK: What's that?

LIZ: It'll be a bit awkward working out which one's the monkey.

JACK: Shit, Liz.

LIZ: Laugh, Jack.

JACK: Ha ha. That picture cost me thirty bob.

LIZ: It's funny, though.

JACK: I can't bear people coming up to me asking me for money in the street. Like that bloke with that monkey. Pinching bloody money. Or people asking me for a poppy. I don't begrudge giving it. It's just when they come up to you in the street, it's embarrassing.

LIZ: Let's go in here, Jack.

JACK: Where?

LIZ: Fortune-teller's, Madame Petrunia.

JACK: Madame Shit.

LIZ: I bet it's good, that.

JACK: Give over.

LIZ: She's a world-famous Gypsy.

JACK: Is she, bloody hell.

LIZ: She is. It says so.

JACK: She's probably from Fleetwood or somewhere.

LIZ: Look, she's been with Johnny Ray. Frankie Lane. There's some pictures of her holding hands with the stars.

JACK: She wouldn't be able to read my hands, nowt but calluses.

LIZ: I wonder what she'd say.

JACK: If she told you you was going to be rich and famous, you'd believe her, wouldn't you?

LIZ: Yeh.

JACK: And if she told you you were going to walk under a bus, you wouldn't believe her.

LIZ: It could be true, though.

JACK: It's shite, Liz.

LIZ: It's summat different.

JACK: I thought we'd come to buy yer mam sommat.

LIZ: We have . . .

JACK: Well, then . . .

LIZ: I know, but . . .

JACK: I'm not chucking my money away.

LIZ: It's holiday, Jack.

JACK: I'm not crossing somebody's palm with silver to be told sommat I already know.

LIZ: But you don't know what future'll hold for us, or are you bloody psychic?

JACK: I know this much . . . I'm gonna be working with a shovel in my hands for fifty-two bloody years, and no Madame Pinnochio'll alter that.

LIZ: He was right an' all, weren't you, love?

JACK: Ar.

LIZ: He's got blue marks all over his legs and back.

JACK: Liz?

LIZ: That's with pit work, dust gets in your cuts . . . they go blue. First time I saw one I was nearly sick. You get used to it.

JACK: I've never been one for charms and that.

LIZ: You mek your own luck.

JACK: I've not made much of my bugger.

LIZ: At least the weather's held off.

JACK: Now that is luck . . .

LIZ: It was stifling. I had my summer dresses on all the time. I'd brought some cardigans with me from Marks but I didn't need them.

JACK: Everybody was sunburnt.

LIZ: Except Jack.

JACK: I got my forearms brown.

LIZ: An Italian-looking bloke came around the sands every day selling sunglasses. I bought a pair. Sunday, Monday and Tuesday it was beautiful. I had that Blackpool sea air on my face, I was looking well and my legs were going brown.

JACK: Wednesday morning we were back ont sands. I wa' gerrin' used to t' sun. I undid top button of my shirt.

LIZ: He had this hanky on his head that he wouldn't take off, said it stopped him gerrin' sunstroke. I think he thought he was in Africa or somewhere.

(*They are reclined in their deckchairs.* LIZ *is wearing sunglasses.* JACK *has a knotted hanky on his head.* LIZ *is applying suntan oil. This lasts for a moment.*)

JACK: Burn!

LIZ: Tek yer shirt off.

JACK: Shuttit. Burn.

LIZ: I might tek my top off.

JACK: Leave it on.

LIZ: Rub some oil on me, Jack.

JACK: Rub it yersen.

LIZ: Come on.

JACK: An't you got any hands?

LIZ: Sun's caught me, you know?

JACK: Has it?

LIZ: I think it's clouding over.

(LIZ *administers some lotion to her arms.*)

Do you want some lotion?

JACK: No, I'm natural . . . Where's it gone?

LIZ: Behind a cloud.

JACK: Ar.

LIZ: I thought you weren't bothered about sun?

JACK: No.

LIZ: It's clouding over.

JACK: Ar.

LIZ: Sea's bringing it in.

JACK: Ar.

LIZ: It's gonna rain.

JACK: Ar.

LIZ: It's gunna chuck it down.

JACK: Bugger it.

LIZ: Jack?

JACK: What?

LIZ: Hold my hand.

JACK: What?

LIZ: Hold me hand for a bit.

JACK: What for?

LIZ: I like it.

JACK: I don't.

LIZ: Please.

JACK: No.

LIZ: Please!

JACK: I'm not.

LIZ: Don't you like me?

JACK: Ar.

LIZ: Hold me hand, then.

JACK: No.

LIZ: Why?

JACK: Don't want to.

LIZ: Are you embarrassed or sommat?

JACK: No.

LIZ: You don't like me, do you?

JACK: Ar.

LIZ: You never hold me hand.

JACK: Don't start.

LIZ: I've had enough of you.

JACK: I think it's spotting of rain.

LIZ: I'm fed up on it, Jack.

JACK: Ar.

LIZ: I am.

JACK: It's raining.

LIZ: It's finished, Jack.

JACK: Why?

LIZ: You don't care.

JACK: Oh, ar.

LIZ: Do you?

JACK: Get the stuff. It gunna chuck it down.

LIZ: No, listen.

JACK: Look how black it is. Every bugger's going. We're gonna get drenched.

LIZ: No, I'm not going until you listen.

JACK: Look at the bloody weather. Get yer chair.

LIZ: Jack?

JACK: I'm gerrin' saturated.

LIZ: I am.

JACK: Come on, then.

LIZ: You never take any notice of me, do you?

JACK: What do you want me to say?

LIZ: I don't want you to say owt. I want you to listen.

JACK: I'm listening.

LIZ: No, you're not.

JACK: Christ, Liz.

LIZ: It's over, Jack . . .

JACK: Is it?

LIZ: It's over.

JACK: Good.

LIZ: I'm finished with you . . .

JACK: Thank God.

LIZ: I'm finished, Jack, bloody lousy finished.

> (JACK *has left* LIZ. *The lights have gone very dark. She is standing on stage, rain in the background. She begins to cry. Ken Dodd sings, 'If I had my Way . . .' Music plays through the interval.*)

ACT TWO

Ken Dodd records have been playing throughout the interval. The lights dim and the music fades. LIZ *is sitting on two chairs. She has a raincoat on and her hair is soaked through. A dim blue spotlight picks her out, as does a dim light overhead.*

LIZ: 'When I was a young man courting the girls ...' That's what Jack'd sing when we fell out.

    'I played me a waiting game.

    If a maid refused me with tossing curls,

    I'd let the old earth take a couple of whirls.

    Then I'd ply her with tears in place of pearls.'

    Not this time, Jack.

    'And as time went along she came my way

    As time went along she came ...'

    'And it's a long long time from May to December,

    And the years grow short when you reach September.'

    I must have walked for miles. All the way up north ... It was still throwing it down. I was soaked. I'd had enough, what with one thing and another. I really wasn't bothered if I never saw him again. I knew it would only get worse and it did from time to time. I looked at the sea. It was cold and grey, the tide was in, the wind had got up, and the waves were coming over on to the prom ... I'd marvelled at that before. Now I wanted to die ... everything was grey, nothing had any colour ... he always takes ... he gives nothing ... That's what I was thinking.

    (JACK *enters. He too is soaking wet and is wearing a raincoat. He has obviously been walking for ages. He sits at the side of* LIZ, *but she ignores him — he is not there. Silence for many a moment.*)

JACK: Hey up. Are we talking, Liz? I've been looking all over for you. Every shelter ont front. I thought you might have gone to t' Fun House. I've been in there looking for you. Look, Liz. Aren't you talking or what?

LIZ: Nowt to seh.

JACK: You are talking, then.

LIZ: It's over, Jack.

JACK: It shite over.

LIZ: And you can stop swearing.

JACK: What're you doing up here?

LIZ: I'm sat.

JACK: I know that.

LIZ: I wish I wa' dead, Jack.

JACK: Tha dun't.

LIZ: I'm wet through.

JACK: Tha's right.

LIZ: Am I?

JACK: Look at bloody weather, eh?

LIZ: Ar.

JACK: You wouldn't've thought it, would you? I'll lose my tan.

LIZ: What tan?

JACK: I'm not bothered about t' rain, is tha?

LIZ: Have you been looking for me?

JACK: Ar.

LIZ: All this time?

JACK: I went to see if I could get some tickets.

LIZ: What for?

JACK: A show or sommat.

LIZ: Oh, yeh?

JACK: I thought I'd treat yer.

LIZ: Did you get any?

JACK: I got these for t' *Student Prince* in t' Winter Gardens.

LIZ: I've seen *Student Prince*, Jack.

JACK: I have but I know tha likes it.

LIZ: It's thee that bloody likes it, Jack.

JACK: Tha likes it an' all, dun't tha?

LIZ: 'S all right.

JACK: Come on, we'll get a tram back to t' Beverley, get dried off a bit.

(*They begin to take off their wet clothes.*)
It rained and rained, by the time we'd got dried off and went
up to the Winter Gardens we were as damp again.

LIZ: When I think back, most of the dos we had were all over
nothing really . . . it must have rained every September. That's
where we got the song from. 'September in the Rain', Jo
Stafford. Allus reminded me of Blackpool.

JACK: I'd paid good money for these seats in the Winter Gardens.
We were sat with all the folks who had a bob or two, you could
tell.

LIZ: I felt underdressed. They were all posh, and dolled up.

JACK: Sod 'em, I thought, my money's as good as theirs.

LIZ: Only difference is that they've got more of it.

JACK: I love *The Student Prince* . . . a great show.

(*There is a blackout. Spotlight picks out* LIZ *and* JACK, *sitting
in the stalls at the Winter Gardens.*)
This is where he goes back to her.

LIZ: I know . . .

JACK: 'Golden Days' is coming up . . .

LIZ: I know . . .

JACK: Good set, in't it? It's good how they've done it.

LIZ: Yeh . . . just watch it for a bit.

JACK: I am watching it . . .

LIZ: You've not stopped telling me what's gonna happen.

JACK: Well, I want you to enjoy it.

LIZ: I am.

JACK: Who's shussing me? Watch play . . .

(*They watch the play for a bit and* JACK *begins to cry. He
takes out his hanky and blows his nose.*)

LIZ: 'S up?

JACK: Eh?

LIZ: What's up?

JACK: Nowt.

LIZ: Are you crying?

JACK: No.

LIZ: Jack.

JACK: I can't help it.

LIZ: Bloody hell.

JACK: It gets me . . .

LIZ: Bloody hell.

JACK: It's good, in't it?

LIZ: People are looking at yer.

JACK: It's nowt.

LIZ: Blow yer nose.

JACK: I'm right now.

LIZ: Tha like a big kid.

JACK: Nowt wrong wi' crying. I'll pee less, that's all, save my kidneys.

LIZ: Every time we see *Student Prince* one of us has a little cry.

JACK: I did enjoy it that night.

LIZ: We came out of the Winter Gardens singing all the songs.

JACK: 'Drink, drink, drink, to eyes that are bright as . . .'

LIZ: 'When it's summer time in Heidelberg there's beauty every-where . . .'

JACK: 'Golden days . . .'

LIZ: 'I'll walk with God from this day on,
His helping hand I'll lean upon,
This is my prayer . . .'

JACK: All the way down the front.

LIZ: We were soaking . . .

JACK: We went into Stanley's fish shop . . . had fish and chips.

LIZ: We had them 'sat down'.

JACK: And came out without paying.

LIZ: We went to bed and slept like a log. I suppose we couldn't grumble about the weather.

JACK: No, we'd had an hour's sun.

LIZ: We'd had more . . . It wa' brown. It wa' sommat to show Mrs Witton when we got home.

JACK: We nearly didn't make it . . .

(*Blackout.*)

Lights straight back up. They are standing at the foot of the Tower, looking up at it.

JACK: No.

LIZ: Please?

JACK: No.

LIZ: What about yesterday?

JACK: That's got nowt to do with it.

LIZ: Come on, let's go up t' Tower.

JACK: No.

LIZ: My mam's been up . . .

JACK: Ar.

LIZ: You're not frightened, are you?

JACK: Me?

LIZ: Yeh.

JACK: No.

LIZ: You are.

JACK: We've to pay to get int Tower then to pay to go up.

LIZ: Once we're in though we can spend all day looking round. We're out of t' wet.

JACK: I'd sooner just walk round a bit.

LIZ: It's no good coming all these years . . . Didn't you go up as a kiddy?

JACK: No.

LIZ: Not going up t' Tower, well, it's a bit like going to Bath and not seeing t' Spa.

JACK: I can see t' Tower . . . it's theer.

LIZ: Give me some money. I'm going up it.

JACK: Go.

LIZ: I am and you can shite . . .

JACK: Don't expect me to catch thee when it falls down.

LIZ: Don't talk rubbish.

JACK: It wa' a year ago today that somebody fell off that Tower.

LIZ: Tha's been reading Billy's *Weekly Liar*.

JACK: It's right.

LIZ: A big fella like you, dare go up, bloody hell, wait till I tell our Betty and Albert.

JACK: Tell 'em.

LIZ: You never do bloody owt.

JACK: Right then . . . come on . . . and don't blame me if you're badly. I had to go through with it now. I got in the lift and

there was sweat running down my legs. I didn't tell her. It wa'
bloody foulest day I'd known. Stuck up theer.
> (*Blackout.*)

*A spotlight picks them out as they stand at the very top of the Tower.
There is a large fence around the outside of the Tower which the actors
can hold. If they stand right near the audience they can perhaps better
create the sense of height.*

LIZ: Oh, bloody hell, Jack.

JACK: Don't you like it?

LIZ: I daren't move.

JACK: It's grand.

LIZ: I'm scared, Jack.

JACK: I could stop up here all day.

LIZ: Is it moving?

JACK: Aye, it'll be swaying a bit int breeze.

LIZ: Jack, it's bloody moving.

JACK: I think that's where that bloke threw himsen into roof o' ballroom.

LIZ: Jack?

JACK: Aye, it is, that must be where he fell in. They've had to put a
new roof on. That's why this fence's up, stop anybody trying to
throw thesen off.

LIZ: Coming up's bad enough.

JACK: You wanted to come up.

LIZ: Let's get down now. We've been up long enough.

JACK: 'S up with yer?

LIZ: I'm bloody frightened. That's what's up.

JACK: You wanted to come up.

LIZ: I know I did.

JACK: You'll have to wait for t' lift.

LIZ: You're off again.

JACK: Ar.

LIZ: Can't you see that I'm shaking?

JACK: Come here.

LIZ: You lousy fella.

JACK: It's nowt.

LIZ: I'm not arguing over it.

JACK: What're you doing, then?

LIZ: Shit, Jack.

JACK: You shit.

LIZ: Don't talk to me.

JACK: I wonder if I could throw you over this fence.

LIZ: You mek me bloody sick.

JACK: I ask you. Arguing up there. If they put it in a book nobody'd believe it. I wa' wet through wi' sweat when we got down, inside and out.

LIZ: I wa' badly. It's nice to say that you've been up, but never again in this world.

JACK: I'd never known it be as bad in September. If I've ever been near dying, it was up that bloody Tower.

LIZ: I was glad to get down.

JACK: Let's have a drink . . .

    (*Blackout.*)

LIZ: In the Tower Lounge people were huddled together.

JACK: It was packed.

LIZ: I had a brandy and lime. Jack had half of Sam Smith's.

JACK: Not a big drinker.

LIZ: At a table near to us a group of people were smoking.

    (JACK *and* LIZ *sit waiting for their drinks to come. As they wait the smoke from the opposite table begins to drift over to their table.* JACK *makes a cough, and* LIZ *wipes her eyes. The smoke is bad.* JACK *begins to waft the smoke away with his hand.* LIZ *helps out by using a hanky. This is insufficient. So* JACK *begins to blow the smoke back in the direction it came, making large blowing gestures.*)

JACK: Hey up? Can you keep that smoke up there, pal?

LIZ: Don't say owt, Jack.

JACK: Hey up.

LIZ: Jack, don't start owt.

JACK: Who's smoking them cigs, me or you?

LIZ: Jack.

JACK: I don't want that bloody filth down my lungs, pal, I've enough of that at work.

LIZ: Jack.

JACK: I'm not bloody bothered.

LIZ: You shouldn't say owt. They're happen on their holiday and all.

JACK: They're sat there smoking it, and then puffing it over here.

LIZ: They're going now.

JACK: I'd pull his bloody arms off soon as look at him.

LIZ: Settle down now.

JACK: I bloody would.

LIZ: Give over . . . enjoy yourself.

JACK: I shouldn't have said owt. I should have hit first and asked questions second.

LIZ: Let it bloody rest now.

JACK: I ought to have given him a bloody woncer.

LIZ: When Jack got in 'that' mood . . .

JACK: Which mood?

LIZ: He was unbearably dangerous. It's lovely here, in't it?

JACK: 'S right.

LIZ: You can see all t' names ont roof.

JACK: Ar.

LIZ: They must be different composers.

JACK: Yeh.

LIZ: I like it here . . . right relaxing.

JACK: 'S all right.

LIZ: I like it.

JACK: Good.

LIZ: Good service, in't it? He's a nice waiter, an' all.

JACK: Yeh.

LIZ: Pleasant.

JACK: Ar.

LIZ: He's got a good tan, an't he?

JACK: Ar.

LIZ: I bet he lives here.

JACK: Ar.

LIZ: He's a big smart fella, that waiter. Jack.

JACK: What?

LIZ: That waiter's a smart-looking fella.

(*Silence.*)

He's attractive, he is. Why don't you look like that?

JACK: Like what?

LIZ: Like him who's been serving us.

JACK: Do you mean that thing that's been hovering about?

LIZ: He's nice.

JACK: He's shite.

LIZ: Oh, he is.

JACK: When he comes back, I'm gunna kill him.

LIZ: Jack?

JACK: I'm gunna kill him.

LIZ: I'm only joking.

JACK: I'm not.

LIZ: I only said it . . .

JACK: You said it, you bloody said it.

LIZ: I wa' only having a laugh.

JACK: He's dead when he comes for these glasses.

LIZ: Please, Jack.

JACK: Don't 'please, Jack' me.

LIZ: Jack . . .

JACK: When I get in that mood, I'm wicked, I am, I'm evil. I'm six foot of idiot jealousy. I work in a bloody hole in the ground, and she's got the cheek to call an article like him smart, attractive. I'd be bloody smart and attractive if I had his job. I can't help it when it comes over me, the mood, that is. It's like a fog that covers me from head to toe. Nobody'll get me out of it. She leaves me alone and I come round. I'm not bothered about owt, only my family, everybody else can shite. I like my privacy, I like to be on my own sometimes. She knows what I'm like.

LIZ: Jack.

JACK: What?

LIZ: I'm sorry.

JACK: Ar.

LIZ: It rained non-stop, Thursday, so we spent a lot of the time in a shelter on the front. We'd brought a flask, made some coffee and had a bit of a picnic. We did a bit of shopping and I bought our Betty a shoe that hangs on the wall and it's a calendar. Bought

my mam some slippers from Marks ... and Jack a white fur
cover for the steering wheel.

JACK: Never bloody used it.

LIZ: I bought myself a shopping bag. There were some dead cheap
so I treated myself to one.

JACK: Rest of the time we walked up and down, eating fish and
chips in shop doorways, mixing my vinegar with rain water.

LIZ: Ugh!

JACK: 'S all right.

LIZ: We went to Tussaud's.

JACK: Ar, we did.

LIZ: That wa' a wash out.

JACK: Wa' it heck.

LIZ: I didn't think much of the Hall of Fame.

JACK: She couldn't tell who they were.

LIZ: I don't think they're all that realistic.

JACK: We trailed round with a group of about fifty others all
smelling and wet through in their Pacamacs like us.

LIZ: Then we went into the Horror section.

JACK: Horror.

LIZ: That wa' better.

JACK: I'd show 'em bloody horror. Days regular, that's bloody
horrible.

LIZ: If you wanted, you could go downstairs to the Anatomy
section.

JACK: This was just for adults.

LIZ: So we went down.

JACK: Well, bloody hell, they had specimens of bloody everything.

LIZ: What's that Jack?

JACK: Dunno.

LIZ: Looks like a ...

JACK: Yeh, it does, dun't it?

LIZ: Oh, look at it ...

JACK: Come on ...

LIZ: Oh, look at that ... There was this model of a hermaphrodile.

JACK: Hermaphrodite.

LIZ: I felt badly.

JACK: I felt bloody badly. Everywhere you looked there wa' different diseases of the body. Some models showed diseases where I didn't think you could get diseases.

LIZ: I wanted to get out.

JACK: And me . . . fancy paying good money to go and see bits of people's liver on show.

LIZ: It wa' only wax.

JACK: I'm not bothered. I'd a sooner sat ont front in a shelter.

LIZ: And we did.

JACK: I've never seen as many people walking about in the rain.

LIZ: The pubs must have made a fortune.

JACK: I don't like going in at dinner times.

LIZ: It dawned on me that there was nowt to do.

JACK: What about talent contest ont pier?

LIZ: What about when we took our Pam?

Lights.

JACK: Now then, we've got a smashing little lady up here. Haven't we?

LIZ: Yeh.

JACK: What's your name, love?

LIZ: Pamela.

JACK: Pamela. And where are you from?

LIZ: Don't know.

JACK: You don't know?

LIZ: No.

JACK: Are you from this earth or Fuller's?

LIZ: Don't know.

JACK: Don't know. Talkative, are you, Pamela?

LIZ: There's my mam.

JACK: Is that your mam?

LIZ: Yeh.

JACK: What are you going to do?

LIZ: That's my dad.

JACK: What is it that you're going to do? Are you going to dance? Or are you going to sing? Pamela, come back to us . . .

LIZ: I want to sit down.

JACK: You want to sit down?

LIZ: Yes.

JACK: Aren't you going to sing for us?

LIZ: Yes.

JACK: Oh, you are going to sing for us . . . that'll be good. Won't it?

LIZ: Yeh.

JACK: What are you going to sing?

LIZ: 'My girl's a Yorkshire girl'.

JACK: 'My girl's a Yorkshire girl'.

LIZ: My dad sings it . . .

JACK: Your dad sings it, does he . . . in the bath . . . ?

LIZ: In the house.

JACK: Oh, in the house, eh? Are you ready then? Right, off you go. 'My girl's a Yorkshire girl'.

LIZ: My girl's a Yorkshire girl,
Yorkshire through and through.
My girl's a Yorkshire girl . . .
Ee by gum she's a champion . . .
Though she's only a factory lass and wears no fancy clothes
I'm short of a Yorkshire relish for my little Yorkshire rose . . .

Lights.

JACK: Well, I could have bloody eaten her, bless her. She stood there like a matchstick and sung. There was bloody tears running down my face . . . She didn't win . . . but she still talks now about being in that talent contest. She's more guts than me . . . I daren't do owt like that.

LIZ: He's a big kid is Jack when it comes to owt like that.

JACK: It's nowt to be ashamed of, Liz. Some folks can stand up and do stuff. Others prefer to watch.

LIZ: It took me a bloody hour and half to get him ont big dipper.

JACK: I like to stand and watch 'em now, ont big dipper. You can see 'em get on all smiling faces and candy floss. I like to see 'em, when they get off, being sick, legs all wobbly.

Lights.

LIZ: Are you strapped in, Jack?

JACK: Ar.

LIZ: All right.

JACK: I wish I bloody wasn't strapped in.

LIZ: Right, we're off.

JACK: It's slow, int it?

LIZ: It's slow until we get to t' top.

JACK: Hey up, how bloody high does it go?

LIZ: To t' top.

JACK: This is bloody stupid.

LIZ: Hold on . . .

JACK: Bloody hell . . .

> (*They are at this stage on their way down one of the slopes on the big dipper. The actors lean back in their seats and scream.*)

Bloody hell . . .

LIZ: It's great . . .

JACK: I'm gonna be sick . . .

LIZ: Here's another one . . . whoooooooooo!

JACK: Arrrrr!

Lights.

JACK: I like to watch 'em . . .

LIZ: Going on the donkeys is about Jack's limit.

JACK: That's one thing that allus gets me about Blackpool, them donkeys. They're bloody filthy.

LIZ: He can't stand filth.

JACK: One year I took our Pam, and this donkey stunk.

LIZ: I wanna go on this one, Dad.

JACK: Our Pam allus picked the oldest scruffiest donkey.

LIZ: I wanna go on Bluebell.

JACK: No, go on this one . . . Dandy.

LIZ: No . . .

JACK: Tha don't wanna go on that one . . .

LIZ: I do . . .

JACK: Pam, it stinks . . .

LIZ: It dun't.

JACK: It's old, that one. Look, Dandy's young. It'll go faster.

LIZ: Don't like Dandy.

JACK: It'll be a better ride . . . .

LIZ: Don't want a better ride.

JACK: When we got up and had a close look at Bluebell you could see the flies on it . . .

LIZ: She loved going ont donkeys, our Pam.

JACK: I'm not kidding, they're pinching money up and down the country with donkey rides. Our Pam went on Bluebell. It only went about twenty yards, then it came back, it wa' ninepence a go . . . I told him . . .

LIZ: Leave it.

JACK: You don't get your money's worth on here . . .

LIZ: Leave it.

JACK: Well, they've only gone two bloody yards . . .

LIZ: He was allus exaggerating.

JACK: I'm telling you . . . they're that bloody old Jesus must have rode on 'em.

LIZ: Jack?

JACK: You snipe-nosed pig.

LIZ: He was allus causing trouble, them days.

JACK: Who wa'?

LIZ: You.

JACK: You've got to stand up for yourself.

LIZ: He wasn't happy until things were in a turmoil.

JACK: You'd let people shit on you, you would.

LIZ: You can't tell him owt.

JACK: That's what she tells every bugger we meet.

LIZ: I don't.

JACK: I've told her, say nowt to no bugger. But she tells everybody her business. I tell her, you can't trust anybody, only t' family.

LIZ: An' you can't trust them all t' time.

JACK: Saturday morning, it wa' lovely that year . . .

LIZ: Not that year it wasn't.

JACK: It was, because I said to you, 'Look at it. We've had a lousy week and it's bloody lovely now we're going back.'

LIZ: It wa' allus like that.

JACK: Not allus.

LIZ: Sometimes I sit at home and when the wind's blowing and the rain's hitting the window I think of Blackpool.

JACK: I like stew meat and chips in weather like that, and bread with butter on that you can dip in your gravy.

LIZ: I'll make you some of that when we get back.

JACK: Ar.

LIZ: We've been thinking about changing coast for next year. Have a few days up in the North East. Geordies.

JACK: Very friendly like us . . .

LIZ: You're not bloody friendly . . .

JACK: I am when you get to know me.

LIZ: Catherine Cookson lives that way on.

JACK: Grace Darling . . . her wit' lifeboats, she's from up there.

LIZ: Anyway . . .

JACK: Ar.

LIZ: Time is it?

JACK: Time we wa' gerrin' off.

LIZ: We've a bus to catch . . . We like to sit and watch the sea. Soothing.

JACK: Ar?

LIZ: Like to have a bit of a think.

JACK: It's all water under the bridge, Liz . . .

LIZ: It is.

JACK: Water under the bridge . . .

LIZ: I get a bit depressed when I think about my age . . .

JACK: It's one-way traffic now, Liz . . .

LIZ: I hope it's not busy ont motorway. I shouldn't want owt to happen.

JACK: Bus don't go while eight. There'll be nowt ont road.

LIZ: I think we'll have an hour int Tower before we go.

JACK: Can do.

LIZ: I hope you have a better week.

JACK: An't it been lousy?

LIZ: Typical Blackpool weather.

JACK: You've got to keep wrapped up.

LIZ: It's a good job I put you them cardigans in.

JACK: Ar.

LIZ: I wouldn't mind a dance . . .

JACK: No.

LIZ: Are you all right?

JACK: Ar.

LIZ: You look a bit flushed . . .

JACK: I'm all right.

LIZ: Are you warm?

JACK: I'm rate, Liz.

LIZ: You're boiling . . .

JACK: I'm bloody smothered wit' clothes . . .

LIZ: Your face is red raw.

JACK: Sea air on it.

LIZ: I don't know, Jack. What are we gonna make of you?

JACK: Bloody nowt.

LIZ: Shall we have a walk? I don't want you drinking.

JACK: A drink'd set my blood pressure off.

LIZ: I wouldn't mind a dance.

JACK: Ar . . . I wouldn't.

> (*Lights. Music plays and they are standing centre stage waltzing together slowly.*)

LIZ: I could never get him off the floor sometimes.

JACK: I liked a dance.

LIZ: It's more of a steady walk now.

JACK: It was still raining when we came out of the Tower.

LIZ: The nights were drawing in. It was dark and wet.

JACK: That sea breeze had turned a bit nippy.

LIZ: I don't think we'll come here again.

JACK: Money's awkward anyhow.

LIZ: Shall we get that bus?

JACK: Ar.

LIZ: We walked down the prom.

JACK: In the rain.

LIZ: For the last time.

JACK: When I die they can scatter my ashes on them sands.

LIZ: And mine.

> (*They pick up their cases.*)

All the lights were shining . . .

JACK: The Tower was lit up . . .

LIZ: People were sauntering along, not bothered about the weather.

JACK: We walked past the Manchester Hotel down to the bus station.

LIZ: We stopped outside the Manchester to listen to an organ playing.

JACK: Listen, Liz.

LIZ: Shall we go in?

JACK: Just stand and listen.

LIZ: It allus reminds me of Blackpool.

JACK: She sings it well. Come on, we'll have a last drink, bugger it!

LIZ: (*Singing*) The leaves of brown came tumbling down.
Remember, that September
In the rain.
The sun went out just like a dying ember.
That September in the rain.
To every word of love I heard you whisper
The rain drops seemed to play a sweet refrain.
Though spring is here to me it's still September,
That September in the rain.

> (*They stand singing in the rain. Rain sound is heard and above their singing is the singing of Jo Stafford. This plays as the lights fade. The lights come back up. The actors bow and leave their cases on the stage. Ken Dodd sings 'Tears for Souvenirs'.*)

HAPPY JACK

CHARACTERS

JACK
LIZ

Happy Jack was first presented professionally by the Hull Truck Theatre Company in 1985 with the following cast:

JACK   Andrew Livingston
LIZ   Jane Clifford

Directed by John Godber

ACT ONE

An empty space. There are two chairs on stage. A backcloth with worn wallpaper gives shape to the stage. An old gramophone is standing at the back of the stage. A clothes rack is full of clothes that the actors will use during the play. Kitty Kallen's 'Little Things Mean a Lot' plays as the audience enters. The actors enter very slowly. The house lights are up and bright light fills the stage. The actors speak directly to the audience.

LIZ: Blow me a kiss from across the room . . .

JACK: Say I look nice . . .

LIZ: When I'm not. Brush my hair . . .

JACK: As you pass my chair.

LIZ: Little things mean a lot.

JACK: *Happy Jack.*

LIZ: The cast . . .

JACK: With —— as Jack . . .

LIZ: And —— as Elizabeth.

JACK: Page one, the introduction.

LIZ: Jack Munroe was born in 1914, seventy-odd years ago to this very month. He was the only son of Amanda Munroe and lived all of his life in Upton, a small mining village in the West Yorkshire coalfield. Jack was a miner, a father, a brawler, sometime poet, thug, con-man lover and comedian.

JACK: He was a big chap, about 230 pounds, and over six feet tall. Big for a miner. He started work at Frickley Colliery at the age of fifteen . . .

LIZ: Fourteen.

JACK: (*Looks at her, and continues.*) He came straight out of the Board school and straight into the pit. Some would say he was lucky, he worked through both wars. Jack would say . . .

LIZ: 'That's the way things 'appen.'

JACK: By the time he was seventeen he had twenty men working under him.

LIZ: But he always remained a collier, never went to management.

JACK: In his own two-fisted animal way, Jack commanded respect . . .

LIZ: If they didn't respect . . .

JACK: He would hit people. In fact when he was in one of his . . .

LIZ: 'Moods' . . .

JACK: As Elizabeth would call them, he would hit anyone.

LIZ: Even his wife.

JACK: Only when they were first married.

LIZ: She was born Elizabeth Cooper.

JACK: They were the same age.

LIZ: More or less. They had always known each other . . .

JACK: Lived down the same street . . .

LIZ: Carr Lane . . .

JACK: Went to the same school . . .

LIZ: Northfield Board School . . .

JACK: They would always be together.

LIZ: At the age of twenty-two, when she returned from 'service' in Bradford, they were married.

JACK: He never recalled calling her 'Elizabeth'.

LIZ: Always 'Liz'.

JACK: Jack worked at the pit for forty-two years. He was to suffer from knee trouble, kidney trouble and finally pneumoconiosis. The strenuous work of a fit young man, the tests of resilience and feats of strength were to batter his body.

LIZ: A fact that he didn't realize until later life.

JACK: The Coal Board awarded him a thousand pounds for his dust.

LIZ: That's forty-two years' coal dust on his lungs.

JACK: They lived all their married life in Saxon Terrace. One street in a large area of terraced houses, all pointing in the same direction – towards the pit. In later years the two of them struggled to buy their house, when many of the others had been knocked down.

LIZ: The house was spotless. 'Cleanliness . . .'

JACK: Liz would say . . .

LIZ: '. . . is next to godliness.' She struggled daily to keep the house in sparkling condition. As the years drew on the house was to become less neat, more lived in, untidy, this was to irritate Liz through her later years. She wasn't up to the sort of cleaning of her 'service' days. In 1975 she died, of a stroke, and despite an operation in her fifties her body was riddled with cancer. She died in hospital, with Jack characteristically by her side.

JACK: She often referred to him as . . .

LIZ: 'Happy Jack'.

JACK: It was her little joke. Sometimes she used it with tenderness, and sometimes to have a dig at him. Most of the time she regarded him as 'Pa', but if she wanted something special doing it would be 'Jacko'. Her favourite and lasting expression though was 'Happy Jack'. She felt quite pleased at awarding him this title. He was always miserable or, more to the point, appeared to be so.

LIZ: It was a quirk of the Munroe household that you didn't express any love or caring or affection directly to anyone who you happened to love or care for. Jack was a master at this, and had developed it further.

JACK: So much so that the person who you loved the most you demonstrated the most disdain and contempt for.

LIZ: But beneath it all, over the years, there had been enough love to sink a mine shaft.

JACK: Neither would admit that.

LIZ: In 1978, three years after Liz, Jack died.

JACK: Those years almost killed him. He was to diminish in stature as well as spirit.

LIZ: For the first time he had to make decisions, to make his meals, make the beds, collect the pension and sleep alone.

JACK: His health deteriorated.

LIZ: After having walked fifty yards, he would be out of breath; going upstairs to bed would leave him exhausted; often he would lay awake at nights crying for Elizabeth and trying to catch his breath.

JACK: He refused to move into a bungalow, and lived at Saxon Terrace until he had forcibly to be moved to his daughter's, where he died. Of a stroke. His kidneys had collapsed. Years of hard physical graft had taken their toll.

LIZ: He was a wreck.

JACK: He was dead.

LIZ: He was buried next to Elizabeth and they shared the same headstone, just as they had shared everything else.

JACK: If you were to ask Jack, 'Would you do it all again?'

LIZ: I'm sure he'd say . . .

JACK: Yes.

LIZ: Page six, scene one. The Munroes' household. Two large easy chairs and a gramophone. Jack is seated, he is . . .

JACK: Sixty-one.

LIZ: And Elizabeth.

JACK: Liz.

LIZ: Is sixty. They are sat in the dark listening to a collection of their favourite records. They are very content and relaxed. Jack may sing to the records. Liz sits by the fire and gazes into the range, watching the shapes that the flames make. They often sat like this, thinking of the years together.

JACK: Little things mean a lot.

LIZ: They would play all their favourites, Steve Conway, Bing, the Ink Spots . . .

JACK: Louis Armstrong.

LIZ: Louis Armstrong, Dean Martin . . .

JACK: Al Jolson . . .

LIZ: Al Jolson, Alma Cogan, Johnny Ray.

JACK: Jack's favourite singing star of all was . . .

LIZ: Mario Lanza.

JACK: They would sit for hours and listen to Mario sing . . .

The lights have gone dim during the last sequence. The actors are 'in' the Munroes' living room. Mario Lanza singing 'Golden Days' plays. JACK *and* LIZ *may sing to some of it.*

JACK: Beautiful. Tha can't lick Mario for singin'. I once thought that John Hanson was good but, I've gi' o'er.

LIZ: He is good, but he's gerrin' on a bit now is John Hanson.

JACK: Who, Mario?

LIZ: John Hanson.

JACK: Wi' Mario it comes easy. Mind you, it went to his head.

LIZ: And he got fat.

JACK: What?

LIZ: Mario got fat.

JACK: He was fat in *The Great Caruso*. Fat as a pig.

LIZ: That was why he couldn't be the prince.

JACK: Eh?

LIZ: In *The Student Prince*. He was too bloody fat. Would've looked a bit daft having a fat prince. Big fat pig. It was his voice that did the singing though, but he was too fat for a prince. You don't see any fat princes.

JACK: Great film.

LIZ: 'Golden Days', Jacko. Can you remember?

JACK: I bloody can.

LIZ: When he goes back to Kathy at the Inn, where he's been a student, and he can't marry her, coz he's a prince. Well ... I cried my bloody eyes out.

JACK: Good film.

LIZ: Cried for an hour.

JACK: Mind you, tha can't lick Mario.

LIZ: I've allus liked John Hanson.

JACK: He's not a patch on Mario.

LIZ: Ohhh, but he's good though.

JACK: He ought to pack it in, did John Hanson.

LIZ: Can you remember when we saw him at Leeds Grand? Eee, it wa' a laugh.

JACK: He wa' int *Desert Song* then, Liz.

LIZ: Wa' he? Oh, aye, he wa', Pa, you're right.

JACK: He wa' t' Red Shadow. He looked like a bloody shadow, skinny as a bean. Bloody 'ell, he looked older than me. He is older than me.

LIZ: It wa' good, though.

JACK: He ought to pack it in.

LIZ: That was the best bit, when it started snowing.

JACK: Oh, bloody 'ell!

LIZ: Somebody must've left a skylight open int roof.

JACK: Talk about laugh.

LIZ: I had to have a little titter to myself. Can you remember? He was up there singing ... what is it? 'My Desert is Waiting', that's it, and they're all in Arab stuff, supposed to be in the desert and that, and there's all this snow that starts blowing in. I had to laugh. Best thing about it wa' that everybody wa' just ignoring it.

JACK: *Desert* bloody *Song*, int middle of soddin' December.

LIZ: I enjoyed it, though. Oh, but I did have to laugh.

JACK: Aye, he ought to pack it in did John Hanson. They get money for nowt some of 'em. Money for nowt. They're good for a couple of years and then they just go on and bloody on. Same as Mario, he wa' good but it all went to his head. Mind you, Bing wa' all right, he wa' ...

LIZ: He was supposed to be fat in *The Great Caruso*, anyway.

JACK: Who?

LIZ: Mario, in *The Great Caruso*, he was fat, supposed to be.

JACK: I know, Liz. I've seen it five times.

LIZ: And it was Edmund Purdom who spoke the words. A smart fella wa' Edmund Purdom.

JACK: It wa' t' only film he made.

LIZ: I once saw John Hanson as the Student Prince.

JACK: Blackpool.

LIZ: Aye, it wa' Blackpool. Winter Gardens.

JACK: Can you remember?

LIZ: I can now.

JACK: Four pounds it cost us. We'd seen it a bloody dozen times, even then. I'll never know why you wanted to see it again.

LIZ: Four pounds and we had these seats behind a big pillar, can you remember? And we both had to lean to each side all the way through. It wa' a laugh, though.

JACK: It wa' a laugh. I couldn't hold me head up straight for a fortnight.

LIZ: I just sat and listened after a bit. I like to sit and listen. He was good in that was John Hanson.

JACK: Aye, he was.

LIZ: Put another record on, Jacko.

JACK: Who?

LIZ: Put Mario on again. I like to sit and listen to Mario.

JACK: Tha' can't lick Mario.

> (JACK *goes to the gramophone and the lights fade. Both the actors freeze until the lights are off. A small extract of music is played.*)

White light.

JACK: Scene two. Page eleven. They are both fifty.

LIZ: The Munroes had an unparalleled ability for argument.

JACK: Not logical cohesive argument, just argument.

LIZ: The Munroes' kitchen.

JACK: Jack is stood in front of the fire.

> (*A spotlight cuts out the two actors.*)

LIZ: Are you warm?

JACK: Yeh.

LIZ: Why don't you shift?

JACK: Why?

LIZ: Shift and let some heat come out.

JACK: I'm cold.

LIZ: I am.

JACK: Go in the room then and put the fire on.

LIZ: It's cold in the room.

JACK: It'll not be cold if you put the fire on.

LIZ: Shift, my legs are cold.

JACK: My arse's cold.

LIZ: Shift out of the way and let some heat come out.

JACK: I'm not.

LIZ: Bloody shift.

JACK: I'm gerrin' warm.

LIZ: You're like a big kid.

JACK: You are when you can't get your own way.

LIZ: Shit, Jack.

JACK: And you shit an' all.

> (*Blackout.*)

The actors sit on the chairs as if they are having a meal. Lights.

JACK: What's this I've got here?

LIZ: Dinner.

JACK: I know it is.

LIZ: What did you ask for then?

JACK: What is it?

LIZ: Lamb.

JACK: I don't like lamb.

LIZ: Gerrit.

JACK: You know I don't like . . .

LIZ: Gerrit eaten, and gi' up moanin'.

JACK: Where's the sirloin?

LIZ: They had none.

JACK: I'm not eatin' this.

LIZ: Leave it then.

JACK: Where's my steak?

LIZ: Couldn't afford it.

JACK: What?

LIZ: Eat that now you've gorrit.

JACK: I don't like it.

LIZ: It's best lamb is that.

JACK: I'm not bothered.

LIZ: It cost me nearly a pound that.

JACK: I'm not eating it.

LIZ: Leave it then. I'll have it.

JACK: It's going ont fire back in a minute is this.

LIZ: Yes, you do.

JACK: Bloody lamb. Bloody lamb!

LIZ: I've eaten mine.

JACK: You can shit, you can.

LIZ: And you can.

   (*Blackout.*)

JACK: *is seated.* LIZ *is standing.*

LIZ: I've had to get up, have I?

JACK: What are you on about?

LIZ: You know that I'm badly.

JACK: What have you got up for then?

LIZ: Well, I didn't hear much action down here.

JACK: I thought you said you weren't well.

LIZ: I'm not.

JACK: Well, go back to bed then.

LIZ: I can't.

JACK: Why?

LIZ: I can't trust you to clean up properly.

JACK: Liz, just go back to bloody bed.

LIZ: Well, what have you done? You've been up an hour and I've not heard any movement down here yet.

JACK: I've been taking the ashes out . . .

LIZ: And you've made a mess and all . . . look at it . . .

JACK: Liz.

LIZ: It's no good, I'll have to do it myself.

JACK: You won't. I'll get everything done. You get back up them stairs.

LIZ: I ask you to have a day off and you can't be bothered to help me. I'll have to do it.

JACK: Listen, why don't you leave the bloody housework? It'll be here when you aren't.

LIZ: You know I have a good clean on Wednesdays. Have you done the brasses?

JACK: Not yet.

LIZ: Well, what you been doing?

JACK: I've had a wash, cleaned my teeth, and taken the bloody ashes out and I've had a shit. Is there anything else that you want to know?

LIZ: You make me bloody sick, you do.

JACK: Do I?

LIZ: I've got the step to do. I've got the lino to wash down.

JACK: Why don't you leave it for today?

LIZ: Coz I thought you were going to give me a hand.

JACK: Jesus Christ. I've had a day off work to help you, woman, and . . . and you can do it your bloody self. I'm going out. Where's my coat?

LIZ: Yes, you go out and you'll never come back in here again.

JACK: We'll see.

LIZ: Yes, we will bloody see.

JACK: You're bloody house mad.

LIZ: I'll bloody swing for you, Jack. Look at me hands, look at my bloody arthritis.

JACK: I'm bloody off to work. I'm not staying here. I don't get this at t' pit.

> (JACK *exits.* LIZ *picks up a cloth.*)

LIZ: You foul fella, you're not coming back in this house.

> (LIZ *begins to cry and begins to wipe the stage floor. She is still crying when* JACK *returns.*)

JACK: Come here, give us that cloth.

LIZ: No.

JACK: Give us it.

LIZ: No, I'll do it.

JACK: I'll bloody well do it.

LIZ: Get off me, don't touch me . . .

JACK: I'll go.

LIZ: Don't touch me or I'll stab you.

JACK: You daft old sod . . . Come here . . .

> (*He takes the cloth.*)

LIZ: Oh, you foul fella . . .

JACK: Put kettle on . . . get a cuppa tea and go lay down.

LIZ: Jack, I hate you sometimes.

JACK: Only sometimes? I must be getting soft in my old age.

> (*They share a laugh through tears.*)

LIZ: You bloody thing.

> (*Blackout.*)

Both actors sit in chairs and face the audience.

LIZ: It makes me wonder which is for the best. It gives me the creeps thinking about it.

JACK: Makes little difference. Tha'll not know owt about it when it comes.

LIZ: It's deciding though, isn't it?

JACK: It's same whatever you do.

LIZ: You wonder though, don't you?

JACK: I don't want any flowers sendin'. I'll have 'em now.

LIZ: Jack, don't be so crude.

JACK: They can do what they want to me. Put me in a bag and leave me int garden, or chuck me int dyke.

LIZ: Jack!

JACK: I'll not know owt about it.

LIZ: You're a bloody animal.

JACK: That's what they do with animals.

LIZ: I've never liked cremation.

JACK: Nor me. I've seen enough coal being burnt.

LIZ: We've got five hundred int Halifax. That should take care if sommat happens.

JACK: If. What're you on about *if*? There's no 'if' about it.

LIZ: It gives me the creeps thinking about it.

JACK: Well, I only hope that it's me that goes first. Coz if it's you I've bloody had it by meself.

LIZ: Well, that's lovely, that is.

JACK: I couldn't live without you, Liz.

LIZ: How do you think I'd get on without you?
>   (*Blackout.*)

Lights. LIZ *is sitting.* JACK *has turned away from the audience.*

LIZ: What're you doing?

JACK: Shhh!

LIZ: Are we going to our Betty's or what?

JACK: Hang on . . . nearly finished it . . .

LIZ: What're you bloody doing?

JACK: Writing . . .

LIZ: Bloody hell.

JACK: A poem about t' house.

LIZ: Let's have a look, then.

JACK: No.

LIZ: Come on, let's have a look.

JACK: No, gi' up.

LIZ: I bet it's rubbish.

JACK: I'll read it to you.

LIZ: Tha's like a big kid.

JACK: Right, listen . . .

LIZ: Hurry up then, coz we're already late.

JACK: It's about all t' things we've had int house, you know,
right . . .
A telephone table,
A lampshade blue . . .

LIZ: We've only just got that telephone table, Jack.

JACK: I know.

LIZ: What are you starting off with that for?

JACK: Are you going to listen or what?

LIZ: Hurry up then.

JACK: And don't be bloody interfering wi' my poem . . .

> (JACK *begins in earnest*.)

A telephone table,
A lampshade blue,
A pack of cards,
Two fireguards,
A picture from a zoo,
A miner's lamp,
A cushion slightly worn,
A chandelier,
A three-speed gear,
A brass and copper horn,
An old school bell,
An elephant with a broken leg,
A plastic rose,
A plant that grows,
A gypsy doll named Peg,
An imitation oil lamp,
A purple dressing-gown,
A mirror, cracked,
A paper rack,
A Paisley eiderdown,
A reproduction Dovaston, a poker like a sword,
A scuttle of coal, a goldfish bowl, a statue of our Lord,
Add many years of happiness, the right amount of love,
A few fears,
The same tears,
Trust in up above,

A thirty-year-old council house,
A husband
And a wife . . .
A family spent . . .
They represent
Years of married life.

> (*A silence.* JACK *and* LIZ *look at each other.*)

LIZ: It's good.

JACK: Ar.

LIZ: It is.

JACK: Ar, it's nowt. Daft, in't it?

LIZ: Why don't you send it off to somebody?

JACK: Like who?

LIZ: Somebody.

JACK: Ar, it's nowt. It's only a poem.

> (*Blackout.*)

JACK *stands over a chair shaving:* LIZ *comes to him.*

LIZ: Have you been to look at what they've done, next bloody door?

JACK: What?

LIZ: Have you seen what them snipe-nose pigs have gone and bloody done next door? It looks an eyesore, it does.

JACK: What's up now?

LIZ: Next door. I'm not kidding, it used to be all right round here, but it's a tip. You save up, you save up and buy your own bloody house and it gets worse. Have you seen what they've done? Of all the bloody lousy rotten tricks. Cut all the soddin' privets down.

JACK: So what?

LIZ: Well, just look at it. They didn't want touchin'. It was just nice and private in our backs, and they've cut the buggers down.

JACK: So?

LIZ: So I want something doin' about it.

JACK: But listen, love . . .

LIZ: No, you're not talking me out of it.

JACK: Just listen . . .

LIZ: Jack, I've had e–bloody–nough.

JACK: Will you bloody listen!

LIZ: What?

JACK: Liz, they are not our privets.

LIZ: They're on our part.

JACK: They are not.

LIZ: Jack, some of them privets are on our part.

JACK: Well, even if they are . . .

LIZ: They are our bloody privets.

JACK: Look, just settle down. You're gerrin' all worked up over some bleedin' privets.

LIZ: Do you know, you never back me up with anything, do you? I always have to battle it meself, ball comin' in t' garden, paper lad cuttin' through hedges.

JACK: What is it that you want me to do?

LIZ: I want you to back me up.

JACK: Right. Yes, it looks a bugger with them privets cut down, I agree with you.

LIZ: Swine.

JACK: Look, Lizzy, they are their privets. If they want to cut them down they can, if they want to grow them they can, if they want to burn all the bloody lot and stick the ashes up their soddin' arse they can.

LIZ: Shit you.

JACK: Liz, be reasonable.

LIZ: Shit.

JACK: You shit and all.

LIZ: We've paid for this house and you're not bothered, are you?

JACK: Course, I'm bothered. What d'you want me to do?

LIZ: Go round and tell 'em.

JACK: Tell 'em what?

LIZ: Shit, Jack, just shit.

JACK: For Jesus Christ's sake be bloody reasonable, woman.

(*Blackout.*)

A tight spotlight picks up LIZ. JACK *stands behind her. Faces only.*

LIZ: I used to be all right, no troubles, no worries. I never got depressed or fed up about my life. It was our Pam who started it. She wouldn't eat when she was younger. She'd just sit there, staring, not touching her food. I thought she'd die. She wa' that thin. She has bad asthma, she's so frail. Jack's so big and she's so thin and weak. I can't understand it. I didn't need the tablets to begin with. The more it's gone on the more I need them. I get all flustered, all worked up. I need them to calm me, to comfort me, to control me . . .

JACK: Tek a tablet.

LIZ: I get depressed. I get fed up of it, the routine, the house, these four walls. This is my world in here. Like a prisoner in solitary. I never see anyone, or talk to anyone, just listen to the wireless, all day long, I'm stuck in this bloody house listening to the soddin' wireless. I'm a prisoner, Jack, in this house.

JACK: Get yourself out.

LIZ: I have these funny dos.

JACK: Get yourself out.

LIZ: I feel dizzy.

JACK: Have a walk to the shops.

LIZ: Jack, I feel badly.

JACK: Get out more often.

LIZ: I feel as dizzy as a goof.

JACK: What?

LIZ: Nobody knows how I feel. I come over all dizzy. I feel like fainting, but I just go a bit groggy. I get these bloody headaches, and pains in my stomach. I'm in t' change. I get migraines, I'll be getting all ready to go out shopping and I'll get a migraine. I get it so bad that I can't see. I have to lie down. My head throbs and my neck. I feel as if I'm going to die.

JACK: Tek a bloody tablet.

LIZ: My fingers are killing me. Look at 'em, all bent and twisted. That's with having my hands in water. Every morning I pull the washer out. I wash every morning. He has clean on every day – socks, trousers, vest, underpants – every day.

JACK: They're not mucky.

LIZ: Every day I clean this house from kitchen to bedroom, from cellar to attic. All the ledges and cupboards and carpets need cleaning. While I'm cleaning, the washing's drying on the line, or if it's a bad day I have to dry 'em around the fire, and then when it's dry I iron it, and then I watch telly and then it's bedtime and then I tek a tablet because I can't sleep. My mind's all active.

JACK: Go to sleep, Liz.

LIZ: What is there for me?

JACK: What is there for me?

LIZ: What has there been in my bloody life? I've never been out of this house. I've never been abroad, to France or Spain or anywhere. London I went to once, years ago. I've been to Leeds shopping and that's it. I've been inside all the time, out of the way. It's too late now to start to complain.

JACK: Shuttit.

LIZ: What have I got to look forward to? The house, the routine?

JACK: What about my life?

LIZ: I might as well be dead. I might as well be bloody dead.

JACK: Tek a tablet, Liz.

　　　(*Blackout.*)

Lights.

LIZ: He gets me all churned up.

JACK: I don't.

LIZ: If they're playing with the ball outside, or if the kids are making a noise, he's up at the bloody window looking.

JACK: You never know what they're up to.

LIZ: He can't relax, he can't sit still. He's on the bloody move all the time. He's like a cat on hot bricks.

JACK: I'm not.

LIZ: He'll end up in Charlie Fox's sooner than he thinks.

JACK: Undertakers.

LIZ: He will.

JACK: I'm rate.

LIZ: He's allus bloody arguing, wanting to hit somebody.

JACK: I'm past that now.

LIZ: He's a bloody liar. On Mischief Night they were throwing eggs at our window.

JACK: I ask you, bloody kids chucking eggs, they must have money to burn.

LIZ: Jack went out to see 'em . . .

     (JACK *goes out to the kids.*)

JACK: Oi, bugger off! Go play down your own end. You cheeky sods.

LIZ: They gave him a mouthful.

JACK: Bloody kids. I'll tell your father.

LIZ: (*As kids*) He'll not do owt.

JACK: We'll see.

LIZ: Jack went down the street to see their dad, Taffy Jones.

JACK: I'd never liked him.

     (JACK *walks around the stage.*)

    Are you there, Mr Jones?

LIZ: (*As Taff*) Aye.

JACK: Ar, well, I've had a bit of a do with your lads.

LIZ: How do you know they were my lads?

JACK: Coz I saw 'em. They've been doing mischief.

LIZ: Well, it is Mischief Night.

JACK: Ar, I know, but they've been throwing eggs at our windows. Our lass's been cleaning them all day. I mean, it's not fair.

LIZ: Well, what do you want me to do about it?

JACK: Well, if you could have a word with 'em, I mean, I tried to talk to 'em but I got nowt but abuse of 'em.

LIZ: My kids do what they want down this street.

JACK: Well, it's not fair, is it?

LIZ: They do what they want.

JACK: Could you have a word with 'em?

LIZ: No, I bloody can't. They're only kids, what's up wi' yer?

JACK: Well, if I see the buggers I'll give 'em what for.

LIZ: You'll leave your hands off my kids or I'll bloody have you.

JACK: You'll what?

LIZ: I'll have you.

JACK: You little worm. I'll knock your bloody head off.

LIZ: And he did.

JACK: Straight over their coal bunker.

LIZ: Taffy was thirty-seven.

JACK: Jack was in his fifties.

LIZ: Taffy Jones went to the police station to report Jack, but the police just laughed at him.

JACK: But, I mean, chucking eggs, when you're proud of your house. It's not fair, is it? Our kids never did owt like that.

LIZ: We brought them up proper.

JACK: And if they had done I'd've gi'd 'em a good hiding.

LIZ: Our kids wouldn't've got caught, Jack.

(*A beat.*)

JACK: Ar, you're rate theer, crafty sods. I don't know where they got it from.

LIZ: Every year when the kids were young we went to Blackpool. We went to Blackpool for fifteen years on the trot. We all loved Blackpool, me, Jack and the kids, loved it. The Golden Mile, it was different then. Winter Gardens. The Tower. Blackpool changed, everything changes. Then we went to Cleethorpes and then to Whitley Bay.

JACK: It's nice and quiet.

LIZ: We started in a big posh hotel at Blackpool on honeymoon on the sea front, then we went to a little guest house down Waterloo Road, and then a bed and breakfast near the Coliseum bus station and now in a caravan at Whitley Bay.

JACK: Nice and quiet.

LIZ: My nerves get bad, they get bloody awful. We have a week a year to get away from it.

JACK: It's grand to get away.

LIZ: From the house.

JACK: From the pit.

LIZ: From the routine.

JACK: And the muck.

LIZ: From the soddin' washing.

JACK: Soddin' arguments.

LIZ: My nerves are bad, bloody awful. Before we ever go away I get all upset, even when I'm packing the cases. I get nervous, being on the road and all that. I enjoy it when I'm there. I wish to Christ we could afford more time away. When I'm there, when I'm away from home, I don't ever want to come back.

(*Blackout.*)

White lights up.

JACK: Page twenty. Whitley Bay. The Schooner Nightclub.

LIZ: A large wooden shell of a building with a large audience.

JACK: It is the last night of their annual holiday.

LIZ: The Munroes demonstrated little . . .

JACK: If any . . .

LIZ: . . . exhibitionism. Their barometer of enjoyment was perma-
nently frozen up. However, Liz would allow herself, once a
year, a few brandy and limes, a bag of crisps, a foxtrot, a
Broadway quickstep . . .

JACK: A saunter together . . .

LIZ: . . . and she was well on her way to a good night out. She even
learnt sequence dancing especially for this week's holiday. On
the Friday night of the week's holiday the caravan site would
celebrate with a . . .

JACK: 'Mr and Mrs' competition.

LIZ: Jack was a reluctant entrant, but Liz loved it.
     (*Music. Lights.*)

JACK: In this scene I play a typical site-club compère.

LIZ: And I play a slightly inebriated Elizabeth Munroe.

JACK: (*As compère*) Right. Sh sh, listen, be quiet at the back. Listen,
be quiet, my dad's in bed. Sh! Right then. Now, you know
what we've done. We've sent her husband into the sound-proof
box. Well, to be honest, the lovely Adele takes them out
through this door and into the car round the back. And they sit
with the car radio on, but anyway. Now then, now then, we
have here, Elizabeth.

LIZ: Yes, that's right.

JACK: Are you enjoying it here?

LIZ: Yeh, it's smashin'. We allus come every year.

JACK: Great, that's what we like to hear, my love. Now then, are
you here for a fortnight?

LIZ: No, we're going back tomorrow.

JACK: Oh shame, never mind, my love, I bet you'll be back next
year?

LIZ: Hope so.

JACK: And we hope so as well, Elizabeth, we do. Can I call you Liz?

LIZ: Yes, you can call me what you want.

JACK: Now then. Liz, now then. Doesn't she laugh a lot! Look at her laughing! Are you shy? Ohhh! She's shy, aren't you? Now then, listen, this is not hard. You know what to do, don't you?

LIZ: Yeh.

JACK: Have you got anybody out there?

LIZ: No.

JACK: Any family?

LIZ: Daughter and a son.

JACK: Lovely, are they grown up?

LIZ: Yeh.

JACK: Lovely, smashin'. Right then, now then. You know what the idea of the game is. I'm going to ask you what did your husband, Jack . . . is it Jack?

LIZ: Yeh.

JACK: What did your husband Jack say that *you'd* say to these questions? You get a point for each correct answer and a tenner for all three correct. Is that clear?

LIZ: Yes, I know what to do.

JACK: I'm glad somebody knows what's going on. Right then, are you ready? Right, this is your first question. I asked Jack: 'If you had to travel somewhere on holiday, let's say abroad, how would you want to travel? By train, by car, by bus? How would you travel: car, bus or train? Think carefully. What did Jack say that you would prefer to do – car, bus, train?

LIZ: I think he'd say, bus.

JACK: *Yes.* Well done, my love, well done. That's one out of one. Are you going away again this year?

LIZ: No, no, we're not.

JACK: Shame. Anyway, now then, one out of one, not bad, not bad at all. Right then, second question. I asked Jack. What is the last item of clothing that you take off before you get ready for bed? What did your Jack say was the last item?

LIZ: D'you mean before I put my nightie on?

JACK: Yes, my lovely, yes. What did he say?

LIZ: Ohhh! I daren't say it.

JACK: She says she daren't say it. What is it that you wear?

LIZ: My whatsit.

JACK: 'My whatsit'?

LIZ: Bra, brassière.

JACK: Is exactly what he said, my love, exactly. Well done, Liz, my
love. That's great, really great. Two out of two, smashin'. Right
then, now then, last one. Are you ready?

LIZ: Yes.

JACK: Last one. Take your time and think very carefully. Do you
keep bits of paper in the house? After you've unwrapped
something, a present or anything, do you keep, do you keep the
paper? Think carefully what did Jack say. Do you keep them,
yes or no?

LIZ: Yes, I keep everything tidy.

JACK: Liz. That is exactly what he said. Well done. My lovely
Adele, bring Jack out of the car. Elizabeth you have just won
for you and your husband a ten-pound note, and a bottle of
champagne.

LIZ: Whoooo!

JACK: Whoooo! She says. A bottle of champers. Well done, my love,
well done. Give her a big hand, everybody.

> (*Blackout.*)

JACK *goes and changes his costume at the hat stand.* LIZ *stands still.*
She brings a chair downstage, stands behind it.

LIZ: During the afternoon Jack and Liz would have a steady walk
down to St Mary's lighthouse.

> (JACK *is taking off his coat.*)

JACK: They would stand and watch the tide come in, covering up
the road to the lighthouse.

LIZ: In this scene, it is dusk.

JACK: Both of them are leaning over the railings, you know, as
people do.

> (*The chairs have been turned in such a way as to resemble prom
> railings. Both* JACK *and* LIZ *lean over. The lights slightly dim.*)

LIZ: Eee, I love it, Jack.

JACK: I do.

LIZ: Blackpool wa' nice, but . . .

JACK: Well, it's quieter.

LIZ: I've always liked up North East.

JACK: I have.

LIZ: I've never been on a boat, Jack.

JACK: No, I haven't.

LIZ: Can you remember when we went paddling at Blackpool?

JACK: I can. We've had many a happy hour paddling.

LIZ: And I couldn't stop sneezing that night, could I?

JACK: Water wa' like ice.

LIZ: Can you remember seeing *Gigi*?

JACK: Ar.

LIZ: One of my favourites.

JACK: Ar.

LIZ: What did he say?

JACK: Who?

LIZ: Maurice . . . Chevalier, when they're sat by the sea . . .

JACK: Oh, ar. I can remember. Ar, did it go . . .

       (LIZ *begins to sing.*)

LIZ: We dined alone.

    We dined with friends.

    A tenor sang . . .

JACK: No, no, that's not rate . . .

LIZ: That's it, Jack.

JACK: Is it, hell. I can remember it as if it were yesterday . . . (*As Chevalier*) We met at nine.

LIZ: We met at eight.

JACK: I was on time.

LIZ: You were late.

JACK: Oh, yes, I remember it well.

LIZ: We dined with friends.

JACK: That's it.

LIZ: We dined alone.

JACK: A tenor sang.

LIZ: A baritone.

JACK: Oh, yes, I remember it well. That dazzling April moon.

LIZ: There was none that night. And the month was June.

BOTH: That's right, that's right.

LIZ: It warms my heart to know

That you remember still,

The way you do . . .

JACK: Oh, yes. I remember it well.

LIZ: Then they talk for a bit.

JACK: He talks because she's just sat listening.

LIZ: She talked funny, didn't she?

JACK: Well, they wa' French.

LIZ: No, I didn't mean that.

JACK: That carriage ride.

LIZ: You walked me home.

JACK: You lost a glove.

LIZ: I lost a comb.

JACK: Oh, yes, I remember it well.

That brilliant sky.

LIZ: We had some rain.

JACK: Those Russian songs.

BOTH: From sunny Spain?

JACK: Oh, yes, I remember it well.

You wore a gown of gold.

LIZ: I was all in blue.

JACK: (*Stops. A beat.*) Am I getting old?

LIZ: (*Looks.*) Oh no, not you.

How strong you were,

How young and gay,

A prince of love,

In every way.

JACK: Oh, yes, I remember it well.

(*Blackout.*)

Lights.

LIZ: It's a nice house. It's warm. It gets bloody lonely. When you're by yourself for a long time in the same house, in the same rooms, you start to think about things. You can't help it. Ideas take over your mind, become massive, uncontrollable. Something that's been said, the smallest words that have been said take on more and more significance. They keep ringing in your head, getting louder and louder. It's like if Jack's home late from the pit. I imagine things that might happen to him. I can't help it. He may have had a car crash. His driving's getting worse. Maybe there's been an accident at the pit. There's a lot of accidents. Sometimes I've thought that he might be seeing another woman. I get all churned up inside. Or I think that he's fighting again. I mean, you don't know where he is, do you? Two miles under the ground, that's a long way away, a long way. It's funny, you wouldn't think it about Jack, but he's a kind bloke. We fall out, we argue, I call him all the lousy names under the sun, but he'd do owt for me. I never show him any affection but, you know? I used to. I used to love him physically, I mean really love him. I wa' proud of him being a big ignorant fella, a tough nut, not-give-a-damn attitude. When we were younger in bed it wa' like sleeping with a mountain, sleeping at the side of a mountain. I wa' snug and asleep in the valley and Jack wa' the mountain keeping the cold and wind off me, keeping me warm and safe. I thought that if he's here I'm not scared of dying, and that's what I'm most frightened of. I'm not allus right to him. It takes a lot. I waste all my time doing other things, cleaning the house, occupying my mind. When it comes to the important things like sitting down together, taking time over each other, I haven't got the energy. I don't feel like doing it. I just take him for granted. He keeps on going to work and I assume that everything's OK. I know it's not the best way to run things, but in this life we just go on. Things affect us, but me? I just keep going.

You wouldn't believe me if I told you that Jack wa' soft. He is, as soft as a brush. When our Ian wa' born the nurse asked him if he wanted to come and see the birth. He nearly fainted. I nearly died. He stood outside in the corridor, writing a poem. What a sight, a bloke the size of Jack scribbling a poem on a bit of envelope. The poem was about the pit, not me. He said that he just wanted to write about the pit, how proud he was, just how proud he was. He's still got that poem somewhere in the house. I think he's written one or two, all about the pits. He's as soft as a brush.

I go in hospital. I wanted to tell you, I've been meaning to tell you this last five minutes. I go in on Wednesday. I've had some tests. It's been coming this has for years. I've got an ulcer. I think it's a growth. As I said, you think about a lot of things when you're by yourself. I imagine this thing inside me. It's awful. It's in my womb. I asked the doctor, 'Is it malignant?' He said, 'No.' But you're never satisfied, are you? . . . I'll need that week's holiday when I come out. It's not that I'm worrying about going in. Once you've had kids you're not bothered about much. It's just that I wish I'd been in and come out. I wish, I wish to God it was all over and done with and I wa' back here in this house, my home.

(*Lights fade.*)

ACT TWO

White light. JACK *and* LIZ *are putting the chairs together to make a sort of bath seat. They do this through* JACK'S *speech.*

JACK: Jack really paid little attention to his son Ian, especially when he was in his infancy. It wasn't until Ian was sixteen that Jack discovered how quickly he'd grown up, and how little actual time he had spent with his son.

LIZ: Consequently when Ian married and had a son, Jack assumed it as his own. The child would stay with his grandad for weekend after weekend. Jack made him a hut, and a tree house and a barrow to help in the garden.

JACK: The child loved it.

LIZ: Particularly when his grandad gave him his Satd'y night bath.

JACK: Page thirty-five. The bathroom at Saxon Terrace.

LIZ: The walls are emulsioned, the floor covered with oilcloth.

JACK: Jack has the task of bathing his grandson.

LIZ: In this scene I play an 'unlikely' grandson.

JACK: And I play a very contented 'Happy Jack'.
    (*They are 'in' the situation.*)

LIZ: (*As grandson*) *More water!* Grandad, more water.

JACK: You know what yer gran's said.

LIZ: Come on.

JACK: Look out. Let me get these sleeves rolled up and we'll gi' thee a wesh.

LIZ: Don't splash us.

JACK: Dun't splash thee, dun't splash thee. Dun't tha want to be hard like thee grandad?

LIZ: Yeh.

JACK: Put thee muscle up and let's have a look at it.

LIZ: I 'ant got any muscle.

JACK: Thy has, let's have a look. Oh, ar! It's theer, it's comin' on is that.

LIZ: Is it?

JACK: Like knots in cotton.

LIZ: Can we have some more water in? I'm freezin'.

JACK: Aye, we can do, but dun't tell thee gran. If she finds out that I'm running off her hot water, she'll play 'ell wi' me. Theer, is that enough?

LIZ: Yeh, it's warm.

JACK: It wants to be.

LIZ: Tell us a tale, Grandad.

JACK: No, I'm busy weshin' thee.

LIZ: Tell us a tale.

JACK: I've teld thee 'um all.

LIZ: Tell us one agen, Grandad, tell us one.

JACK: Which one? I've got that many.

LIZ: Tell us about when you nearly got picked to play football for England.

JACK: No, I'm not tellin' thee that 'un. I get shown up.

LIZ: Tell us about when you wa' in Africa.

JACK: No, look, I'm not tellin' thee one. Tha's heard too many stories thy has.

LIZ: Tell us one.

JACK: Bloody no! And that's swearin', now be teld.

LIZ: Tell us.

JACK: No.

LIZ: Tell us, Grandad. I love thee.

JACK: How much?

LIZ: (*Making a sign*) About that much.

JACK: That's not much.

LIZ: Tell us.

JACK: No.

LIZ: Right then. I'm tellin' me gran.

JACK: What?

LIZ: You've let me have some more water in an' she said I could only have a drop in. And then she'll shout at yer, and you swore at me, you. You called me bloody, and she'll shout at yer for that when I tell her.

JACK: When did I swear?

LIZ: You called me 'bloody'.

JACK: You little sod.

LIZ: (*Shouting*) Gran! Me grandad's just swored at me.

JACK: Sh, sh, you little bugger.

LIZ: You bugger, you bugger.

JACK: I'll tell thee sommat that I've never teld anybody else int world.

LIZ: What?

JACK: When I ran away.

LIZ: Did you run away?

JACK: Yeh. I ran away to a circus.

LIZ: When?

JACK: Whooo! When I was as old as you. One day I left me mam and dad and I caught a bus and a ran away to a circus in London.

LIZ: What for?

JACK: Sommat to do, adventure.

LIZ: Wa' it good?

JACK: Great. I was the youngest lion-tamer in the world. I'd be put in the ring wi' this lion, and it'd look at me, and I'd look at it, and then I'd grab it by its fur, all its fur round its neck, an' I'd pick it up wi' me muscles, and I'd swing it. Round me head. An' when I thought that it wa' dizzy enough, I'd let it go.

LIZ: What did it do, Grandad?

JACK: It tried to stand up, and it looked at me and then it walked off, a bit dodgy and teld all them other lions to look out for me. An' all crowd wa' clappin' an' goin' mad, an' chuckin' money. An' these lions would do owt I teld 'um.

LIZ: What did you used to seh to 'um?

JACK: I'd seh, 'Ungowa. Get in that cage.'

LIZ: How long did you be a lion-tamer for?

JACK: Only a week, an' then I came back because I was hungry. It's not right good pay being a lion-tamer.

LIZ: What about all that money that they chucked at yer?

JACK: What money?

LIZ: You said that they all went mad an' chucked money.

JACK: Oh, yeh, that money, Ohh I, er, had to give it to the bloke in charge, an' that. Anyway I had to come back because I missed my schooling.

LIZ: Urgh! School.

JACK: What's up?

LIZ: School stinks of baba.

JACK: Na' then.

LIZ: Did you go to school then, Grandad?

JACK: Once or twice, nip, once or twice. Do you want some more hot water?

(*Blackout.*)

LIZ *remains where she is.* JACK *goes to the hat stand. In the dark we hear screaming.* (*A spotlight on* JACK. LIZ *maybe remains.*)

JACK: Ar, once or twice, it's rate an' all is that bugger. I never put much store by book learning, didn't seem to make much sense to me. I've got two hands, and I can handle a shovel, and I know how coal gets made. That's about the sum total of my schooling. Mind you, I can print really well. That's all I can remember from school, having to print out letters all the bloody time. I've learnt this much: if you want owt, you've got to work for it, nobody's gonna hand it to yer on a plate. I've worked for everything we've got ... and that's not much by other standards. Before Liz had our Ian I never had a day off from the pit ... never had a laker ... I thought I was working for sommat, sommat important. Huh? I must have been bloody loose. We wa' scratin' and saving up trying to mek sommat for ussens. I never had time to see that I wa' getting older, slowing down. I'd been doing the same amount of work at forty as I was doing at twenty ... ar ... working? Working for what? For who? National Coal Board. (*Laughs.*) I've upset some people in my time, lad, I've upset some of the buggers.

(*A beat.*)

Don't thee be like thee grandfather Thee go and mek sommat of thee life. Don't thee be a bloody miner. For God's sake, make sommat for yersen.

(*Blackout.*)

LIZ: Jack! Jack! For God's sake! The lights of the theatre were bright and warm, blinding. I was soaking with sweat. All I can remember is that my knees were up in the air, and I could just about see the large hillock that was to become our Ian. The (*Screams out of the blue*) pain was excruciating.

JACK: Jack was stood outside. He was nervous. 'What had I done?' he thought. I hope she's gunna be all right. You don't think about this side of it.

LIZ: She had been rushed to the hospital in an ambulance.

JACK: Jack was twice sick in the ambulance. He felt an urge to put some idea down on paper, all he had was the back of an envelope. (*Writing*) Do you ever stop to think?

LIZ: I am pushing, I'm trying my best.

JACK: Have you ever thought about a miner?

LIZ: I'm trying, aren't I? I'm tryin'.
      (*She screams.*)

JACK: Christ! I'm glad I'm not a woman.

LIZ: I am pushing. It was a difficult birth.

JACK: Have you ever stopped to wonder?

LIZ: (*Screaming*) Jack!

JACK: Have you ever stopped to wonder,
      When you think about our coal,
      How a miner leaves his loved ones
      To descend the Devil's hole?

LIZ: It was a big baby. Like having twins.

JACK: Have you ever stopped to wonder of inequalities in life,
      How easily found underground is pain and sweat and strife?
      Have you ever stopped to wonder, with your life so fine,
      That a miner's education takes place deep, down a mine?

LIZ: Ten pounds and three ounces. Liz was in great pain.

JACK: Have you ever stopped to wonder?

LIZ: (*Whispering*) Jack?

JACK: Have you ever stopped to wonder?

LIZ: (*Louder*) Jack?

JACK: Have you ever stopped to wonder,
      When ambition they have none,
      That society has left them,

With all ambition gone?
Have you ever stopped to wonder
Why they show but small respect,
That years of exploitation
Leaves something to suspect.

LIZ: It was a beautiful baby boy. Blue eyes, blond hair. She immediately called him Ian.

JACK: Ian John Munroe.

LIZ: Liz was very ill for several days. She was to have a blood transfusion. She almost lost her life. Ian John Munroe was four days old before Liz saw him. And Jack . . . still in the corridor.

JACK: Have you ever stopped to wonder?

(LIZ *stands besides* JACK.)

LIZ: Why I'm on the miners' side?

BOTH: We were born beneath a muck stack
And we speak of it with pride.

Lighting change.

JACK: Page forty-one. The honeymoon. It was the week of the St Leger when they decided to take their honeymoon. Four days at Blackpool. They stopped in the Metropole on the sea front near the north pier. Liz had always wanted to stop at the Metropole. It was a dream come true.

LIZ: Those four days were full of mixed emotions, for both of them. Seeing Jack away from the pit was like seeing a fish out of water. They spent most of the time looking around the shops, walking on the pier and keeping out of the rain. One evening they paid to see Reginald Dixon play the organ in the Tower Ballroom.

(*The actors have proceeded to set up the Tower Ballroom.*)

JACK: It happened like this. I wanted to see Reginald Dixon. I had always admired his playing. It was raining so we decided that a few hours in the Tower Ballroom would be a good idea. I was shocked at the price, two and six, but it was my honeymoon so I thought, sod it! This big commissionaire fella took me and Liz and about twenty more people to this room, opened the door, in we went, then he shut the door. About ten minutes later organ music started to seep into the room. (*Reginald Dixon: 'Begin the Beguine'*.) The noise wa' comin' through speakers in the wall. Everybody looked amazed, but no one said a word. We'd all paid to *see* Reg play and we were in a room listening to him.

LIZ: For about ten minutes no one spoke or looked at each other, then Jack said.

JACK: Hold on a minute, we're not havin' this.

LIZ: And he left the room telling everyone else to . . .

JACK: Wait theer!

LIZ: He went up to the woman behind the box office.

JACK: Excuse me, love. Can you tell me where the commissionaire is?

      (LIZ *has become the woman behind the till.*)

LIZ: I'm sorry, love, but he's not here.

JACK: Where is he, love?

LIZ: I don't know, love.

JACK: Well, what's the game, love?

LIZ: What d'you mean?

JACK: I mean, what's game here? We've paid five bob to see Reg Dixon and we're stuck in a soddin' chicken box listening to him.

LIZ: Well, you see . . .

JACK: If I'd've wanted to listen to him I'd've bought his records.

LIZ: Well, what d'you want me to do?

JACK: I want to know why we're in theer.

LIZ: Well you see the BBC are recording him today.

JACK: Tha what? And you've got twenty people in a soddin' box?

LIZ: It's not my idea.

JACK: Whose idea is it?

LIZ: I don't know.

JACK: I want my money back.

LIZ: I'm sorry, sir, but we can't give you a refund.

JACK: Tha what!

LIZ: I'm afraid we can't refund.

JACK: D'you mean to tell me that you've willingly took me money and made us listen to someb'dy coz soddin' BBC's recording?

Well, I'll tell you sommat. You couldn't run a bloody raffle.
Get me the bloody manager, and get him me quick.

LIZ: There's no need to shout at me. You know I'm only doing my job.

JACK: I know it's not your fault, love, but isn't it all right, eh?

LIZ: You know, I don't think that the manager will see you.

JACK: Well you'd better go and try an' get him, love, or I'll pull you
through that soddin' grille . . . *The manager came, and Jack got
his money back. In fact all twenty or so got their money back.
The manager wasn't pleased, but there was little he could do.*

LIZ: In those days Jack really wasn't bothered about anyone. No
matter what position they held he would hold them with the
same ignorant, arrogant disregard, as he said . . .

JACK: Even t' Queen Mother shits. She's no different to me.

LIZ: Two days later in the Manchester Hotel, a large pub at the
corner of Lytham Road, the barman had short-changed Jack of
threepence. The barman was an enormously fat arrogant Lan-
castrian. I thought that Jacko had met his match.

    (LIZ *is behind a chair washing glasses.*)

JACK: Oi.

LIZ: (*As barman*) Oi what?

JACK: Oi, can I have a word?

LIZ: Tha'll get more than a word.

JACK: Oh, aye?

LIZ: Yeh!

JACK: Tha wants to lose some weight before tha starts threatenin'.

LIZ: Tha wants to learn to talk before tha starts arguing.

JACK: (*To the audience*) Jack gave him one of his heavy depressed
and dangerous looks.

    (*He does so.*)

LIZ: (*Changing approach*) What's up?

JACK: I'll tell thee what's up. I'm threepence short.

LIZ: You what?

JACK: Tha's short-changed me of threepence.

LIZ: Give over.

JACK: Aye up. I'm tellin' thee, tha's short-changed me.

LIZ: I 'aven't.

JACK: Thy has. I've just reckoned it up.

LIZ: Right, what did you have?

JACK: Never mind what I had, just gimme me money.

LIZ: Look, pal . . .

JACK: Don't 'look pal' me, pal. Tha's done me for threepence. Na' is tha' gunna give it me or what?

LIZ: How much did you give me?

JACK: That dun't matter. I've worked it out. I want threepence.

LIZ: Well, look . . .

JACK: Thee bloody look. I'll pull thee over that soddin' bar if tha' dun't gi' me it.

> (*Blackout.*)

Lights straight back up.

LIZ: It was a good honeymoon, Jack being so reasonable with everyone. Jack created experiences and electric situations, especially with Liz.

> (JACK *and* LIZ *sit together as if eating a meal. A spotlight picks them out. They mime eating for a while.* JACK *eats throughout the dialogue until it is no longer possible.*)

LIZ: It's lovely in here, isn't it?

JACK: 'S all right.

LIZ: Good service.

JACK: 'S all right.

LIZ: I like it.

JACK: Good.

LIZ: Good service. He's a nice waiter. Very pleasant.

JACK: Yeh, all right.

LIZ: I bet he's got that tan living here.

JACK: Yeh.

LIZ: I think he's good-looking, that waiter.

JACK: Ar?

LIZ: I think he's *sexy*.

> (*There is a deafening silence.*)

Jack, I think he's attractive, that waiter.

JACK: Who?

LIZ: Him that's been serving us.

JACK: That thing that's been **hovering about**?

LIZ: He's nice.

JACK: When he comes back, I'm gunna kill him.

LIZ: Jack?

JACK: I'm gunna kill him.

LIZ: I only said . . .

JACK: You said it. You bloody said it.

LIZ: I didn't mean it. I only said it to see what you'd say.

JACK: He's bloody dead when he comes for the sweet orders.

LIZ: Please, Jack.

JACK: Don't 'please Jack' me. I'm six foot of idiot jealousy. I work in a bloody hole in the ground. I'm massive. Eight hours a day in pitch black, and you say that an article like that is 'sexy'. I'd look sodding sexy working at the seaside all year. You say that he's sexy again and I'll crucify you.

(*A moment.*)

I could beat him at everything. Name one thing that he could beat me at. Jesus Christ, Liz, you've got an enormous bloke with you, who'll do everything you want, and you've got the cheek to call him sexy. He couldn't pick his pit cheque up.

(*A moment.*)

All right then, tek off. Tek off with your sexy waiter.

LIZ: I don't want to.

JACK: Well, don't then.

LIZ: He's like a streak of pump water anyway.

JACK: He's like a skull on a stick.

LIZ: It took Liz a long time to realize that Jack's absurd jealousy was an expression of his absolute devotion. She was quite pleased when the honeymoon was over. As far as the waiter was concerned, they left after the main course without paying, before Jack had a chance to carry out his threats.

JACK: Which she knew he would.

LIZ: Their wedding was a quiet but pleasant affair. Held at the local parish church. Liz was all dressed in white and Jack looked smart, if a little bit choked in his wedding suit. Everything was going very smoothly until we came to the wedding photos.

(LIZ *holds* JACK *by the arm and they smirk as if posing for a photo.*)

Smile, Jack.

JACK: I am smiling.

LIZ: You're not.

JACK: I can't smile, rate. It looks daft.

LIZ: It doesn't. It looks nice. Smile.

JACK: Gi' up.

LIZ: (*Whispering*) Bloody smile.

JACK: I am.

LIZ: (*Whispering*) Smile more.

JACK: Oh, bloody all . . . all right.

> (JACK *gives a big daft smile, a light flashes, and that's their*
> *wedding photo.* JACK *leans forward and touches* LIZ.)

Jack had the undoubted ability to express himself through
actions rather than words.

LIZ: When he was twenty he would travel thirty miles every other
weekend to see Liz, who was in 'service' for Wilsons Mill Firm
in Bradford. He would collect her from her digs, and they
would walk around the city, looking in the shop windows,
thinking of what to buy, though they never bought anything. In
the late afternoon they would go to the cinema.

JACK: In the next scene Jack gives Liz her first ever present.

LIZ: A quarter-pound of coconut mushrooms.

JACK: They would go to the Gaumont no matter what was showing.

> (*During the last dialogue the actors have put the chairs together*
> *facing the audience. They then go and stand upstage left. They*
> *open a door and are blinded by the darkness.* LIZ *tries to hold on to*
> JACK, *probably by a sleeve or jacket pocket only. They hobble*
> *down an aisle, and see two seats. These seats are behind the 'real'*
> *seats. They shove their way to the seats and then decide to move to*
> *the 'real' seats. They move into the aisle once again. They reach*
> *the row of seats with the two real seats on them.* JACK *tells an*
> *imaginary gent,* Excuse me, pal. *We imagine him standing and*
> *both* LIZ *and* JACK *squeezing past him and others to their place.*
> *They mime taking off their outside coats, which is a big job. They*
> *sit in their respective seats for a moment, getting comfortable, then*
> LIZ *announces,* I can't see. JACK, *being the gent, decides to change*
> *seats. It is an effort to move in this confined space. Eventually they*

get comfortable. JACK *prods an imaginary person in front of him with his hand.* Tek your feet down I can't see owt. That's better. *The two actors begin to cough in an attempt to simulate the whole of the cinema. Intermittently they will turn around and tell the 'other' members of the cinema to* be quiet, shuttit! *etc. Finally they begin to watch the film in earnest. At varying intervals* JACK *may burst into enormous horse laughing.* LIZ *may laugh as well but she gives* JACK *scolding looks when he laughs loudly. He may touch her leg in the most masculine manner. She looks at him and smiles. She may touch his hand. He looks at her.*)

JACK: I've bought thee sommat.

LIZ: What?

JACK: Sommat tha likes.

(JACK *turns around, answering someone in the audience.*)
Shut thee soddin' mouth or I'll have thee head off.

LIZ: Don't, Jack.

JACK: Coconut mushrooms.

LIZ: Thanks, Jack.

JACK: Tha likes 'em, dun't tha?

LIZ: Course I do.

JACK: Oh.

LIZ: Thanks a lot.

JACK: Aren't you going to open them?

LIZ: Yeh, I can do.

JACK: Give us one.

(*She gives him a sweet.*)
MMMmmmm, they're nice are these, my favourites.

LIZ: Liz enjoyed Jack's fortnightly visits. It was the only time she came out of her digs. Before she went away to Bradford they were always together. They would often walk down Sandy Lane and sit and talk for hours.

JACK: Liz was a never-ending revelation to Jack, her innocence and inquisitiveness fascinated him.

(*They sit, as if on grass.*)

LIZ: Jack?

JACK: What?

LIZ: Do you know what I've been thinking?

JACK: If I knew that I'd be on at the City Varieties at Leeds.

LIZ: You know when you're down the pit?

JACK: Yeh . . .

LIZ: Where do you go?

JACK: What are you on about?

LIZ: Well, do you come back up or do you go down there?

JACK: Go where?

LIZ: Well . . . toilet?

     (JACK *laughs*.)

JACK: Bloody hell, woman.

LIZ: What's up?

JACK: There's no lavs down t' pit. You have to go in a corner.

LIZ: Oh, bloody hell, Jack.

JACK: Listen, guess where we put our snap tins.

LIZ: In lockers?

JACK: In corners. Half t' time when you get your snap tin somebody's messed all over it.

LIZ: I thought you could come back up.

JACK: You can . . . after eight hours.

LIZ: That's disgusting is that.

JACK: Ar.

LIZ: It's bound to get better, Jack, in't it? You know, as years go on.

JACK: Oh, ar it's bound to get better.

LIZ: On Sundays the pair of them would have a walk up to Burntwood. They would never hold hands, but Liz felt a close bond between them. Jack would often impose his poetry on Liz.

JACK: Granted, it was rough, badly written poetry. Jack had penned it during his quarter of an hour break down the pit. The paper it was written on was filthy. But they both enjoyed trying to decipher what Jack had thought in that black hole two miles deep.

     (*Seated on chairs; overhead spotlight.*)

LIZ: From down the mine so perilous

    I heard a collier calling to us,

    One clear call from the bowels of the earth,

JACK: 'Pay the miner what he's worth.'

BOTH: 'Hey there, hey there, you up there,
       Pay the miner his rightful share.'
JACK: Pray for him when underground,
      Exploited for the capitalist pound,
      Toiling away his working hour,
      Meagrely selling his labour power.
LIZ: He moves to his workplace through the murk,
     Where the roof is mesh and dangers lurk.
     With muscles taut and a sight that's failing,
     I heard a miner hailing,
JACK: Hailing.
BOTH: 'Hey there hey there, you up there,
       Pay the miner his rightful share.'
      Down the mine wherein dwells death
      The collier works with hard-fought breath.
      Gleaming bodies, legs that ache,
      Sweat and strain, back fit to break.
      When danger calls they'll tighten ranks.
      They ask no pity, they ask no thanks,
      And all we ask of you up there.
LIZ: Is pay the miner his rightful share.
JACK: Page sixty, the final scene.
LIZ: Their first encounter.
JACK: Jack first asked Liz to 'go out' with him when they were seven-
      teen.
LIZ: Though, as we have said, they had known each other for years.
JACK: He was on his way back from the pit, taking a short cut by
      coming down the side of West Street.
LIZ: She was in West Street Co-op, just coming out . . . Hello, Jack.
JACK: Hello, Liz. How are you?
LIZ: I'm fine, thanks, Jack. How're you?
JACK: I'm all right.
LIZ: Have you just finished work?
JACK: I'm on days regular. Where've you been?
LIZ: I've just been in the Co-op.
JACK: Oh, yeh.
LIZ: You're all dirty.

JACK: Yeh. I haven't hed time for a bath today, I'm going to the Miners' Welfare dance tonight.

LIZ: Oh, I wish I could go.

JACK: Aren't you going?

LIZ: No.

JACK: That's a nice dress you're wearing.

LIZ: Oh, thank you.

JACK: It suits your eyes.

LIZ: Does it?

JACK: Can I ask you something?

LIZ: Yes, of course.

JACK: Well, it's just that, we've known each other for a long time, haven't we?

LIZ: Yes, we have.

JACK: Since we were kids.

LIZ: That's right.

JACK: We've always been friends and played together, all our lives.

LIZ: Yes.

JACK: And I've always liked you, as a friend.

LIZ: I've always liked you, Jack.

JACK: Have you?

LIZ: Yes, always. You've always been a good worker, and honest. You've got broad shoulders, and you're kind.

JACK: I can't explain what I feel for you, Liz, you're the only woman in my life.

LIZ: I love you, Jack.

JACK: Why don't I take you to the dance? D'you want to come?

LIZ: I'd love to.

JACK: I'll nip up home and get fettled. Liz, I'm really glad that you like me.

LIZ: I do.

JACK: I'll see you tonight then?

LIZ: Will you call for me?

JACK: Yeh, about sevenish?

LIZ: Right.

JACK: Good.

LIZ: See you about sevenish then. That was actually fictional dialogue.

JACK: A dramatization, if you like.

LIZ: Pretence.

JACK: You see, it didn't happen quite like that.

LIZ: Though we believe that perhaps they wished that it had.

JACK: Maybe it did happen like that in their minds.

LIZ: But just to put the record straight . . .

JACK: And to deal with the facts . . .

LIZ: It happened like this . . .

> (LIZ *and* JACK *re–act the last scene.*)

JACK: Oi.

LIZ: Oi what?

JACK: Look at thee, about as much fat on a chip.

LIZ: Look at theesen first – more mouth than muscle.

JACK: Tha what?

LIZ: Tha wants a rate good wash.

JACK: Shut thee rattle, Elizabeth Cooper, and get your body over
here.

> (LIZ *walks to him.*)

LIZ: What's tha want?

JACK: What's tha doing toneet?

LIZ: Nowt, why? Who's interested?

JACK: Me.

LIZ: Oh, yeh?

JACK: 'S tha wanna come up to t' Welfare wi' me?

LIZ: Are you asking me out with you?

> (*A beat.*)

JACK: Ar, I suppose so.

LIZ: Well, ask me then.

> (*A moment's hesitation.*)

JACK: Will tha go out wi me?

> (*A beat.*)

LIZ: Yeh, Jack Munroe . . . I can do.

> (*They freeze. Steve Conway plays* 'Good Luck, Good Health,
> God Bless You'. *Costumes are taken off and placed on the
> chairs.*)

READ MORE IN PENGUIN

In every corner of the world, on every subject under the sun, Penguin represents quality and variety – the very best in publishing today.

For complete information about books available from Penguin – including Puffins, Penguin Classics and Arkana – and how to order them, write to us at the appropriate address below. Please note that for copyright reasons the selection of books varies from country to country.

In the United Kingdom: Please write to *Dept. JC, Penguin Books Ltd, FREEPOST, West Drayton, Middlesex UB7 0BR*

If you have any difficulty in obtaining a title, please send your order with the correct money, plus ten per cent for postage and packaging, to *PO Box No. 11, West Drayton, Middlesex UB7 0BR*

In the United States: Please write to *Penguin USA Inc., 375 Hudson Street, New York, NY 10014*

In Canada: Please write to *Penguin Books Canada Ltd, 10 Alcorn Avenue, Suite 300, Toronto, Ontario M4V 3B2*

In Australia: Please write to *Penguin Books Australia Ltd, 487 Maroondah Highway, Ringwood, Victoria 3134*

In New Zealand: Please write to *Penguin Books (NZ) Ltd,182–190 Wairau Road, Private Bag, Takapuna, Auckland 9*

In India: Please write to *Penguin Books India Pvt Ltd, 706 Eros Apartments, 56 Nehru Place, New Delhi 110 019*

In the Netherlands: Please write to *Penguin Books Netherlands B.V., Keizersgracht 231 NL–1016 DV Amsterdam*

In Germany: Please write to *Penguin Books Deutschland GmbH, Friedrichstrasse 10–12, W–6000 Frankfurt/Main 1*

In Spain: Please write to *Penguin Books S. A., C. San Bernardo 117–6° E–28015 Madrid*

In Italy: Please write to *Penguin Italia s.r.l., Via Felice Casati 20, I–20124 Milano*

In France: Please write to *Penguin France S. A., 17 rue Lejeune, F–31000 Toulouse*

In Japan: Please write to *Penguin Books Japan, Ishikiribashi Building, 2–5–4, Suido, Tokyo 112*

In Greece: Please write to *Penguin Hellas Ltd, Dimocritou 3, GR–106 71 Athens*

In South Africa: Please write to *Longman Penguin Southern Africa (Pty) Ltd, Private Bag X08, Bertsham 2013*

READ MORE IN PENGUIN

A SELECTION OF POETRY

American Verse
British Poetry Since 1945
Caribbean Verse in English
Contemporary American Poetry
Contemporary British Poetry
English Poetry 1918–60
English Romantic Verse
English Verse
First World War Poetry
German Verse
Greek Verse
Irish Verse
Japanese Verse
Love Poetry
The Metaphysical Poets
Modern African Poetry
New Poetry
Poetry of the Thirties
Scottish Verse
Spanish Verse
Women Poets

READ MORE IN PENGUIN

POETRY LIBRARY

Arnold	Selected by Kenneth Allott
Blake	Selected by W. H. Stevenson
Browning	Selected by Daniel Karlin
Burns	Selected by Angus Calder and William Donnelly
Byron	Selected by A. S. B. Glover
Clare	Selected by Geoffrey Summerfield
Coleridge	Selected by Richard Holmes
Donne	Selected by John Hayward
Dryden	Selected by Douglas Grant
Hardy	Selected by David Wright
Herbert	Selected by W. H. Auden
Jonson	Selected by George Parfitt
Keats	Selected by John Barnard
Kipling	Selected by James Cochrane
Lawrence	Selected by Keith Sagar
Milton	Selected by Laurence D. Lerner
Pope	Selected by Douglas Grant
Rubáiyát of Omar Khayyám	Translated by Edward FitzGerald
Shelley	Selected by Isabel Quigley
Tennyson	Selected by W. E. Williams
Wordsworth	Selected by Nicholas Roe
Yeats	Selected by Timothy Webb

READ MORE IN PENGUIN

INTERNATIONAL POETS – A SELECTION

Octavio Paz Selected Poems
Winner of the 1990 Nobel Prize for Literature

'His poetry allows us to glimpse a different and future place ... liberating and affirming' – James Wood in the *Guardian*

Fernando Pessoa Selected Poems

'I have sought for his shade in those Edwardian cafés in Lisbon which he haunted, for he was Lisbon's Cavafy or Verlaine' – Cyril Connolly in the *Sunday Times*

Yehuda Amichai Selected Poems
Translated by Chana Bloch and Stephen Mitchell

'A truly major poet ... there's a depth, breadth and weighty momentum in these subtle and delicate poems of his' – Ted Hughes

Czesław Miłosz Collected Poems 1931–1987
Winner of the 1980 Nobel Prize for Literature

'One of the greatest poets of our time, perhaps the greatest' – Joseph Brodsky

Joseph Brodsky To Urania
Winner of the 1987 Nobel Prize for Literature

Exiled from the Soviet Union in 1972, Joseph Brodsky has been universally acclaimed as the most talented Russian poet of his generation.

and

Paul Celan	Selected Poems
Tony Harrison	Selected Poems *and* Theatre Works 1973–1985
Heine	Selected Verse
Geoffrey Hill	Collected Poems
Philippe Jaccottet	Selected Poems
Osip Mandelstam	Selected Poems
Peter Redgrove	Poems 1954–1987

READ MORE IN PENGUIN

INTERNATIONAL WRITERS – A SELECTION

The Butcher's Wife Li Ang

Inspired by a murder case, Li Ang's novel has won international acclaim and made a profound impact on contemporary Chinese literature. With compelling power and daring it unravels the motive, the raw pain and the desperation that drove a woman to murder her husband. 'Fascinating ... the story never loses the reader's sympathy' – *Guardian*

Marbles: A Play in Three Acts Joseph Brodsky

Imprisoned in a mighty steel tower, where yesterday is the same as today and tomorrow, Publius and Tullius consider freedom, the nature of reality and illusion and the permanence of literature versus the transience of politics. In a Platonic dialogue set 'two centuries after our era' in ancient Rome, Nobel prizewinner Joseph Brodsky takes us beyond the farthest reaches of the theatre of the absurd.

Scandal Shusaku Endo

'Spine-chilling, erotic, cruel ... it's very powerful' – *Sunday Telegraph*. '*Scandal* addresses the great questions of our age. How can we straddle the gulf between faith and modernity? How can humankind be so tender, and yet so cruel? Endo's superb novel offers only an unforgettable bafflement for an answer' – *Observer*

Love and Garbage Ivan Klíma

The narrator of Ivan Klíma's novel has temporarily abandoned his work-in-progress – an essay on Kafka – and exchanged his writer's pen for the orange vest of a Prague road-sweeper. As he works, he meditates on Czechoslovakia, on Kafka, on life, on art and, obsessively, on his passionate and adulterous love affair with the sculptress Daria.

A Scrap of Time Ida Fink

'A powerful, terrifying story, an almost unbearable witness to unspeakable anguish,' wrote the *New Yorker* of the title story in Ida Fink's award-winning collection. Herself a survivor, she portrays Poland during the Holocaust, the lives of ordinary people in hiding as they resist, submit, hope, betray, remember.

READ MORE IN PENGUIN

A SELECTION OF PLAYS

Edward Albee	Who's Afraid of Virginia Woolf?
Alan Ayckbourn	Joking Apart and Other Plays
Dermot Bolger	A Dublin Quartet
Bertolt Brecht	Parables for the Theatre
Anton Chekhov	Plays (The Cherry Orchard/Three Sisters/ Ivanov//The Seagull/Uncle Vania)
Henrik Ibsen	A Doll's House/League of Youth/Lady from the Sea
Eugène Ionesco	Rhinoceros/The Chairs/The Lesson
Ben Jonson	Three Comedies (Volpone/The Alchemist/ Bartholomew Fair)
D. H. Lawrence	Three Plays (The Collier's Friday Night/ The Daughter-in-Law/The Widowing of Mrs Holroyd)
Arthur Miller	Death of a Salesman
John Mortimer	A Voyage Round My Father/What Shall We Tell Caroline?/The Dock Brief
J. B. Priestley	Time and the Conways/I Have Been Here Before/An Inspector/The Linden Tree
Peter Shaffer	Lettice and Lovage/Yonadab
Bernard Shaw	Plays Pleasant (Arms and the Man/ Candida /The Man of Destiny/You Never Can Tell)
Sophocles	Three Theban Plays (Oedipus the King/ Antigone/ Oedipus at Colonus)
Wendy Wasserstein	The Heidi Chronicles and Other Plays
Keith Waterhouse	Jeffrey Bernard is Unwell and Other Plays
Arnold Wesker	Plays, Volume 1: The Wesker Trilogy (Chicken Soup with Barley/Roots/I'm Talking about Jerusalem)
Oscar Wilde	The Importance of Being Earnest and Other Plays
Thornton Wilder	Our Town/The Skin of Our Teeth/The Matchmaker
Tennessee Williams	Cat on a Hot Tin Roof/The Milk Train Doesn't Stop Here Anymore/The Night of the Iguana